O9-BTO-702

GILDED LIVES,
FATAL VOYAGE

GILDED LIVES, FATAL VOYAGE

The Titanic's
First-Class Passengers
and Their World

HUGH BREWSTER

CROWN PUBLISHERS
NEW YORK

Endpapers: Passengers stroll on the decks of the *Titanic*'s near-identical sister ship, the *Olympic*.

Page i: The *Titanic*'s sinking was a huge news story.

Page ii: A photograph of the near-identical sister ship, *Olympic*, leaving port on sailing day evokes the *Titanic*'s departure on April 10, 1912.

Copyright © 2012 by Hugh Brewster

All rights reserved.
Published in the United States by Crown Publishers, an imprint of the Crown
Publishing Group, a division of Random House, Inc., New York.
www.crownpublishing.com
Simultaneously published in Canada by Collins Canada,
an imprint of HarperCollins Publishers Ltd.

CROWN and the Crown colophon are registered trademarks of Random House, Inc.

Library of Congress Cataloging-in-Publication Data

Brewster, Hugh.
Gilded lives, fatal voyage: the Titanic's first-class passengers and their world /
Hugh Brewster.
Includes bibliographical references and index.
1. Titanic (Steamship).   2. Titanic (Steamship)—Biography.
3. Upper class—United States—Biography.   4. Ocean travel—Anecdotes.
5. Shipwreck victims—Biography.   6. Shipwrecks—North Atlantic Ocean.
I. Title.   II. Title: The Titanic's first-class passengers and their world.
G530.T6B73 2011
910.9163'4—dc23   2011037159

ISBN 978-0-307-98470-8
eISBN 978-0-307-98471-5

Printed in the United States of America

Book design by Gretchen Achilles
Front jacket illustration: Corbis; photographs, from left: Randy Bryan Bigham
Collection, American Academy of Arts and Letters Collection, Randy Bryan
Bigham Collection, Library of Congress Photographic Archive
Photograph and illustration credits appear on page 323.

10 9 8 7 6 5 4 3 2 1

First Edition

To George Behe,
Randy Bryan Bigham,
and
Don Lynch,
with thanks

"It was a brilliant crowd . . . a rare gathering of beautiful women and splendid men."

—*First-cabin passenger* LILY MAY FUTRELLE

CONTENTS

GILDED LIVES, FATAL VOYAGE

A RARE GATHERING

Caught in the lights of the submarine was a small statue of a Greek goddess. She lay on the soft abyssal mud surrounded by lumps of coal, porcelain sinks, silver serving trays, filigreed windows, a china doll's head, champagne bottles, and much more. No light had ever before been shone on this extraordinary underwater cabinet of curiosities.

But with more of the *Titanic*'s wreck site left to explore, the submarine *Alvin* soon left the debris field and moved on. By early August of 1986, explorer Robert Ballard and his team were back at the Woods Hole Oceanographic Institution in Massachusetts with miles of film footage and hundreds of still photographs. My job for the next year was to edit and compile Dr. Ballard's images and data into a book about his discovery and exploration of the lost liner.

Fortunately, to share the task there was Ken Marschall, the world's foremost painter of the *Titanic* and a font of knowledge about the ship. When I asked him about the Greek goddess, he produced a photograph of the first-class lounge, one of the most elegant of the liner's public rooms. On its marble fireplace stood a statuette that was a match for the one on the ocean floor. It proved to be a reproduction of the *Artemis of Versailles*, a renowned Roman sculpture, from a Greek original, that Louis XIV had once installed in his palace's Grande Galerie. The statuette was an appropriate piece of décor for the *Titanic*'s lounge which was described in a 1912 shipbuilding magazine as "a noble apartment . . . the details being taken from the Palace of Versailles." The *Artemis* of the

Titanic, however, had been made of an inexpensive zinc alloy known as spelter, and then gilded. On the ocean floor, its gilding had been eaten away, leaving only the dull, gray metal underneath. For a ship that has come to represent the sunset of the Gilded Age, the spelter statuette seems an apt symbol.

The *Titanic*'s story, however, has lost none of its sheen. On the eve of its centenary it remains what Walter Lord, the author of *A Night to Remember,* once labeled "the unsinkable subject." It has inspired hundreds of books, movies, and websites, and one hesitates to launch another craft into such crowded sea-lanes. Yet in most accounts of the disaster, the *Titanic* is the protagonist and her passengers merely supporting players, identified with tags like "millionaire John Jacob Astor," "crusading journalist W. T. Stead," and "fashion designer Lady Duff Gordon." Yet who were these people? And what had brought their lives to this fateful crossing?

To Lily May Futrelle, her fellow travelers were "a rare gathering of beautiful women and splendid men." A rare gathering it was—liner historians report that no other passenger list of the period ever featured quite as many celebrated names. For Lady Duff Gordon, the *Titanic* was "a small world bent on pleasure." And it was indeed a smaller world than ours—the populations of the United States and Canada were a third of what they are today (and Great Britain's a third less), and wealth and influence were concentrated in much tighter circles. Those who made ocean crossings regularly usually found acquaintances on the first-class passenger list.

But "bent on pleasure"? There was certainly a contingent of the transatlantic leisured rich on board, a recently evolved class of Americans who kept homes in Paris or regularly made the crossing for the winter "season" in London or on the Continent. But many of the liner's first-class cabins were occupied by hardworking high achievers. The artist Frank Millet, for example, was on his way to Washington to help decide on the design for the Lincoln Memorial. His friend, White House aide Archie Butt, was heading home to prepare for a grueling presidential election campaign. Railroad president Charles Hays was returning to Canada for the opening of his company's new Château Laurier Hotel in

Ottawa. Lady Duff Gordon herself was a leading British couturiere who had urgent business to tend to at her New York salon. Within their lives and those of others on board can be found a remarkable convergence of the events, issues, and personalities of the age, forming what Walter Lord called "an exquisite microcosm of the Edwardian world."

In America, the *Titanic* is often described as a cross-section of the Gilded Age, an era of rapid industrialization and wealth creation in the United States that began in the 1870s and ended with the introduction of income taxes in 1913 and the outbreak of World War I the following year. Her sinking is sometimes viewed as the warning bell for a complacent society steaming toward catastrophe in the trenches of the Western Front. As the poet and actress Blanche Oelrichs observed, it was "as if some great stage manager planned that there should be a minor warning, a flash of horror" before the greater calamity to come.

When Robert Ballard's book *The Discovery of the Titanic* was nearing publication in 1987, I asked Walter Lord, the dean of *Titanic* historians, to pen an introduction. In it he pondered the enduring mystique of the *Titanic* and concluded:

> The thought occurs that the *Titanic* is the perfect example of something we can all relate to: the progression of almost any tragedy in our lives from initial disbelief to growing uneasiness to final, total awareness. We are all familiar with this sequence and we watch it unfold again and again on the *Titanic*—always in slow motion.

As the tragedy of the *Titanic* unfolds once again on these pages, the remarkable characters who people it, will, I trust, help illuminate a world both distant and near to our own, and convey anew the poignance of this epochal disaster.

The train from Paris pulled in behind Cherbourg's dockside station on the afternoon of April 10, 1912. On board was the well-known artist and writer Francis D. Millet.

AT THE CHERBOURG QUAY

The *Titanic* was going to be late.

To the first-class travelers aboard the *Train Transatlantique*, now chugging to a stop at Cherbourg's quayside terminus, this would be dismaying news. The six-hour journey from Paris had been quite long enough. How many hours, they wondered, would now have to be spent in this small, smoke-grimed station before White Star's new steamer could arrive to take them to New York?

As the passengers descended from the train, the scene on the platform was frenetic, according to a young American named R. Norris Williams, who recalled "the porters scurrying around, the crowding and jostling . . . excited people with lost luggage, porters asking for a larger *pourboire,* Thomas Cook's representatives trying to placate some irate would-be-important-looking person—in short—pandemonium."

One representative trying to placate amid the pandemonium was Nicholas Martin, the manager of White Star's Paris office, who had taken the train to Cherbourg to be a calming presence for just this kind of circumstance. As trolleys piled high with steamer trunks and leather suitcases were pushed along the platform, he circulated among knots of passengers, offering reassurances that although the *Titanic* had been delayed while leaving Southampton, she was now en route across the Channel and the tenders would be ready for embarkation by half-past five.

The most important person Martin had to appease was a tall, thin man with a large black mustache and an impatient expression. The

American millionaire John Jacob Astor IV was not only the wealthiest passenger waiting to board the *Titanic*, he was also a friend of the White Star Line's chairman, J. Bruce Ismay. Astor and his young wife, Madeleine, had, in fact, made the crossing from New York with Ismay on the *Titanic*'s sister liner, *Olympic*, just ten weeks before. Astor, according to one acquaintance, "made a god of punctuality" and had a habit of compulsively reaching into his waistcoat to check the time on his gold pocket watch. Fueling Astor's impatience on this occasion was the uncertain health of his wife, now several months pregnant. Concern for her had caused him to hire a nurse to be in attendance for the voyage home. Martin no doubt made sure that the Astor party, which included the nurse, a lady's maid, a valet, and an Airedale terrier, was quickly ushered into the station.

Far less demanding of the White Star manager's attentions were the more than one hundred third-class passengers, Lebanese and Syrian emigrants, mostly, along with a few Croatians and Bulgarians, who were arranging themselves docilely on wooden benches beside their wicker cases and carpetbags, occasionally calling out to their playing children to stay near. They had been traveling for days since they had left their villages, and a few hours more made little difference.

To a seasoned traveler like the celebrated artist and writer Frank Millet, delays, likewise, were something to be taken in stride. But spending several hours in a stuffy waiting room amid the braying voices of his fellow Americans was a more daunting prospect. Like many U.S. expatriates, Millet had an acquired disdain for his less sophisticated countrymen—and women. "Obnoxious, ostentatious American women," in fact, would be singled out for special scorn in a letter he penned the next morning from the *Titanic*. "[They are] the scourge of any place they infest and worse on shipboard than anywhere," he wrote to his old friend Alfred Parsons. "Many of them carry tiny dogs and lead husbands around like pet lambs. I tell you, when she starts out, the American woman is a buster. She should be put in a harem and kept there."

Such crankiness was not typical of Frank Millet, a man known for his geniality and disarming smile. His friend Mark Twain used "a Millet" as a label for a warm and likeable fellow. "Millet," he once wrote, "makes all men fall in love with him" and is "the cause of lovable qualities in people." Millet's less than lovable mood on this April day in Cherbourg can be put down to exhaustion. He had just completed a month in Rome where, as he described to Parsons, he had had "the Devil of a time." As the head of the new American Academy of Art in the Eternal City, Millet had found himself mediating a stream of administrative squabbles. And his final week there had been monopolized by paying court to J. Pierpont Morgan, the American financier who was to help fund the Academy's new building.

Now Millet was required back in America where more meetings awaited. In Washington, the Commission of Fine Arts, for which he was vice chair, was eager to finalize agreement on a Doric temple design for the Lincoln Memorial. Next came the American Academy's annual board meeting in New York followed by a trip to Madison, Wisconsin, where he had won a commission to paint murals for the state capitol building. It was a punishing schedule for a man who would be sixty-six in November but Frank Millet had never been content doing just one thing. As one of his oldest friends observed, "Millet was an artist but constantly subject to a great temptation, that of making excursions into other fields. Thus he led more or less the life of a wanderer."

During his wandering life Millet had shown an almost uncanny knack for being present at many of the landmark occurrences of his day. Where things were happening, Millet was invariably to be found—from the U.S. Civil War, where he had served as a drummer boy, to the building of the White City for the 1893 Chicago Exposition, to the conflict in the Philippines during the Spanish-American War, to the boarding of the *Titanic* on its maiden voyage. As an English art critic wryly noted in 1894, "Inertia is not one of Millet's faults; he is ever in movement, a comrade in the world of art. Are the heavens to be decorated? See Millet. Is there to be a banquet for the gods? See Millet. Has the army moved? Yes, and Millet with it. He breathes the air of two hemispheres . . . he is contagious in art and manly enthusiasm."

The name by which Millet's era is known was coined by his friend

Mark Twain in his first novel, *The Gilded Age,* a satire he cowrote with a friend in 1873, on the greed and corruption underlying America's post–Civil War boom. On March 11, 1879, Twain had stood beside Millet at his wedding in the Montmartre *mairie* [town hall]. The other witness was sculptor Augustus Saint-Gaudens, and the bride was Elizabeth "Lily" Merrill, the younger sister of one of Frank's Harvard classmates. Lily was a beautiful, if strong-minded, young American woman—drawn from the very ranks of those whom her husband would later claim "should be put in a harem and kept there."

In 1885 Lily and Frank became the center of an artists' colony in the village of Broadway in Worcestershire. This unspoiled Cotswold village had beguiled Frank on a visit from London in the spring of that year and he had rented an old stone house on the village green. His artist friends came to visit and some chose to stay. Henry James put Broadway on the map by extolling it in *Harper's Monthly* as "this perfection of a village." The novelist, then forty-two, had been drawn there by the presence of one of his protegés, a twenty-nine-year-old artist with soulful eyes and a cropped black beard named John Singer Sargent. In 1886 Sargent painted a portrait of Lily Millet looking ravishing in a white dress and mauve shawl with her black hair swept high. Twenty-six years later she still wore her hair that way, though it had by then turned an elegant white.

In April of 1912, Frank, too, showed signs of his years and his once-handsome face had assumed the mien of a genial owl. As he walked through the tiled concourse of Cherbourg's dockside station, his features likely also reflected the fatigue he felt after his challenging month in Rome. Lily had joined him toward the end of his time there, and they had left together for Paris two days ago and stayed at the Grand Hotel before departing on separate trains. By now Lily would be across the Channel and on her way back to Broadway, to Russell House, the large stone manse where, years before, his circle of artistic friends—Sargent, James, Lawrence Alma-Tadema, Edwin Austin Abbey, Edmund Gosse, Alfred Parsons, and others—had enjoyed rollicking evenings of what Frank called "high Broadway cockalorum."

In recent years, however, Russell House had been more home base than home for Millet. It had really been Lily's home, where she had raised his daughter and two sons, decorated the house, and designed the large gardens. Millet's absences most often took him to the United States, where his murals of mythical and historical figures were well suited to the rotundas of the domed and pillared public buildings going up in the burgeoning capitals of his homeland.

America's fondness for grandiose neoclassicism would reach its apotheosis at the 1893 World's Columbian Exposition in Chicago. Around a large boat basin where Venetian gondolas would glide was erected the White City, a staggering display of domes, porticos, colonnades, and loggias all covered in a white finish and lit at night by white electric bulbs. Frank Millet was the man who made the White City white. As the exposition's director of decorations he had come up with the right mix of paint to cover the rough, temporary finishes of the pavilions. To help his "Whitewash Gang" apply it within a very tight schedule, he had even invented an early form of spray painting, using a compressor and a hose with a nozzle fashioned from a gas pipe. Millet also created murals for the New York State pavilion and painted some large winged figures on the ceiling of the Palace of Fine Arts, which housed the largest exhibition of American art ever seen in the United States.

J. Pierpont Morgan

The brilliant showcasing of American paintings and sculpture at the Chicago exposition spurred the idea of creating an academy in Rome where American artists could soak up classical inspiration. Charles F. McKim, one of the partners in the famed architectural firm McKim, Mead and White, spearheaded the academy project, and Frank Millet agreed to be the secretary of its first board. With all the funds for the American Academy having to be privately raised, McKim sought out the greatest moneyman of the age, J. Pierpont

Morgan. On March 27, 1902, McKim breakfasted with the financier at his home at 219 Madison Avenue and came away with more than he had expected. Morgan had agreed to give financial support to the American Academy but had also asked McKim to draft plans for a private library to house his collection of rare books and manuscripts on land next to his Madison Avenue brownstone. "I want a gem," Morgan declared, and McKim's Italian Renaissance design for the Morgan Library still stands as one of New York's architectural treasures.

J. P. Morgan traveled and acquired for his collections constantly, but at sixty-five showed no signs of lessening his business interests. "Pierpont Morgan . . . is carrying loads that stagger the strongest nerves," wrote Washington diarist Henry Adams in April of 1902. "Everyone asks what would happen if some morning he woke up dead." Among Morgan's many "loads" at the time was a scheme to create a huge international shipping syndicate that could stabilize trade and yield huge returns from the lucrative transatlantic routes. By June of 1902 he had purchased Britain's prestigious White Star Line for $32 million and combined it with other shipping acquisitions to form a trust called the International Mercantile Marine. In 1904 Morgan installed White Star Line's largest shareholder, forty-one-year-old J. Bruce Ismay, son of the line's late founder, as president of the IMM. The second-largest shareholder was Lord William J. Pirrie, the chairman of Harland and Wolff, the Belfast shipbuilders responsible for the construction of White Star's ships. Pirrie had been the chief negotiator with Morgan's men and was placed on the board of the new trust.

The British government had acceded to Morgan's flexing of American financial muscle in the acquisition of White Star but had also provided loans and subsidies to the rival Cunard Line for the building of the world's largest, fastest liners, *Lusitania* and *Mauretania*—with the proviso that they be available for wartime service. By the summer of 1907, the *Lusitania* had made its record-breaking maiden voyage, and Pirrie and Ismay soon hatched White Star's response. They would use Morgan's money to build three of the world's biggest and most luxurious liners. Within a year Harland and Wolff had drawn up plans for two giant ships,

Lord Pirrie (top left, at left) and J. Bruce Ismay inspect the *Titanic* in the Harland and Wolff shipyard (top right) before her launch on May 31, 1911 (above).

and by mid-December the keel plate for the first liner, the *Olympic,* had been laid. On March 31, 1909, the same was done for a sister ship, to be called *Titanic.* A third, initially named *Gigantic,* was to be built later.

There is a now-famous photograph of J. Bruce Ismay walking with Lord Pirrie beside the massive hull of the *Titanic* shortly before its launch on May 31, 1911. The tall, mustachioed Ismay, sporting a bowler hat and a stylish walking stick, towers over the white-whiskered Pirrie, who wears a jaunty, nautical cap. Missing from the photo is J. P. Morgan, who had traveled to Belfast with Ismay and would shortly join him and other dignitaries on a crimson-and-white-draped grandstand. To the crowd of more than a thousand onlookers, Morgan would have been instantly recognizable from countless newspaper cartoons depicting him as the archetypal American moneybags—his walrus mustache and giant purple bulb of a nose, the product of a skin condition called rhinophyma, being easily caricatured.

For the launch ceremony, there was no beribboned champagne bottle to smash against the bow and no titled dowager to pronounce "I name this ship *Titanic.*" That was not how White Star did things. Instead, at five minutes past noon, a rocket was fired into the air, followed by two others, and then the nearly 26,000-ton hull began to slide into the River Lagan to cheers and the blowing of tug whistles. A white film from the tons of tallow, train oil, and soap used to grease its passage spread over the water as the ship was brought to a halt by anchor chains. Soon, the *Titanic*'s hull gently rocked in the river while the newly completed *Olympic* waited nearby.

The launch had gone off just as planned and a highly pleased Lord Pirrie hosted a luncheon for Morgan, Ismay, and a select list of guests in the shipyard's offices, while several hundred more were entertained at Belfast's Grand Central Hotel, where a third luncheon was held for the gentlemen of the press. During the speeches at the press luncheon, the construction of the "leviathans," *Olympic* and *Titanic*, was hailed as a "pre-eminent example of the vitality and the progressive instincts of the Anglo-Saxon race." That American money had paid for them was made a positive by the observation that "the mighty Republic in the West" and the United Kingdom were both Anglo-Saxon nations that had become more closely united as a result of their cooperation. While the Belfast men toasted their success and the primacy of their race, a shipyard worker named James Dobbins lay in hospital, his leg having been pinned beneath one of the wooden supports for the hull during the launch. Dobbins would die from his injuries the next day.

Following the luncheon, J. P. Morgan and Bruce Ismay boarded the

Olympic along with other guests and sailed for Liverpool. Exactly seven months later, on December 31, 1911, Morgan would walk up the *Olympic*'s gangway once again, this time in New York bound for Southampton. From England he went on to Egypt, where he spent the winter at a desert oasis called Khargeh supervising the excavation of Roman ruins and an early Christian cemetery. By mid-March, Morgan was in Rome, and on the morning of April 3, 1912, he stood with Frank Millet atop the Janiculum Hill, reviewing the plans and site for the new American Academy building. Like the Morgan Library, this was to be another of Charles McKim's Italian Renaissance palaces, built from a design drawn up by the architect before his death in 1909. Millet was keen to see McKim's dream realized and Morgan told the *New York Times*, "I hope that here will eventually be an American institution of art, greater than those of the other countries, which are already famous." The next day the financier went on to Florence, where Millet soon joined him, perhaps to lend an informed opinion on Morgan's ceaseless acquiring of art and antiquities. "Pierpont will buy anything from a pyramid to a tooth of Mary Magdalene," his wife had once noted. Morgan was no doubt pleased that Millet was sailing on the maiden voyage of the *Titanic*. He had planned to be on board himself before changing his plans in favor of a stay at a spa at Aix-les-Bains with his mistress.

WHILE MORGAN TOOK the waters in Aix on April 10, Millet waited on the Normandy coast for Morgan's newest ship to arrive. Eschewing the loud Americans crowding the waiting room, he may have chosen to stretch his legs after the long train ride from Paris. In front of the small, Mansard-roofed Gare Maritime stood the White Star tenders, *Traffic* and *Nomadic*, on which luggage and mail sacks were being loaded. The two tenders had been built at Harland and Wolff to service the new *Olympic*-class liners which were too large to dock in Cherbourg, the first stop after Southampton on White Star's transatlantic route. The quay in front of the Gare Maritime led to a long jetty with an ancient stone tower at its end. It was a mild spring day with scudding clouds allowing bursts of sunshine, so Frank might have walked out on the jetty to see if there was any sign of the liner on the horizon. The walk would have helped to clear his mind of the institutional politics that had plagued him in Rome. As he wrote to Alfred Parsons the next day: "If this sort of thing goes on I shall chuck it. I won't lose my time and my temper too."

It would be a big disappointment for Lily Millet if Frank chose to "chuck" his post as head of the American Academy. She was enchanted with the Villa Aurelia, the ochre seventeenth-century cardinal's palace that went with the job. Now that her children were grown, Lily was establishing a career as an interior designer and had great plans for the villa and its gardens with their sweeping views of Rome. Here she could imagine the serene evenings of their twilight years, reconciled and reunited with her wandering husband.

Frank's friend Archie Butt, too, had admired the villa when the two men had stayed there together before Lily arrived. Since 1910, Frank's more-or-less permanent base had been Washington, D.C., where he had shared a house with Major Archibald Willingham Butt, the president's military aide, known to all as "Archie." It was Frank who had persuaded an exhausted Archie to come with him to Rome the month before and take some rest-and-recovery time before the fall presidential election. President Taft needed his closest aide to be in fighting trim for the coming campaign, and had arranged letters of introduction for Archie to the pope and the king of Italy to grant an air of officialdom to his trip. According to a March 31 social column in the *New York Times*, Major Butt had "had the entrée to every house worth while in Rome," and "by doing exactly what the doctors forbade," as Archie himself had put it, he was in splendid condition and ready to return home. Major Butt had gone on to visit embassies in Berlin and Paris before continuing to England to see his brother. At about the same time that Frank was departing from Paris on the *Train Transatlantique*, Archie had boarded the Boat Train at London's Waterloo Station for the noontime departure of the *Titanic* from Southampton.

After five o'clock that afternoon, with the luggage loaded aboard the Cherbourg tenders, passengers began making their way toward their gangways. As Frank approached the *Nomadic*, his weary mood may have lifted. He could look forward to dining with Archie on the *Titanic* that evening and hearing his droll observations of the other passengers, all delivered in Archie's characteristic Georgia drawl. Millet had often said that he was not a fan of maiden voyages—he preferred liners where the officers and crew were more familiar with the ship. But his meetings in America wouldn't wait. And if White Star's new liner lived up to its billing, there would be a comfortable room and a good dinner for him at the end of this very long day.

Among those boarding the tender *Nomadic* (top, at left) were John Jacob Astor, his young wife, Madeleine, and their Airedale, Kitty.

A *NOMADIC* HIATUS

APRIL 10, 1912, 5:30 P.M.

As Nicholas Martin had promised, the tender *Nomadic* was ready for departure at 5:30. Although the *Titanic* had still not been sighted, Martin had decided to board the passengers and have the tender wait in the harbor. With a late-afternoon chill now in the air, most of the *Nomadic*'s 172 first- and second-class passengers made their way down to the lounge, where roll-backed slatted benches provided plenty of seating. The room was paneled in white and decorated with carved ribbon garlands that gave a hint of the elegance awaiting on the *Titanic*. By contrast, the *Traffic*, now loaded with mailbags and the wicker cases and satchels of steerage travelers, had clean but spartan interiors, in the style of White Star's third-class accommodations.

Soon the floor of the *Nomadic*'s lounge began to vibrate and smoke belched from its single stack as the tender started to move toward the breakwater. It wasn't long, however, before the young American R. Norris Williams began to wonder why they had been sent out on the tender so soon. "Riding the waves in the outer harbor is interesting for a little while," he noted, "but then you get bored; the saloon is stuffy so you wander the decks again, just waiting. Innumerable false alarms as to the sighting of the *Titanic*—more waiting—slight and passing interest in a fishing boat—more waiting." Williams had spotted one of his idols, the U.S. tennis star Karl H. Behr, among the Cherbourg passengers. Behr, aged twenty-six, had been ranked as the number 3 player in the United States and had competed for the Davis Cup and at Wimbledon. Norris Williams was a talented player himself who had

R. Norris Williams and his father, Charles Williams

won championships in Switzerland and France and was planning to play on the U.S. tennis circuit that summer before entering Harvard in the fall. He was traveling with his father, Charles Williams, who was originally from Philadelphia and was, in fact, a great-great-grandson of the most famous of all Philadelphians, Benjamin Franklin. Williams Senior had practiced law in Philadelphia before moving to Geneva with his wife in the late 1880s. Norris had been born and educated there and was fluent in three languages as a result. At twenty-one, he was tall and lanky, with prominent ears and a winning smile seen above the broad collar of his fur coat. Father and son were both wearing large fur coats, which would have caught the eye of Frank Millet as he scanned the room for people he knew.

The Astors with their entourage and Airedale terrier stood out as well. Even their Airedale, named Kitty, had become famous, from the many photographs of the couple with the dog that had been splashed in the newspapers the summer before. Everything the Astors did was news, but the fact that forty-seven-year-old John Jacob Astor IV, whom the gossip sheets preferred to call Jack Astor, or even Jack-Ass (tor), was engaged to a teenaged girl almost thirty years his junior had provided the year's juiciest story. Every detail of the romance had fueled daily headlines. When they would wed and where was a subject of heated speculation.

Astor had confessed to adultery in late 1909 in order to grant his first wife the divorce she so ardently desired. This had eased the case through the courts but had greatly lowered his chances for church-sanctioned second nuptials.

Jack Astor's first marriage, to the Philadelphia society beauty Ava Lowle Willing, had been a disaster from the start. The night before the lavish wedding in February of 1891, the tearful bride-to-be had purportedly begged her parents to call it off. Marrying into America's richest family was clearly not enough to overcome the fact that at twenty-six, Jack Astor was already earning his jackass sobriquet. Within his circle he had a reputation for "pawing every girl in sight," and in 1888 a gossip column had gleefully described him brawling with another young preppy—using both fists and walking sticks—in the cloakroom of Sherry's Restaurant. The fight, unsurprisingly, had been over a girl.

Tall and awkward, with a large head atop a skinny frame, Astor had grown up being cosseted by a domineering mother and four older sisters and ignored by a distant and dissipated father. Boarding school at St. Paul's in New Hampshire was followed by three years of studying science at Harvard, where he left without finishing his degree. "It is very questionable, whether, were he put to it, he could ever earn his bread by his brains," was the observation of the Manhattan gossip sheet *Town Topics*. But Jack was clever with machines and spent many hours tinkering in his home laboratory dreaming up new inventions. Many of these were highly impractical, but a "pneumatic road improver" that could suck up dirt and horse droppings from city streets had won him a prize at the 1893 Chicago Exposition. The next year, he had published a Jules Verne–ish novel, *A Journey in Other Worlds*, which envisioned electric cars and space travel in the year 2000.

Within a year of their wedding, the beautiful Ava (pronounced *Ah-vah*) had dutifully produced a son, William Vincent Astor, but from then on she ignored her husband as much as she could, devoting herself to parties, bridge, and flirtations. (A daughter, Alice, born in 1902, was rumored not to be Astor's child.) Divorce was out of the question as long

as Jack's mother, Caroline Schermerhorn Astor, was alive. The Schermer-
horns had been early Dutch settlers in the Hudson Valley, and it was this
lineage, coupled with her husband's vast fortune, that allowed Caroline
Astor to appoint herself queen of New York society. Her annual ball was
the city's most exclusive affair, and a divorce could cause exclusion from
its gilded guest list. The name "the Four Hundred," for the city's social
elite, was believed to refer to the capacity of Mrs. Astor's ballroom, but it
was, in fact, Mrs. Astor's chief courtier, a drawling socialite named Ward
McAllister, who had coined the term when asked by a reporter how many
people he thought comprised New York society. McAllister had realized
that greater status than his means allowed could come from organizing
the society of a city awash in new money. And he soon saw that Caroline
Astor, whom he dubbed the "Mystic Rose" after the heavenly being in
Dante's *Paradiso*, around whom all others revolve, was in need of a court
chamberlain.

When the Mystic Rose gave a ball, her Fifth Avenue mansion was
decorated with hundreds of American Beauty roses and she appeared fes-
tooned in so many diamonds that her court jester, the outrageous Harry
Lehr, called her "a walking chandelier." Yet by the early years of the
new century the New York/Newport social set was growing tired of Mrs.
Astor's stiffly elegant gatherings. When a stroke diminished her faculties
in 1905, Caroline Astor became a recluse, inspiring a depiction in the
Edith Wharton story "After Holbein" in which "the poor old lady who
was gently dying of softening of the brain . . . still came down every evening to her great shrouded drawing-rooms with her tiara askew on her
purple wig, to receive a stream of imaginary guests."

The death of *the* Mrs. Astor in 1908 marked the end of an era in
New York society, but it also provided an opportunity for her son and his
wife to end their moribund union. The next year, after the most discreet
divorce that money could buy became final, Ava boarded the *Lusitania*
for England, where she was well known in society. She eventually married an English baron, Lord Ribblesdale, and although the marriage did
not last, Ava remained Lady Ribblesdale for life.

Freed from the shadow of two overbearing women, Jack soon demonstrated an uncharacteristic bonhomie. Formerly glum and awkward at social gatherings, he now accepted invitations readily and hosted parties at Beechwood, the thirty-nine-room family "cottage" in Newport, and at the Fifth Avenue Astor mansion. While visiting Bar Harbor in the summer of 1910, he met a seventeen-year-old girl named Madeleine Talmage Force and became instantly smitten. Madeleine and her formidable mother (known in society as "*La Force Majeure*") were soon regular guests on Astor's yacht *Noma*, in his box at the opera, at Beechwood in Newport, at Ferncliff, his Hudson Valley estate, as well as at the Manhattan mansion. All of which must have dazzled a teenager just out of Miss Spence's School for Girls.

Early in 1911, *Town Topics* noted that "Mother Force has let no grass grow in getting her hook on the Colonel [Astor]." By August 2, the *New York Times* had reported that the couple were engaged and described how this had come about. Madeleine's father, apparently concerned about "continued rumors of the attachment between Colonel Astor and his daughter," had called Astor on the telephone to discuss the matter and it had been agreed that Father Force should announce the engagement. *Force majeure*, indeed.

Over the next five weeks, the newspapers feasted on wedding details, particularly as one minister after another refused to officiate. In the end, a Congregationalist pastor presided over a rather short service held in the ballroom at Beechwood in Newport on September 9, 1911. Criticism from the pastor's congregation would soon cause his resignation from the ministry. The newlyweds, too, received a very cool reception from Astor's social set, which may have contributed to their decision to leave in January for a ten-week Mediterranean tour highlighted by a trip down the Nile.

One Newport acquaintance who hadn't snubbed Jack Astor was Margaret Tobin Brown, the estranged wife of Denver millionaire James J. Brown. She was sympathetic to marital woes and escaped her own by traveling. That winter, in fact, Mrs. Brown had joined the Astors on their excursion to North Africa and Egypt. In her pocket as she sat near the Astor party on the *Nomadic* was a small Egyptian tomb figure that she

Margaret Tobin Brown

had bought in a Cairo market as a good luck talisman. The voyage Margaret Brown was about to take would immortalize her in books, movies, and a Broadway musical as "the unsinkable Molly Brown," a feisty backwoods girl whose husband's lucky strike at a Leadville, Colorado, gold mine vaults her into a mansion in Denver, where she is rebuffed by Mile High society. In the 1957 film *A Night to Remember*, Molly Brown is first spotted announcing loudly to her table in the *Titanic*'s dining saloon that her husband "Leadville Johnny" was "the best gol-durn gold miner in Colorado" who had "built me a home that had silver dollars cemented all over the floors of every room!" The rags-to-riches arc of the Molly Brown legend is essentially true, though the details are highly fanciful. The real Margaret Brown, in fact, was never known as "Molly" until after her death, when a greatly embellished biography gave her that tag—and the mansion with silver dollars in the floor was an invention of the same writer.

Feisty she was, however, and Margaret Brown's remarkable energies had already been devoted to such causes as women's suffrage and the establishing of the first juvenile court in the United States. Her self-betterment included learning several languages at New York's Carnegie Institute, and by 1912 any "gol-durns" in her speech had been long banished and she was mixing with society figures at her summer "cottage" in Newport and on her European travels. With her hennaed hair, expensive clothes, and forthright manner, Mrs. Brown might seem a likely candidate to be one of Frank Millet's "obnoxious, ostentatious American women." But some recent news had muted her customary ebullience. While staying at the Ritz in Paris, she had received word that her first grandchild, four-month-old Lawrence Brown Jr., had fallen seriously ill, and she had immediately booked passage home on the earliest available ship. It would therefore have been a rather subdued "Molly" Brown who waited on the *Nomadic* for the ship that would propel her into legend.

Margaret Brown was not the only passenger returning home because of a family emergency. The writer, interior designer, and Washington society figure Helen Churchill Candee had also received an alarming telegram, informing her that her twenty-five-year-old son, Harold, had been injured in an airplane crash. Helen had gone abroad in January to finalize research on a new book about antique tapestries. After spending time in Spain and Italy, she was returning to Paris in early April by way of the Riviera, when a cable sent by her daughter caused her to immediately make plans to sail for home. As she sat alone on one of the *Nomadic*'s slatted banquettes, her petite, elegantly dressed figure topped by a modish hat, Helen, too, was almost certainly preoccupied by anxious thoughts as she wondered what had possessed Harold to get into one of those dangerous new flying machines.

The most somber group of all, however, were the Ryersons of Haverford, Pennsylvania, who were returning home for the funeral of their twenty-one-year-old son, Arthur, a Yale student who been thrown from an open car while motoring on the Easter weekend. The family had received word by telegram in Paris, and Arthur Ryerson Sr. had cabled back to arrange his son's funeral for April 19, two days after the *Titanic* was to arrive. His wife, Emily, was being given comfort by two of her daughters, Suzette, aged twenty-one, and Emily, aged eighteen, while thirteen-year-old Jack Ryerson was tended by his tutor, Grace Bowen. The Ryersons were part of Philadelphia Main Line society, named for the fashionable suburban towns built along the Main Line of the Pennsylvania Railroad and a group that would be well represented on the *Titanic*'s first-class passenger list.

Margaret Brown described her time aboard the tender as an hour or longer of sitting in a "cold, gray atmosphere," which may have referred to more than just the weather, given the number of anxious or grieving passengers on board. The mood on the tender certainly affected Margaret's friend Emma Bucknell, a wealthy widow from Philadelphia, who had also been traveling in Egypt. The matronly, nervous Emma had confided to Margaret that she feared boarding the *Titanic* because of her "evil forebodings that something might happen." Mrs. Brown simply smiled at her friend's premonitions and offered reassuring words to her.

Yet Emma Bucknell was not the only one on board with apprehensions about the voyage. Fashion writer Edith Rosenbaum had at first been looking forward to the crossing, but on reaching Cherbourg she had been gripped by fears and had sent an anxious telegram from the station to her secretary in Paris. Perhaps it was simply nerves, she thought, since this was her first trip to New York as a fashion buyer and stylist, and she was bringing trunks of valuable Paris gowns to show to American clients. Edith also hadn't fully recovered from a car crash the summer before that had killed her German fiancé and severely injured another friend. They had been motoring to the races in Deauville, which Edith was covering for *Women's Wear Daily*, when their automobile crashed into a tree. She had survived with only minor injuries, but the emotional trauma of it lingered.

The accident, however, hadn't diminished her love of France. On her first trip to Paris five years before, Edith had known instantly that it was the city for her. Back home in Cincinnati, marrying a young man from a suitable Jewish family was what was expected of her, but at twenty-eight the prospects for that were growing slim. Over her father's objections, she returned to Paris in 1908, determined to find work in the fashion trade. Her first job was as a salesgirl for Maison Cheruit in the Place Vendôme. Madame Cheruit herself had been impressed by Edith's American verve and *jolie laide* looks—and her claim that in Cincinnati she had always ordered her dresses from Cheruit. After a year, Edith left the fashion house to write about French style for a small periodical distributed by

Wanamaker's department stores, and this led to a job as Paris correspondent for *Women's Wear Daily.* She also drew sketches for the Butterick Pattern Service and later even designed her own line of clothes for Lord & Taylor in New York. But designing, in her words, was "just a sideline." As she would later say, "I never fooled myself that I was going to be another Lady Duff Gordon."

Edith had written about the opening of the Paris branch of Lucile Ltd., Lady Duff Gordon's fashion house, the year before. The idea of an English couturiere establishing an outpost in the capital of haute couture had raised some Gallic design noses skyward, but fashionable French women had soon flocked to Lucile's showroom on the rue de Penthièvre. It was from there that Lady Duff Gordon and her husband, Sir Cosmo, had left that morning to take the train to Cherbourg. Seeing the famous designer sitting calmly on the *Nomadic* in her sable coat and pearl earrings and holding a bouquet of lily of the valley likely helped to calm Edith's fears. She had covered the fashion shows at Lucile's salon but had never actually met the famous couturiere in person, though the lounge of the tender did not seem quite the right place to approach her. Introducing oneself, she had learned, was not the done thing on this side of the Atlantic.

His Swiss-educated manners, similarly, may have inhibited Norris Williams from approaching Karl Behr on the *Nomadic.* The American tennis star, in any case, was no doubt preoccupied by thoughts of the girl he would soon see on the *Titanic.* Nineteen-year-old Helen Newsom was a friend of Karl's younger sister, and a romance had recently blossomed between them despite some objections from Helen's mother and stepfather, Sallie and Richard Beckwith. It wasn't that Karl was unsuitable—he was from a prosperous New York family, after all, and was a Yale graduate and a lawyer, as well as a tennis champion, and had good looks and charm to spare. But at nineteen Helen still seemed a little young for serious courtship. In a bid to cool things down, the Beckwiths had decided to take her on an eight-week tour of Europe in February. On boarding the *Cedric,* however, they had discovered that Karl Behr was a passenger as well, traveling to Europe on a business trip, or so he claimed.

Helen Newsom and Karl Behr

During the crossing the Beckwiths' attitude had softened toward Karl and he was able to spend some quiet time with Helen, something he looked forward to repeating on the crossing home.

Norris Williams was out on deck when the *Titanic* was finally sighted. Shortly before 7 p.m. her funnels were seen beyond the breakwater and the word quickly spread to the passengers in the lounge. Norris noted how majestically the great liner steamed toward them. To Edith Rosenbaum it looked like a six-story house; to Margaret Brown it was "the master palace of the sea." Mrs. Brown recalled the *Nomadic* then putting on steam and steering out into the waves of the outer harbor. She also remembered that when the *Nomadic* reached the choppy seas beyond the breakwater, some of the passengers became "actively ill."

In Edith Rosenbaum's highly colored recollection, however, the rocking of the tender was caused entirely by the wake of the huge *Titanic*, since the sea until then had been calm. As the *Nomadic* drew alongside, she described how "the tender [began] pounding against her sides with such force that I feared she would break in half." According to Edith, it took ten men to hold down the gangway "as it shook and swayed in every direction." Edith also claimed to be the last person to leave the tender since the "uncanny upheaval" of the *Titanic*'s wake had stirred her fears anew.

Yet never in her most tremulous imaginings could Edith Rosenbaum have predicted that 50 of the 172 travelers who sat with her aboard the *Nomadic* were embarking on the final voyage of their lives.

On stepping into the *Titanic*'s first-class reception room,
Edith Rosenbaum instantly felt uneasy.

THE PALM ROOM

N orris Williams would never forget his first view inside the *Titanic*, He remembered stepping into a white-paneled vestibule with a black-and-white-patterned floor that appeared at first to be solid marble, though he soon realized it wasn't. Yet he found the entrance foyer to be so imposing, and so unlike anything he had ever seen on a ship, that it gave him, in his words, "a very distinct start." Edith Rosenbaum had an even stronger reaction. On setting foot inside the *Titanic* she immediately decided that she wanted to go back to Cherbourg. She asked Nicholas Martin, the White Star agent who had come out on the tender with the passengers, about the possibility of locating her luggage. "All right, take another boat," she recalled Martin saying, "but your baggage must remain." When Edith inquired about insurance for it, he replied, "Ridiculous, this ship is unsinkable." Edith thought of the expensive gowns she was taking to New York and concluded, "My luggage is worth more to me than I am, so I better remain with it," and decided to stay.

Arriving on the *Titanic* was also unforgettable for Ella White. A wealthy widow from New York, the short, stout, and rather pug-faced Mrs. White suffered from leg trouble and had fallen and twisted her ankle on the swaying gangway. The ship's doctor was quickly summoned to the reception room, and Mrs. White was then helped by her chauffeur and maid to a C-deck cabin, where she would spend the rest of the voyage. From there, she would occasionally dispatch her younger, slimmer companion, Marie Young, to check on the two prized French roosters and two hens that they had purchased for the farm at her Westchester estate. The poultry were housed near the *Titanic*'s galleys, and several passengers would report the curious sound of roosters crowing on the ship.

Inside the richly carpeted reception room, uniformed stewards awaited to guide the Cherbourg passengers to their rooms. "At the entrance there were like 50 butlers," an Argentinian businessman noted in a letter sent the next day. The *Titanic*'s first-class reception room was actually a large, U-shaped hallway that encompassed the curved balustrades of the grand staircase landing and the entrance to the first-class dining saloon. But it was also one of the most popular public rooms on the ship, where passengers gathered before dinner and met for coffee afterward while the orchestra played. It was known as the Palm Room due to its cozy groupings of wicker chairs and tables set amid potted plants in fashionable Palm Court style. White-paneled walls with arched leaded windows and a ceiling with Jacobean-styled plasterwork helped complete the theme, as did a string and piano quintet that regularly played tunes reminiscent of a Palm Court orchestra.

On stepping into this convivial scene, the weary Cherbourg passengers may have felt like latecomers to a party. For the grieving Ryersons it must have seemed incongruous. White Star chairman J. Bruce Ismay greeted Arthur Ryerson and his family and insisted on providing them with an extra stateroom to the two they had already booked and arranging for the services of a personal steward. Ismay no doubt chose also to greet John Jacob Astor and his party upon their arrival. Astor and Ismay make an interesting pairing since they were curiously similar men. Both were tall, dark, late fortyish, and generously mustached; both were scions of prominent families and had inherited their positions in life; each is remembered as having an aloof and sometimes brusque manner, a likely cover for shyness. Did Astor pull out his gold watch to remind Ismay of the late hour of their boarding? One can imagine Ismay casually responding that the *Titanic* had been held up by another liner swinging into her path while leaving Southampton—all regrettable but quite unavoidable.

In reality, the incident in Southampton harbor earlier that day could have been rather more serious. Just after noon, as the tugs had begun to move the *Titanic* away from Ocean Dock and down the narrow channel, they approached two smaller steamers, the *Oceanic* and the *New York*, moored together farther down the pier. Due to water displacement caused by the passing of the huge new liner, the *New York*'s steel mooring cables had "snapped like thread" with "cracks like pistol shots" in the words of *Titanic* passenger Francis Browne, and her stern had swung out toward the *Titanic*. Browne, a keen photographer, had leaned over the railing of the boat deck with his camera at arm's length to capture the *New York*'s stern coming within four feet of the *Titanic*. "A voice beside me said, 'Now for a crash' and I snapped my shutter," he recalled. Browne then quickly dashed farther aft, "only to see the black hull of the *New York* slide gently past." A sudden burst of water from the *Titanic*'s port propeller following a "Full Astern!" order from the bridge had avoided the predicted crash—though only narrowly. Tugboats attached lines to the *New York* and pulled her away to moor elsewhere, but the near collision delayed the *Titanic*'s departure by an hour or more.

At luncheon afterward there had been much discussion of the recent excitement, with some passengers wondering aloud if passenger ships had just become too big, while others noted that this was an unfortunate omen for a maiden voyage. By late afternoon, however, the talk was all about the size and splendor of the new liner as passengers trooped up and down the grand staircase exploring her decks and public rooms. "You would never imagine you were on board a ship" was a much-overheard comment. That evening Frank Millet, too, became caught up in the general enthusiasm and wrote to Alfred Parsons the next morning that being on the *Titanic* was "not a bit like going to sea. You can have no idea of the spaciousness of this ship. . . . She has everything but taxicabs and theatres."

Bruce Ismay would not have delayed the Astors for long given Madeleine's weakened condition, and as they were escorted to their large and elegant suite on C deck, *Titanic* stewardess Violet Jessop managed to catch her first glimpse of Madeleine Astor. "Instead of the radiant woman of my imagination, one who had succeeded in overcoming much opposition and marrying the man she wanted," she later wrote, "I saw a quiet, pale, sad-faced, in fact, dull young woman arrive listlessly on the arm of her husband, apparently indifferent to everything about her."

Clearly, Madeleine Astor was feeling the effects of her pregnancy and a long day's journey. Violet penned an even more unflattering depiction of a wealthy American matron coming on board but discreetly used the pseudonym "Mrs. Klapton."

> My heart sank as Mrs. Cyrus Klapton, clutching her pet Pekinese, bore down towards my section followed by a downcast maid. She had invariably reduced each successive maid to submission ere she boarded the ship. Although in many ways my job was not that prestigious, I could consider myself lucky when I looked at that maid and saw what her position had done to her.

It is suspected that Violet Jessop's moneyed dragon is based on Charlotte Drake Cardeza, a Philadelphia heiress who had booked an even grander suite than the Astors and arrived on board with even more luggage. Her fourteen steamer trunks, four suitcases, and three packing crates contained seventy dresses, ten fur coats, eighty-four pairs of gloves, and thirty-two pairs of shoes as well as feather boas, parasols, ermine muffs,

Charlotte Cardeza and her son, Thomas, on board her yacht, the *Eleanor*

and ivory hair combs. In her jewel case was a diamond and Burmese ruby ring worth $14,000 ($300,000 today) as well as a seven-carat pink diamond from Tiffany's worth $20,000 ($450,000 today). Mrs. Cardeza had booked one of the two ultra-deluxe B-deck parlor suites, each of which had a sitting room with a marble fireplace and a private fifty-foot promenade deck decorated with greenery and Tudor-style woodwork. (The other deluxe parlor suite had been booked by J. P. Morgan but was now occupied by J. Bruce Ismay.) Charlotte Cardeza was on her way home to Montebello, her walled stone mansion in the fashionable Main Line town of Germantown, Pennsylvania. Yet she apparently did not mingle much in Philadelphia society. The short and stocky fifty-eight-year-old widow was happiest hunting big game and had, for a time, owned her own steam yacht, the *Eleanor*, which was large enough to take her to Africa for yearly safaris. Her son, thirty-six-year-old Thomas, who had been living in a hunting lodge in Hungary, was returning home with her for medical treatment. Charlotte may have thought that relaxing in seclusion on their private promenade deck would be good for her son's health, but Thomas would instead use it as a place to host floating poker games.

Although Charlotte Cardeza seems another likely candidate for Frank Millet's "obnoxious, ostentatious" category, she was not one of those women he observed carrying tiny dogs, despite Violet Jessop's portrayal of "Mrs. Klapton" toting a Pekingese. But Myra Harper, the wife of Henry Sleeper Harper of the New York publishing family, did carry a Pekingese, topically named Sun Yat-sen, for the new president of China. Another lapdog called Frou Frou was carried by newlywed Helen Bishop, aged nineteen, who was returning to Dowagiac, Michigan, after a four-month honeymoon trip with her husband, Dickinson Bishop, who was twenty-five. And a Pomeranian belonging to Elizabeth Rothschild, and her husband, Martin, a New York clothing manufacturer, could also have caught Frank Millet's eye as he waited on the tender.

Though Millet admired the *Titanic*'s spacious staterooms, the small inner cabin that he had booked down on E deck was not one of them. Frank was a frugal Yankee who, as a rule, did not like to spend much money on shipboard accommodations. Yet with empty first-class staterooms available, a number of passengers managed to trade up to better rooms and Frank may have been among them. Norris Williams and his father were quite content with their two-berth cabin and found it to be larger than they had expected. Norris immediately began describing it in a quickly jotted letter to his mother that he sent back on the tender to Cherbourg. "Of course there is room after room—smoking-reading-lounge-palm room," he noted, "you can imagine that there are many other rooms but as we have only been on board about 10 minutes . . . we have not been able to see everything."

Edith Rosenbaum was impressed by her luxurious stateroom on A deck and pleased that she could store some luggage in an empty cabin opposite. On her way down to dinner she couldn't help being impressed by the size and luxury of the *Titanic*'s public rooms that to her seemed larger than those in most Parisian grand hotels. Yet in a letter sent to her secretary the next morning, she complained, "It is a monster, and I can't say I like it, as I feel as though I were in a big hotel, instead of on a cozy ship." In signing off, she wrote, "I cannot get over my feeling of depression and premonition of trouble. How I wish it were over!"

Margaret Brown was still feeling chilled from her long wait on the tender and decided to forgo a lavish dinner in the dining saloon for the warmth of her cabin's electric heater and the cozy coverlet on her brass bed. Many of the Southampton-boarded passengers had already been at table in the dining saloon when the Cherbourg tenders arrived, as photographer Francis Browne recalled:

> As we sat down to dinner—we were eight at our table—we could see the newly arrived passengers passing in the lobby [reception room] outside and hear the busy hum of work as the luggage and mails were brought on board. But soon it all quietened down and after a time someone remarked, "I wonder have we started yet." We all stopped for a moment and listened, but noticing no vibration or noise the answer came, "No we can't have started yet." But the waiting steward leant over and said, "We have been outside the breakwater for more than ten minutes, Sir." So gentle was the motion of the ship that none could notice its movement (and there was no drink on the table stronger than Apollinaris!)

Francis Browne was in his second year of theological studies in Dublin, preparing for his ordination as a Jesuit priest. He had been given this trip, his first on an ocean liner, as a treat by his uncle, the bishop of Cloyne, whose cathedral was in Queenstown (now Cobh) in Ireland, which would be the *Titanic*'s next stop. Browne was traveling to Queens-town with the Odells, an English Catholic family known to his uncle, who were taking a motoring holiday in Ireland. Luckily for posterity, Browne had remembered to bring along his camera, another gift from Bishop Browne. Photographs actually taken on board the *Titanic* are few and those from the "Father Browne Album" comprise the largest and most significant part of them.

Browne had begun snapping pictures that morning at London's Waterloo Station before the 9:45 departure of the Boat Train. When it arrived in Southampton, Browne took a sweeping shot from the gangway of the port side of the *Titanic* towering above Ocean Dock. After documenting the near collision with the *New York*, he ate a hurried lunch in the dining saloon since he wanted to be up on deck when they sailed past the Isle of Wight. As he was photographing one of the four round stone forts that stand in the waters of the Solent off Portsmouth, an American passenger bore down on him. In a loud, penetrating voice that, in

Francis Browne photographed author Jacques Futrelle standing beside the gymnasium on the boat deck.

Browne's words, "had not learned its intonation on this side of 'the Herring Pond,' " the American asked, "Could you tell me, Sir, why is the channel so narrow here?"

"I suppose when they built those forts they never calculated on having ships as big as the *Titanic*," Browne replied.

"Oh, I did not mean that. Why is the land so near here?"

With wry Irish wit, Browne responded, "Well, I suppose that they could not shift the Isle of Wight back any further than it is."

Undaunted, the American went on to question him about the distance between Dover and Calais and to ask "Why don't you English cross here?" At this, Browne recalled "a ghost of a geography class" and replied, "Oh, that's not France, that's the Isle of Wight."

"I see. I thought it was France," the American replied and moved off.

Inquisitiveness would have been in character for this large, rumpled American with the Georgia drawl. His name was Jacques Heath Futrelle, and he was the author of a series of mystery novels that had earned him the nickname "the American Conan Doyle." His popular Thinking Machine stories, which featured the brilliant amateur sleuth Professor S. F. X. Van Dusen, had first been serialized in Hearst's *Boston American*, where Futrelle was a staff writer. The public's enthusiasm for the character allowed him to quit journalism and concentrate on writing mystery novels. With his royalties he was able to acquire a large house called "Stepping Stones" on the harbor in Scituate, Massachusetts, for his wife, Lily May, also a writer, and their two children. If Futrelle's faculties were less than keen during his exchange with Francis Browne that afternoon, it was perhaps because he and his wife had not slept the night before. A party with friends in London to celebrate his thirty-seventh birthday had lasted until 3 a.m., and instead of going to bed, the Futrelles had decided to simply pack up and make an early start for Southampton.

Francis Browne soon spied Futrelle again up on the boat deck and took a photograph of him standing outside the arched windows of the ship's gymnasium. Browne then stepped inside the gym and snapped the white-clad instructor happily posed on a rowing machine. He then went down to A deck and took a photograph beneath the ship's bridge that shows Frank Millet's friend, Archie Butt, standing in the distance in

Browne also snapped Archie Butt on the forward end of A deck chatting (at right) with two other men. The boy on the right is eleven-year-old Jack Odell.

conversation with two men. Archie is wearing a black military overcoat over his U.S. Army major's uniform. Sailing day on a maiden voyage was clearly an occasion that warranted his being in uniform. He had worn civilian clothes for his departure with Millet on the *Berlin* five weeks before, which had prompted a *New York Times* article headlined MAJOR BUTT'S SUIT A WONDER. The reporter described Archie as boarding the ship "in a suit of clothes that won the admiration of every passenger on the deck of the liner...."

His cambric handkerchief was tucked up his left sleeve.... He wore a bright copper-colored Norfolk jacket fastened by big ball-shaped buttons of red porcelain, a lavender tie, tall baywing collar, trousers of the same material as the coat, a derby hat with broad, flat brim, and patent leather shoes with white tops. The Major had a bunch of lilies in his buttonhole, and appeared to be delighted at the prospect of going away. He said that he had lost twenty pounds in weight following the President in his strenuous tour through the West.

When asked if it were true that he was engaged to Miss Dorothy Williams of Washington, Major Butt replied sadly: "I wish it were. This bachelorhood is a miserable existence. I have distress signals flying at the fore, and will refuse no reasonable offer to enter the matrimonial field. I'll do the best I can, and if this leap year gets away before I get a wife I shall feel very much discouraged."

The gallant Major did not wear an overcoat, and he winced once or twice when he was posing on the windswept deck for the photographers.

Archie was well known as a dandy—seven trunks had accompanied him to Europe just to carry his wardrobe. But the description of a lavender tie and lilies in the buttonhole suggests a flamboyance bordering on effeminacy. Archie was a good-humored man who enjoyed joking with reporters and feeding them tidbits of White House news—as a former journalist himself, he knew how to please the press. And the fact that reporters from several newspapers were on hand for his departure is an indication of just how well known a Washington figure Archie had become. But he would not have been amused by the *Times* article and one can imagine him venting his pique about it with the same sardonic wit he so often employed in the letters he wrote almost daily to his sister-in-law Clara.

Archie intended his letters to Clara to be compiled and published as a journal of his White House years. They were written quickly, often at the end of very long days, but with considerable flair. "I never reread or correct my letters," he claimed to Clara. "I have decided to postpone that until my old age, if I have one." In their spontaneous form Archie's letters provide a remarkably intimate picture of both the White House and the Washington social scene during the Theodore Roosevelt and Taft administrations. Archie knew his letters would be of interest to historians, and before leaving for Europe, he carefully instructed Clara that "in case of accident of any kind," she was not to edit out any names, "for letters if they have any historic value must be printed as written."

Archie had joined the U.S. Army at the outbreak of the Spanish-American War and had been a highly efficient quartermaster during tours of duty in the Philippines and Cuba. This, coupled with his impeccable manners and creamy Southern charm, had made the forty-two-year-old captain a perfect choice for presidential military aide. The position was primarily a ceremonial one—providing some uniformed pomp for ambassadorial receptions and the like—showing some gold lace, as Archie termed it, though he would parlay the job into something much more. His White House posting began on April 8, 1908, and it wasn't long before Archie had endeared himself to President Theodore Roosevelt, joining him for vigorous games of tennis and on horseback jaunts in Rock Creek Park. The president soon put Archie in charge of the White House stables, including the care of his own horses. The two men also bonded over their shared Southern heritage—Roosevelt's mother had been from Georgia—and soon the ebullient Teddy would be styling Archie and himself as "two old Southern gentlemen" as they swigged mint juleps in their tennis clothes and made jibes about New England Yankees.

First Lady Edith Roosevelt, too, found Archie to be an amiable addition to the White House staff and a suitable escort to take her to the theater or social functions when the president was engaged. In late July she invited him to join the family for a few days at Sagamore Hill, their summer retreat on Oyster Bay, Long Island, and it was here that Archie was virtually assumed into the Roosevelt family. In four letters to his mother, Archie describes balmy days at the "summer White House" with "endless tennis and swimming and boating and riding . . . and I am keen for it."

Archie's high spirits made him popular with the six Roosevelt children, and he describes one family swim after tennis where "everyone joined in the water fight and sides were chosen to see who could clear the float [swim raft]." When Archie climbed out of the water, his leg was bleeding from scratches inflicted by the barnacles under the raft. The president asked Archie how this had happened and he jokingly replied that another guest, a wealthy young New Englander from the State Department named William "Billy" Phillips, was responsible. Roosevelt hooted loudly and later announced to a group of visitors that "Phillips had worn his spurs in the water and that I [Archie] had said that if Phillips was a gentleman he would cut his nails." Archie went on to describe how Phillips, who was "the most ultra-type of a cultured Bostonian, could see no humor in the remark at all."

Billy Phillips and his "water spurs" became a running gag that continued even after their return to the White House. That October, Archie decided to repay his hostess by inviting her and her daughter Ethel to a lunch at his home. As soon as Theodore Roosevelt got wind of this, he invited himself along—instantly making it an occasion of greater import since the president rarely dined outside the White House. Despite his claim that bachelorhood was "a miserable existence," Archie actually managed the domestic details of his life with considerable aplomb. He kept a well-furnished home staffed by a cook and Filipino houseboys, with rooms that he rented to other bachelors. Archie describes the planning of the presidential luncheon in loving detail to his mother—from the table setting (place mats rather than a tablecloth) to the planning of the Southern-style menu and the selection of the other guests. One of these would be the ultra-refined New Englander from the Sagamore Hill visit, Billy Phillips. During the soup course, Archie (with the president's encouragement) had arranged for Phillips to be served a bowl of water in which were placed a pair of spurs with a scroll attached. Phillips gamely unrolled the scroll, which announced:

GEORGIA recognizes New England's right to set a new fashion in warfare, and in token of such recognition Mr. William Phillips of Massachusetts is hereby created KNIGHT of the WATER SPURS by direction of the President with the consent and advice of his Aides.

The stunt was a huge success, as was the entire luncheon, and the presidential couple lingered to admire Archie's Spanish furniture and the collection of Chinese fans he had acquired during his time in the Philippines. Archie's description of this happy occasion, however, would comprise one of the last letters he sent to his mother, who would die only days later. Archie was devastated, for he was the most devoted of sons. His mother, widowed when he was twelve, had taken a library job at the University of the South in Sewanee, Tennessee, to help pay college fees for Archie and his younger brother, Lewis. She had died in England while visiting his older brother, Edward, and this distance made it even harder for Archie. He eventually hand-carried her ashes by train to Augusta, Georgia, for burial in the family plot. Later he would write to Clara that "each day I seem to miss Mother the more and the awful fact that I will not see her again almost paralyzes my brain."

The Roosevelts were extremely kind to Archie in his grief and the first lady arranged a cruise down the Potomac on the presidential yacht for his first day back. The president and his family, however, were soon packing up to leave the White House following the November election of William Howard Taft, Roosevelt's anointed successor. Butt had met Taft when he was governor of the Philippines, and it didn't take long after the inauguration for Archie to be embraced by the new first family. "The big man," as Archie called Taft, would come to regard his military aide "as if he were a son or brother." Taft was a keen horseman and golfer, despite his three-hundred-pound girth, and Archie joined him in these pursuits and on his daily walks. He also accompanied the president, his wife, Helen "Nellie" Taft, and their teenaged daughter, Helen, when they sailed on the presidential yacht *Mayflower* and during visits to their summer home in Beverly, Massachusetts. One White House staffer nicknamed Archie "The Beloved," and Taft came to rely on "The Beloved" even more after Nellie Taft suffered a stroke in May of 1909 and was unable to shoulder many of the first lady's duties for some months afterward.

In 1911 Archie used his closeness to Taft to try to mend the rift that had developed between the new president and his predecessor. Right after Taft's inauguration in March of '09, Roosevelt and his son Kermit had departed for an African hunting expedition, and the former president did not return to America until June of 1910. In the midterm elections that November, the Democrats seized control of both the House and the Senate, which raised serious doubts about Taft's ability to carry the

White House for the Republicans in 1912. Taft soon became convinced that Roosevelt would challenge him for the nomination. The tireless Teddy was not a man for the sidelines and couldn't stifle his disappointment at Taft's timid continuance of his progressivist policies. Archie paid a peacemaking visit to Sagamore Hill on January 28, 1912, and afterward wrote to Clara that he didn't think that Roosevelt would run. But only weeks later Roosevelt announced, "My hat is in the ring."

It is often written that the strain of trying to preserve his allegiances to both men pushed Archie to the brink of a nervous breakdown in early 1912. His letters, however, reveal that the reason for his low mood was a physical ailment brought on by stress and overwork. Archie had been at Taft's side during a grueling precampaign swing through twenty-eight states in the fall of 1911. According to his own tally they were on the road for fifty-eight days and had made 220 stops, with 380 speeches by Taft, who had been seen by "3,213,600 ear-splitting citizens." (Archie was particularly incensed by "saucy little brats" who yelled out "Hello Fatty" to the president.) As he declared to Clara, "Do you wonder that our nerves have been disintegrated and that our innards are all upside down?" Archie's innards were actually in serious trouble from "auto-intoxication," a stress-induced illness that left him unable to digest food properly and caused ever-increasing levels of toxins to be released into his bloodstream. It was this illness that had caused the weight loss of twenty pounds that he had mentioned to the *New York Times* reporter, and it prompted friends to comment on how gaunt and ill he looked.

On February 23, 1912, Archie wrote to Clara of his decision to go to Rome for a little holiday with Frank Millet. "I hate to leave the Big White Chief just at this time, though . . . if I am to go through this frightful summer I must have a rest now." Loyal soldier that he was, Archie had decided to stick with Taft through the fall election. "My devotion to the Colonel [Roosevelt] is as strong as it was the day he left, but this man [Taft] has been too fond of me for the past three years to be thrown over at this time."

In an oft-quoted sentence from this same letter Archie tells Clara, "Don't forget that all my papers are in the storage warehouse and that if the old ship goes down you will find my affairs in shipshape condition."

Major Butt (top, at left) was constantly at Taft's side during official appearances. Following his illness, a thinner Archie (above, at right) accompanies the president on one of his daily walks.

Though this is often cited as a *Titanic* premonition, Archie then adds, "As I always write you in this way, whenever I go anywhere, you will not be bothered by presentiments now." Archie's time in Rome would prove to be restorative but his low and fatalistic moods continued to reappear. While staying with his cousin Rebie Rosenkranz in London before sailing, he had seemed to her husband to be "in a depressed and sad state of mind . . . nerves he called it." On his last full day in England he had suggested a visit to Westminster Abbey, saying, "If I do not see it now I shall never see it." Yet Archie was not fatalistic about the *Titanic*, which he had heard was unsinkable, and in Father Browne's photograph of him he is caught chatting amiably on A deck. So there is every reason to believe that at dinner on April 10, 1912, his customary affable nature was on display.

As an experienced transatlantic traveler, Archie knew to head for the dining saloon shortly after boarding to reserve a good table for the voyage, in this case for himself, Frank Millet, and his Washington friend, Clarence Moore. As the three men sat at table that evening, the conversation likely recapped Archie's audiences with the pope and the king of Italy as well as his subsequent trip to England to see his older brother, Edward, a cotton trader who lived in Chester, near Liverpool. There was undoubtedly some talk of horses and dogs since Clarence Moore was a noted sportsman and former master of hounds at the exclusive Chevy Chase Hunt Club. He had just been scouring the north of England in search of a pack of good hounds and had purchased fifty pairs for the newly formed Rock Creek Hunt Club. Archie, too, was an ardent dog lover and the owner of some pointers that he kept kenneled with Moore's dogs back in Washington.

Clarence Moore was a Washington banker and broker whose wisest investment had been to marry Mabelle Swift, the heiress to a Chicago meat-packing fortune. This helped him to acquire a substantial Beaux Arts mansion on the most fashionable stretch of Massachusetts Avenue and a gaily awninged seaside home called "Swiftmore" near the Taft summer White House at Beverly, Massachusetts. Moore had occasionally joined Archie for rounds of golf with "the big White Chief" at the Beverly country club.

Given Frank Millet's delayed arrival, Archie and Clarence Moore likely chose to dine with him later in the dining saloon, perhaps in one of the room's alcoves where backlit leaded-glass windows added to the atmosphere. "It was hard to realize," another passenger later wrote, "that one was not in some large and sumptuous hotel." The menu, too, was large and sumptuous, reflecting the Edwardian fashion for elaborate multi-coursed meals—from hors d'oeuvres, soup, fish, fowl, and meat to a savory, a salad, and a selection of puddings and sweets. Archie's doctor had prescribed a very restricted diet for him but as a lover of fine food he may have been tempted into "doing exactly as the doctors forbade" in the *Titanic*'s dining saloon.

Archie was an opera lover as well and no doubt recognized the tunes from *Cavalleria Rusticana* and *Tales of Hoffmann* wafting in from the musicians in the Palm Room. Millet, Moore, and Butt may have taken coffee there before repairing to the smoking room on A deck, their regular haunt throughout the voyage. The "smoke room," as it was often called, was a popular place for masculine conversation and cards. Designed to emulate a Pall Mall men's club, it featured mahogany paneling with mother-of-pearl inlay and hand-painted stained glass windows. Dark leather chairs were grouped around green-baized tables where card games were usually in progress. Above the glowing coal-burning fireplace, the only real one on board, was a painting by the maritime artist Norman Wilkinson of ships entering Plymouth harbor. Frank Millet likely gave it a close appraisal since a few years before he had painted a similar scene on the ceiling of Baltimore's Customs House.

After a smoke and a hand of cards, Butt, Millet, and Moore probably called it a night. It had been a long day, after all. As they walked to their cabins, there was barely a movement as the ship made its steady course along the Channel's southern reaches. Up in the crow's nest on the foremast, lookouts Frederick Fleet and Reginald Lee could see the lights of the French coast in the distance and the mast lights of other ships. For a closer look, binoculars would have helped, but the pair they had used in the crow's nest on the trip from Belfast to Southampton had gone missing. This had been reported to Second Officer Charles Lightoller, but he had said there wasn't a replacement set available. No one seemed bothered about it, so the lookouts weren't worried either. Binoculars were not standard equipment in the crow's nest on many ships. And these things just seemed to happen on a maiden voyage.

On board R·M·S·"TITANIC."

April 11   1912

Dear Alfred:— I got yours
this morning and was glad
to hear from you. I thought
I told you my ship was the Titanic.
She has everything but taxicabs
and theatres. Table d'hôte, restaurant
à la carte, gymnasium, turkish
bath, squash court, palm gardens,
smoking rooms for "ladies & gents," intended I fancy to keep the women
out of the mens smoking room which
they infest on the German and
French steamers. The fittings are
in the order of Waddon hall and
are exceedingly agreeable in design
and color. As for the games they

The first page of Frank Millet's letter to Alfred Parsons. (For full text, see page 307.)

"QUEER LOT OF PEOPLE"

Early the next morning, Frank Millet took out a sheet of cream White Star notepaper with the line's red pennant and "On Board R.M.S. 'Titanic'" printed at its top and began penning a letter to his old friend Alfred Parsons. After extolling the comforts of the *Titanic*, Millet described his own accommodations:

> I have the best room I have ever had in a ship and it isn't one of the best either, a great long corridor in which to hang my clothes and a square window as big as the one in the [Russell House] studio alongside the large light. No end of furniture, cupboards, wardrobe, dressing table, couch, etc., etc.

This description bears no resemblance to cabin E-38, the small, inner room listed as being Millet's on the passenger list. It is, however, an accurate depiction of Archie Butt's stateroom, B-38. Archie had paid the same £26 fare as Frank but the White House had pulled strings to have him upgraded to a bigger stateroom. It's possible that Archie had managed to have his friend transferred to a larger cabin as well, although Millet would not have wanted to pay much extra for it. It's also possible that Frank may have simply chosen to keep his small cabin for sleeping and use Archie's larger stateroom during the day for reading and writing. The two men had reportedly shared a cabin on the *Berlin* on the way over in March and had also been housemates in Washington. One of their friends described their closeness as being like that of Damon and Pythias; another noted that "the two men had a sympathy of mind which was most unusual." Expressions such as these have led to speculation as to whether a more intimate relationship existed between Frank and Archie.

Of the two men, Archie Butt, the witty, dandified bachelor with an intense devotion to his mother, seems a more likely gay man than Frank Millet, the decorated war correspondent and married father of three. But it is only from Millet that we have tangible proof of same-sex affections.

Frank Millet, circa 1874

A cache of his love letters to a San Francisco poet and writer named Charles Warren Stoddard have, quite remarkably, survived. They date from 1874, when Millet, then twenty-eight, was enjoying the Bohemian life on the Continent after completing his art studies at the Royal Academy in Antwerp. He had come to Venice that fall to paint and study the Italian masters, particularly Titian. "Charlie" Stoddard, thirty-one, was similarly smitten with wanderlust. During his twenties he had made four voyages to Hawaii and other Pacific islands, and his published account of these journeys, *South Sea Idyls*, contains descriptions of encounters with native men that, to the knowing reader, are unmistakably homoerotic.

In the autumn of 1874, Stoddard was supporting himself in Europe by writing travel pieces for the *San Francisco Chronicle*. One night at the opera in Venice, a young man quietly joined him in his box at intermission. "We looked at each other," Stoddard wrote, "and were acquainted in a minute." The young man was Frank Millet. He soon asked Stoddard what he was doing for the winter and then suggested they share living quarters. Stoddard accepted the offer and remembered that they became "almost immediately very much better acquainted."

It's possible that Millet had already met Stoddard a few months earlier in Rome through Mark Twain, for whom Stoddard had been a kind of secretary and drinking companion. Frank also needed someone to share the rent for "Casa Bunce," an eight-room house overlooking the Grand Canal that he had inherited when another artist had decamped for Rome. But Charlie Stoddard would be more than just a room-mate to Frank—he became the first, and perhaps greatest, love of Millet's life, and their Vene-tian idyll would be fixed forever

Charles Warren Stoddard

in his memory. During the daytime hours, Frank labored diligently on his art, sometimes making copies of works in churches or galleries, or sketching in Piazza San Marco. Charlie smoked, napped, and worked in a dilatory way on his articles for the *Chronicle*. In the evening they might take a gondola ride with Giovanni, their gondolier, cook, and errand boy. In his *Chronicle* pieces, Stoddard would switch genders when writing of "spoons" with " my fair" in a gondola, " . . . but that is between us two."

In late January of 1875, the pair left Venice for a three-week tour of northern Italy. In Padua, Frank was entranced by the Giotto frescoes in the Scrovegni Chapel, and Stoddard, a Catholic convert, was equally awed by the Basilica of St. Anthony and gave Frank a medallion of the patron saint of lost things. They then moved on to Florence, where they paid an after-hours visit to Michelangelo's *David*. After bribing the custo-dian to open a wooden shed behind the Accademia where the statue was being kept, the two men climbed some wooden scaffolding to a platform surrounding the figure's waist. Frank ran his fingers down the swollen veins of the right arm and encouraged Charlie to do the same. He later described wanting to hug the marble image because it seemed as warm as flesh. Frank had seen the *David* in Florence the year before and had fantasized about touching it with Charlie, perhaps imagining the two of them communing with an artist from an earlier time who shared their affinity for the beauty of men.

They then moved on to Siena, where, according to Stoddard, the two lovers slept in "a great double bed . . . so white and plump it looked quite like a gigantic frosted cake—and we were happy." Not long after their return to Venice, however, the happiness began to pale, at least for Charlie. Money was scarce, and Casa Bunce was drafty and hard to heat, causing Frank to come down with rheumatism. Into this scene out of *La Bohème* there suddenly floated a tall, handsome figure in a long, black cloak of "Byronic mold" wearing a large hat with tassels. Charlie dubbed him "Monte Cristo," but he was, in reality, an American artist named A. A. Anderson, who had independent means and a taste for the high life abroad. An entranced Charlie spent days in Anderson's gondola "reading chatting, writing, dreaming or merely drifting. . . ." In his suite at the Hotel Danieli Anderson hosted a dinner that to Charlie was "the realization of a sybarite's dream." The exotic American would soon leave abruptly for Egypt, and a disappointed Charlie would find life at Casa Bunce to be rather drab in the aftermath. By May, Millet's "butterfly," as he dubbed Stoddard, had flown, leaving for Chester, England, and a man he had trysted with a year before.

Millet was utterly bereft and poured out his love and longing for Charlie in letters that only caused his "butterfly" to flutter farther away. "Miss you? Bet your life," he wrote. "Put yourself in my place. It isn't the one who goes away who misses, it is he who stays. Empty chair, empty bed, empty house." Over the door of Casa Bunce he erected a sign, UBI BOHEMIA FUIT? (WHERE HAS BOHEMIA GONE?) and in his letters to Charlie continually proposed scenarios where they could re-create "our little Bohemia." It is rare to find such unabashed male passion freely expressed in nineteenth-century correspondence, and it's clear from Millet's letters that in the world of European Bohemia that he had embraced so completely, the strictures of his Massachusetts Puritan heritage held little sway.

When his strained finances forced a return home to East Bridgewater in the fall of 1875, Frank's letters to Charlie took on a near-obsessive tone as he longed for Europe and Charlie and despaired at the provincialism surrounding him. But it would not be until January of 1877 that his finances permitted him to return to the Old World. Traveling with him to France were the two sisters of his Harvard friend Royal Merrill, along with their mother and a younger brother. While a student, Frank had lived with the Merrill family for a year in Cambridge. In Paris, he would share living quarters with them in Montmartre, though even there his longing for Stoddard continued unabated.

"Come Charlie, come!" he wrote in the spring of '77. "My bed is very narrow but you can manage to occupy it, I hope." This invitation was made despite the two Merrill sisters living only one floor below. Stoddard would finally visit at the end of April just as Millet was departing for Bucharest to cover the Russo-Turkish conflict for the *New York Herald.* From Bulgaria, Frank would attempt to stir some jealousy in Stoddard by writing that he was "spooning frightfully with a young Greek here."

Millet would not return to Paris until mid-April of the following year, arriving sunburned, war-weary, and bearing two crimson military decorations from the Russian czar. The Merrills had eagerly awaited the arrival of "our hero," and by the end of 1878, Frank proclaimed himself to be in love with Elizabeth "Lily" Merrill, the elder of the two sisters. His affection for Lily seems to have been heartfelt, but he would prove to be an often-absent husband and an indifferent father. There would never be other women, however, and there are clues in Millet's short stories and letters to indicate that his sexual attraction to men was more than just a youthful, Bohemian phase.

"Misogynist" was a name often applied to gay men a century ago, and there was certainly a strong streak of misogyny in Millet. He opposed female artists exhibiting at the Chicago Exposition, and even his last letter to Parsons from the *Titanic* is heavily larded with female disparagement. In addition to railing about "obnoxious, ostentatious American women" and proclaiming the young American woman to be "a buster," he notes that the ship has "smoking rooms for Ladies and Gents, intended I fancy, to keep the women out of the men's smoking room which they *infest* in the German and French steamers" [italics mine]. He concludes by calling Olga Mead, the Hungarian wife of architect William Mead, " a B——" [Bitch]. All in all, this reveals more misogyny than can be ascribed to the garden-variety male chauvinism of the period.

Earlier in this rather revealing letter, Millet begins his commentary on the other passengers with a few lines that have always intrigued *Titanic* researchers:

> Queer lot of people on this ship. Looking over the [paasenger] list, I only find three or four people I know but there are good many of "our people" I think. . . .

Although "queer" was already a pejorative term for homosexuality by 1912, Millet was most likely not using it in that context. But who are the "our people" he so enigmatically sets off in inverted commas? If he simply means "our *kind* of people," why did he not say so? And from his condescending references to the American passengers, it seems clear that Millet thinks most of those on board are *not* his kind of people, nor would they be for a refined Englishman like Alfred Parsons.

Parsons was a key member of the "little Bohemia" that had first formed around the Millet household in Broadway during the summer of 1885. In 1900 Millet had sold to Parsons five acres of his Russell House property, on which he built his own house and garden. First known as an illustrator and painter of English pastoral scenes, Parsons later gained a reputation as a garden designer. He assisted Lawrence Johnston in the creation of Hidcote, today one of England's most-visited gardens, and designed the grounds for Henry James's Lamb House in Rye. Like James, Parsons never married and was considered to be a "confirmed bachelor."

Could Millet therefore mean "our people" to be gay people? Parsons was a very close friend of Millet's, and it is not impossible that he could be alluding to their shared affinities. It would be decades before anything like a gay identity would emerge in England or America, but from the writings of E. M. Forster, Edward Carpenter, Hugh Walpole, and others, we know that Edwardian gay men did manage to find one another. Can it be merely coincidence that a good number of the artists and writers drawn to Millet's Broadway Bohemian "colony"—Henry James,

John Singer Sargent, Alfred Parsons, Edwin Austin Abbey, and Edmund Gosse—are believed to have had same-sex affections?

If indeed Millet noted other gay men among the travelers on the *Titanic*, who might they have been? One passenger often thought to be gay was a good-looking, thirty-five-year-old rubber merchant from Liverpool named Joseph Fynney. He was active in youth work at his local church, and the late-night visits of adolescent boys to his home raised the suspicions of neighbors that he was "a Nancy boy." Fynney visited his widowed mother in Montreal yearly and usually brought along a teenaged boy for the trip. This time his companion was a dark-haired, sixteen-year-old barrel maker's apprentice named Alfred Gaskell. Both Fynney and Gaskell, however, were traveling in second class and so would not likely have been seen by Millet during the brief time he had been on the ship.

During the long wait on the tender, however, Frank Millet would probably have noticed a handsome Egyptian manservant who was traveling with Henry and Myra Harper (and their Pekingese). Millet may have been acquainted with Henry Harper, since he was a good friend of his more dynamic cousin, Harry Harper, and had done work for the family's magazines in New York City. Henry Sleeper Harper would later write that the Egyptian manservant was "an old dragoman [guide] of mine who had come with me from Alexandria because he wanted 'to see the country all the crazy Americans came from.' " But Hammad Hassab was actually a young, unmarried dragoman of striking good looks, and despite the fashion for having exotic servants, his presence with the Harpers had a whiff of impropriety to it.

A trio of Canadian bachelors who were known as "the Three Musketeers" could also possibly have drawn Millet's attention, although he would have spotted only two of them, Thomson Beattie and Thomas McCaffry, since their traveling companion, John Hugo Ross, was ill and confined to his cabin. Ross and Beattie were both successful real estate agents in Winnipeg, Manitoba, then a boomtown with Canada's largest per capita population of millionaires. To escape the fierce prairie winters, Beattie and his close friend McCaffry, a Vancouver banker, were in the habit of boarding liners for destinations like North Africa or the Aegean.

This year, they had been joined by Ross, another dapper, witty bachelor, and the three men had departed from New York in January bound for Trieste and a three-month tour of Italy, Egypt, France, and England. After two months of travel, Ross had fallen ill with dysentery in Egypt and his travel-weary companions had become anxious to get home. Beattie had written from Paris to his mother in Fergus, Ontario: "We are changing ships and coming home in a new, unsinkable boat." The usually energetic Ross was so frail he had to be carried aboard the *Titanic* in Southampton and spent the rest of the voyage in his cabin. Beattie and McCaffry, whom the *Winnipeg Free Press* would describe as "almost inseparable," shared cabin C-6, a room with a large window that looked out on the forward well deck.

Though bachelorhood, it must be noted, is not necessarily an indicator of homosexuality, it took considerable resilience to remain single in an era when marriage bestowed manhood. For lesbians the social pressure was less intense since "maiden ladies" living together drew little scrutiny. In America, these alliances between women were sometimes known as "Boston marriages," a term coined from Henry James's 1886 novel *The Bostonians*, which described two "new women" living together in a marriage-like relationship. If Frank had observed the portly and mannish Ella White gesturing with her walking stick to her soft-spoken younger companion, Marie Young, on the *Nomadic*, he may have suspected that the two women had such a relationship. Some "Boston marriages" were platonic, however, and it is not known if there was a sexual component to Ella White's relationship with Marie Young. But the two women lived and traveled together for thirty years, and when Ella White died in 1942, the bulk of her estate was left to Marie Young.

We also cannot know whether Frank's closeness to Archie Butt ever extended beyond the bounds of mere friendship. Archie was far too careful to ever pen anything as indiscreet as Millet's correspondence with Stoddard. Yet within Archie's letters there are enough clues to picture him as a Ragtime-era gay man hiding in plain sight. Archie had the same gift for observation and waspish wit found in gay diarists from Horace Walpole and Henry "Chips" Channon to Cecil Beaton and Andy Warhol. He also had a remarkable eye for the details of women's clothes and jewelry and could, for example, describe from memory a selection of First Lady Edith Roosevelt's gowns and include such details as "black velvet with *passementerie* down the front."

Archie also remarks often on the "pulchritude of the male element" he sees at social gatherings, employing expressions like "as handsome as a young Greek athlete." And although Archie was often named as one of Washington's most eligible bachelors, he was unable to sustain a relationship with any woman other than his mother. To modern eyes, Archie's attachment to Pamela Boggs Butt seems extreme. During his three-year posting in the Philippines, he had pined so much for her that he had arranged to bring her halfway across the world—into a war zone—for an extended visit. Pamela then lived with him when he returned to Washington as depot quartermaster and joined him in Cuba when he was posted there in 1905. Even years after her death Archie thought of his mother daily, surrounded by photographs and mementoes of her.

On the first day of May 1911, Archie wrote that a certain woman "has been camping on my trail for many months now" but then notes that he will not marry her because he is sure he could not love her and "I don't think that my mother would have liked her at all." He then describes the only two women he ever really loved. The first was a girl who had been fond of him when he was in his early twenties but her "cat of a mother" was determined that she should marry a rich man. The second was Mathilde Townsend, the now-married daughter of one of Washington's leading hostesses, who, as he notes, "never really cared for me, not in the way of love." Yet when Mathilde had told Archie in early April of 1910 that she was engaged to someone else, he wrote to Clara that it was "a terrific blow to me . . . and [I] woke this morning as if someone had died in the night."

Archie's distress over losing Mathilde seems a trifle overdramatized given that she had done nothing to encourage his interest. After sitting out a ball with her several weeks before, Archie had recorded that "it was the same old story at the end. An evening wasted in beating my hands against an iceberg." Mathilde, aged twenty-four, had clearly found it awkward that dear old Archie (he was twenty years her senior) was suddenly trying to woo her. Archie also knew that Mathilde's redoubtable mother, Mary Scott Townsend, widow to a railroad baron, had set her eye on "a coronet" [a British dukedom] for her daughter, and that an army quartermaster, his current lofty post notwithstanding, was not in the running. He sympathized with Mathilde's resistance to becoming yet another "dollar princess"—yet his own social ambition is evident when he writes: "I shall not mention her again, save only as one who has passed out of my life into that world of New York and Newport *into which I have peeped but will never enjoy*" [italics mine].

He does mention Mathilde again, however, since on May 26, 1910, he attended her wedding at the vast Townsend mansion on Massachusetts Avenue to see the lovely bride pass down an aisle of lilies in a white satin Worth gown with a three-yard train. By December, Archie is reporting that he had recently had "such fun doing the shops" with Mathilde, now Mrs. Peter Gerry, followed by lunch at the Plaza. Men who are fun to go shopping with are rarely the marrying kind, yet if Archie was indeed homosexual he was likely not effeminate, since no one with any less-than-manly traits could have succeeded in the testosterone-fueled atmosphere that surrounded Theodore Roosevelt. Archie had kept up with Roosevelt in all his physical stunts, from rock climbing and fording icy streams in Rock Cliff Park to making a strenuous one-day, ninety-eight-mile gallop to Warrenton, Virginia, and back through sleet and snow. Roosevelt was quite sensitive regarding effeminacy—he had been dubbed "Oscar Wilde" as a young New York State assemblyman after wearing a purple suit and delivering a speech in a high-pitched voice. As president, he would never allow himself to be photographed in tennis whites—even though his inner circle was dubbed his "tennis cabinet"—preferring to release pictures in which he was posed in buckskin or on horseback.

At the end of March 1910, just before Archie received the news of Mathilde's engagement, he wrote that Frank Millet had taken up residence at his home and that "he is such a good housekeeper that I think I will turn the housekeeping over to him." Frank gave English lessons to the Filipino houseboys before breakfast and, in Archie's absence, wallpapered the second floor with rose-patterned paper that Archie claimed made him feel like Heliogabalus, the Roman emperor who smothered his guests in roses. Despite these hints of domesticity, there is no evidence that the relationship extended beyond companionship. A young naval lieutenant who roomed for a time with the two men would only remember their unusual sympathy of mind and that "on the older man [i.e., Millet] Major Butt leaned for advice and took it."

AS MILLET WAS writing about the "queer lot of people" on the *Titanic*, the man who had spurred an act of Parliament that outlawed homosexuality in Great Britain was also dashing off final notes to family and friends in his C-deck cabin. William Thomas Stead was a trailblazing investigative journalist, known to all as W. T. Stead and often hailed as "the Napoleon of newsmen." Over the past thirty years, Stead had tackled issues that had both outraged and mobilized people in Britain and abroad. In 1890, the *New York Sun* claimed that Stead, "between the years 1884 and 1888 came closer to governing England than any other man in the kingdom." Over the last fifteen years, the veteran journalistic crusader had made world peace one of his causes and this had earned him a nomination for the Nobel Peace Prize in 1903. He was now on his way to New York to give a talk on "Universal Peace" at the Men and Religion Forward Movement Congress in Carnegie Hall on April 21.

W. T. Stead

At sixty-two, Stead was three years younger than Frank Millet but looked older due to his furrowed brow and snowy Old Testament beard. The prophetic look was appropriate to another of Stead's pursuits—communing with the spirit world. He had become the medium for a spirit named Julia, who communicated through automatic writing and séances.

Stead had compiled Julia's messages in a book entitled *After Death* and had also set up a psychic institute called Julia's Bureau. Julia had not communicated any *Titanic* forewarnings to Stead, however, and in a letter sent at Queenstown to his daughter Estelle he enthuses about the size and magnificence of the ship and his "love of a cabin . . . with a window about 4 ft. by 2 ft. looking out over the sunlit sea." He also describes the *Titanic* as "a splendid, monstrous, floating Babylon." The "Babylon" metaphor significantly invokes Stead's most famous—and most notorious—journalistic campaign, a series of articles he wrote in 1885 entitled "The Maiden Tribute of Modern Babylon." As the editor of the London daily newspaper, the *Pall Mall Gazette,* Stead had been approached in May of 1885 by a prominent anti-vice campaigner to help rouse public opinion in support of a bill that was stalled in Parliament. The Criminal Law Amendment Act, which proposed measures to combat child prostitution and white slavery, had gone down to defeat three times in the House of Commons. The anti-vice advocate's stirring stories of exploited children fired Stead's reformist zeal and he plunged into an investigation of London's seamy underworld, interviewing everyone from procurers and pimps to rescue workers and jail chaplains. He even arranged for one of his female staffers and a Salvation Army lass to pose as prostitutes and penetrate brothels, with the assumption that they could make an escape before service was required.

When the first installment of "The Maiden Tribute of Modern Babylon" appeared on July 6, 1885, it caused a sensation. Victorian London had never seen such frank sexual content in print. Headlines like THE VIOLATION OF VIRGINS, THE CONFESSIONS OF A BROTHEL-KEEPER, and HOW GIRLS WERE BOUGHT AND RUINED both titillated and outraged. When W.H. Smith & Son, London's largest distributor to newsstands, refused to sell the papers, volunteers, including members of the Salvation Army, stepped in to help. Even George Bernard Shaw telephoned with an offer of assistance. Over the next four days the *Gazette*'s offices were mobbed as crowds fought to obtain sheets still wet from the press and the police had to be called in to maintain order. Secondhand copies sold at twelve times the normal cost. Soon public meetings and angry demonstrations in support of the Criminal Law Amendment Act took place all over Britain. The Salvation Army amassed 393,000 signatures on a petition a mile and a half long and marched with it in a giant roll to Westminster under a banner saying, [WE] DEMAND THAT INIQUITY SHALL CEASE. Parliamentarians quickly bowed to public pressure and the CLA Act (informally dubbed "Stead's Law") received royal approval on August 14, with Queen Victoria noting that she "had pleasure in giving my assent."

But Stead himself was soon to become a victim of "Stead's Law." One of the most sensational stories in the "Maiden Tribute" series was entitled "A Child of Thirteen Bought for £5." It described how a Cockney girl named "Lily" had been purchased from her drunken mother, taken to a midwife to attest to her virginity, and then to a brothel where she was put to sleep with chloroform. As the story ends, Lily is awakened when her "purchaser" enters the room. "There's a man in the room!" she screams. "Take me home; oh, take me home!" What the article neglected to mention was that Lily's abduction had been engineered as a test case by Stead. He was the man who had entered the room posing as her "purchaser," after which the girl had been spirited off to France in the care of Bramwell Booth, the head of the Salvation Army.

Rival newspapers began to dig into the story and soon Stead's enemies saw their chance. On September 2, 1885, he and those who had assisted him in "buying" the child were arraigned in court on charges of abduction and procurement. Stead defended himself ably but was convicted on a technicality—that he had not secured the permission of the girl's father. The judge's hostility to Stead was evident throughout the trial and his instructions to the jurors left them with little choice except conviction. The judge even told the jury that they should not be prejudiced "because in the streets some months ago were circulated . . . an amount of disgusting and filthy articles." Yet it was Stead's shattering of the language taboo that was perhaps the "Maiden Tribute's" greatest achievement. What had formerly been "disgusting and filthy" could now be written about openly, allowing a widely ignorant public to glean useful information on sexual matters.

On November 10, 1885, Stead began a prison sentence of two months and one week. On every November 10 after his release, he would don his prison uniform and proudly walk about the streets. Yet "Stead's Law" would have wider-reaching consequences than the newsman himself had ever imagined. During the debate on the CLA Act in the House of Commons, a Liberal member named Henry Labouchère had questioned why sexual acts between men should not be included in the bill. The late addition of the Labouchère Amendment made any act of "gross indecency" between men punishable by two years in prison—thus criminalizing homosexuality in Great Britain for the next seventy-two years.

Ten years after the passing of the CLA Act, the poet and playwright Oscar Wilde launched a libel suit against the brutish Marquess of Queensberry for a note he had left at Wilde's club calling him "a posing somdomite [*sic*]." Queensberry was the father of Wilde's lover, Lord Alfred Douglas, and he had been stalking and harassing the playwright for months. When Wilde lost the case, he was charged and convicted of "gross indecency" and sent to prison for the two years of hard labor that the law required. W. T. Stead assailed the hypocrisy of Wilde's conviction, noting that "if all persons guilty of Oscar Wilde's offences were to be clapped into gaol [jail], there would be a very surprising exodus from Eton and Harrow, Rugby and Winchester [elite schools], to Pentonville and Holloway [prisons]."

The harshness of prison life contributed to Wilde's early death in 1900 at the age of forty-six. Stead never reflected in print on the connection between "The Maiden Tribute" and Wilde's fate. However, after reading *De Profundis*, the book Wilde wrote while in prison, he sent a letter to the playwright's friend Robbie Ross in 1904, saying:

> I am glad to remember when reading these profoundly touching pages, that he [Wilde] always knew that I, at least, had never joined the herd of his assailants. I had the sad pleasure of meeting him by chance afterwards in Paris and greeted him as an old friend. We had a few minutes talk and then parted, to meet no more, on this planet, at least.

AS THE DEADLINE for mail to be dropped at Queenstown approached on the morning of April 11, 1912, Millet and Stead would either have summoned a steward or joined the other passengers walking toward the Enquiry Office on C deck with letters and postcards. From there, the mail went down four decks to the post office, where it was sorted and put into canvas mailbags, each of which contained about two thousand letters. An electric hoist then moved the bags to the mail storage room one deck below in preparation for loading onto the Queenstown tenders. Many of these letters were not received till after the *Titanic* had gone down, and a good number were the last communication ever received from those who would not live to see New York. One of these is a letter from the *Titanic*'s chief officer, Henry Wilde, to his sister, in which he says: "I still don't like this ship, I have a queer feeling about it."

Francis Browne was up early on the morning of April 11 to capture
the *Titanic*'s first sunrise on film.

QUEENSTOWN

Norris Williams awoke on Thursday morning to find his father standing by their cabin's porthole looking out at the sun shining brightly on a calm ocean. By then Francis Browne was already up on the boat deck with his camera in hand. At sunrise he had taken a photograph of the sun breaking through the clouds. As an aspiring Jesuit, Browne probably also chose to make his morning meditation on deck at that hour. Certainly, he was eager to fit as much as he could into his last morning on the liner.

At approximately the time that Browne would have returned to his A-deck room before breakfast, a steward was carrying a tray to A-36, the starboard-side cabin opposite Browne's. Each morning at seven o'clock steward Henry Etches brought tea and fruit to the *Titanic*'s chief designer, Thomas Andrews, whom he found always hard at work with plans and drawings spread out over the cabin. Though only thirty-nine, Andrews was already a managing director of Harland and Wolff, and it was his custom to travel on maiden voyages to observe a new liner in service and recommend improvements. He was also in charge of a nine-man "guarantee group" from Harland and Wolff that was on board to assist with any matters requiring special attention. On the rolled-up blueprints beside Andrews's bed, there were sketched-in plans for shrinking the size of the underused reading and writing room to make way for additional staterooms. The papers that covered his desk and night table included notes on everything from reducing the number of screws in the stateroom hat hooks to staining the wicker furniture on one side of the ship a particular shade of green.

Andrews was a nephew of Lord Pirrie, Harland and Wolff's chairman, but there was never a whisper that nepotism had boosted his career.

Thomas Andrews

He had joined the firm as an apprentice at the age of sixteen and had worked tirelessly in virtually every department since then, often arriving for work at 4 a.m. He took special pride in this particular ship and had taken his wife and one-year-old daughter to admire the *Titanic* before she left for Southampton. Andrews was universally popular at Harland and Wolff—his coworkers described him as being "sunny and big hearted" with "a wonderful, ringing laugh." His wife Helen recalled being with him near the shipbuilder's Queen's Island works one evening when a long line of workers filed past. "There go my pals, Nellie," he had said to her, adding later, "and they are real pals, too." Stewardess Violet Jessop remembered that, before sailing, the stewards had given a gift and a vote of thanks to "Tommy" Andrews for the improvements he had made to their "glory holes," the tiny stewards' quarters on the lower decks. "Our esteem for him," Jessop wrote, "already high, knew no bounds."

Downstairs, in the first-class dining saloon that morning, many of those same stewards were already hard at work bringing breakfast to their assigned tables. Saloon steward Jack Stagg wrote to his wife that so far there had been "nothing but work all day long" even though with a mere "317 first" on board he might end up with only one or two tables to look after. "Still one must not grumble," he added, "for there will be plenty without any." (No tables meant no tips, an important supplement to a steward's wages.) Lighter duties may have suited steward William Ryerson who was new to White Star procedures since all his previous jobs had been on Cunard ships. Steward Ryerson was unaware that he shared a family connection with the posh Ryersons up on B deck. He was, in fact, a third cousin once removed to Arthur Ryerson, who was returning home for the funeral of his eldest son.

The thirty-two-year-old Steward Ryerson had been raised in Port Dover, Ontario, a village on Lake Erie, but had left as a teenager to join the British Army, where he saw service in India before returning to London. There he married an English girl and, with jobs being scarce, had signed on as a steward with Cunard. His wealthy distant relative, by contrast, was the son of Joseph T. Ryerson, who had founded a Chicago steel company. Arthur Ryerson had practiced law in Chicago before retiring to a mansion in Haverford, Pennsylvania, and a summer estate overlooking Lake Otsego near Cooperstown, New York.

A surviving menu from the first breakfast served in the first-class dining saloon reveals a wide selection of hearty British favorites—grilled mutton kidneys and bacon, lamb collops, Findon haddock and fresh herrings [sic]—with some nods to the American palate in the offerings of Quaker Oats, boiled hominy, buckwheat cakes, and corn bread. Both W. T. Stead and his American table companion, a New York lawyer named Frederic Seward, would therefore have had no trouble selecting familiar breakfast fare from the menu card. The two men bonded early in the voyage, and the fact that they were both minister's sons likely provided some common ground for table talk. Stead's upbringing as the son of a Congregationalist preacher in a small Yorkshire town was the matrix for much of his reformist zeal. As a young boy, he had once expressed indignation at an injustice by exclaiming, "I wish that God would give me a big whip that I could go round the world and whip the wicked out of it!" In later years Stead's father would inquire wryly, "Aren't you going to leave a little for the Lord Himself to do, William?"

With cards and letters left to write, Stead would not have lingered long over breakfast. Francis Browne, too, soon left the table he shared with the Odell family to go back up on deck for more photographs. A shot he took from the aft end of A deck shows the arc of the *Titanic*'s wake through the water as the ship took a twisting path in order to test her compasses. Browne would label another photograph on the same album page "The Children's Playground" since it shows six-year-old Douglas Spedden spinning a top beside a cargo crane on A deck, while his father, Frederic, looks on.

Frederic Spedden and his wife, Margaretta, known as "Daisy," were both heirs to Gilded Age fortunes and divided their time between their home in Tuxedo Park, a fashionable enclave north of New York City, and a summer "camp" near Bar Harbor, Maine. In the winter the couple boarded the liners for warmer climes, and this year's itinerary had included stops in Algiers, Monte Carlo, Cannes, and Paris. The Speddens were devoted to their only child, Douglas, and a nursemaid, Elizabeth Margaret Burns (nicknamed "Muddie Boons" by Douglas), was traveling with the family along with Daisy's maid. Daisy dabbled in writing and kept a diary in which she had written after boarding the *Titanic* in Cherbourg: "She is a magnificent ship in every way and most luxuriously, yet not too elaborately, outfitted."

In his enthusiastic shooting that morning, Francis Browne made two double exposures that would have been discarded had they not proven to be of such historical significance. One photo showing an unidentified couple taking a stroll on A deck is overlaid with a ghostly view inside the private promenade deck of Charlotte Cardeza's deluxe suite where a "Bon Voyage" bouquet of flowers can be seen standing on a wicker table. The second is of even more significance because it is the only photograph taken inside the *Titanic*'s wireless cabin, or Marconi Room as it was known. Browne snapped two shots in one exposure of the junior Marconi operator Harold Bride sitting at the telegraph key wearing his headphones. Curving downward on the wall in front of him are two brass pneumatic tubes that brought passenger messages up from the Enquiry Office three decks below. For a charge of twelve shillings and sixpence ($3), passengers could leave a message of up to ten words with a charge of ninepence (35 cents) for each additional word. The message was then placed in a cylinder and sent up to the Marconi Room where it dropped out the bell-shaped end of the pneumatic tube into a wire basket.

While Browne continued snapping photographs that morning, Captain Smith made his inspection tour of the ship accompanied by his

Captain Smith (at right) with Purser McElroy

senior officers. Each day at 10:30 a.m. Smith took a walk through all decks of the ship, including the public rooms in all three classes, the dining saloons and galleys, the hospital, workshops, and storage areas, until he finally reached the engine rooms, where he was greeted by the chief engineer. On this first morning at sea, there had been an emergency drill with the sounding of alarm bells and the closing of the steel doors that sealed off the liner's sixteen watertight compartments. An assistant electrician named Albert Ervine described this rehearsal in his last letter to his mother, and concluded: "So you see it would be impossible for the ship to be sunk in collision with another."

Following his daily inspection, Smith returned to the bridge and reviewed with his officers any matters arising from the tour and also checked on the ship's progress, looking over the charts and reading any radio messages sent forward by the Marconi Room. The captain was likely aware that some tension existed among his senior officers, stirred up by his last-minute installation of Henry Wilde as chief officer. This change had caused William Murdoch to be bumped down from chief to first officer while Charles Lightoller was demoted to second officer, and the previous second officer had left the ship in Southampton. According to Lightoller,

> the ruling lights of the White Star Line thought it would be a good plan to send the Chief Officer at the *Olympic*, just for the one voyage, as Chief Officer of the *Titanic*, to help, with his experience of her sister ship. This doubtful policy threw both Murdoch and me out of our stride; and, apart from the disappointment of having to step back in our rank, caused quite a little confusion.

One consequence of this change was the missing binoculars for the lookouts. On the trip to Southampton from Belfast, the lookouts had used the now-departed second officer's binoculars, which he had locked in a drawer in his cabin before he left the ship. When Lightoller inquired about binoculars for the lookouts, he was told that none were available for them.

Lightoller assigned the responsibility for the last-minute officer shuffle to head office rather than to Captain Smith since he remained unfailingly loyal to "E.J." and believed that any man ought to have beeen willing to "give his ears" to sail under him. With his white beard, immaculate uniform, and soft-spoken manner, Captain Edward J. Smith was also a favorite with the passengers, and many frequent travelers would plan their crossings to sail with him. His thirty-eight years of service with the White Star Line had earned him the title of Commodore of the White Star Fleet and the honor of commanding new ships on their maiden voyages.

On this particular morning, Captain Smith likely timed his inspection tour to be back on the bridge to greet the Queenstown harbor pilot, John Whelan, who was well known to Smith and had guided the *Olympic* during its maiden stop in Queenstown the year before. Whelan had spent the night in the pilot's signal tower onshore and, upon sighting the liner flying a red-and-white signal flag indicating that his services were wanted, had climbed into a small whaling boat and been rowed out to the ship.

As Francis Browne watched the approach of the pilot's boat from up on deck, someone standing nearby asked him, "What fort is that?" pointing to a massive structure on the west side of the harbor entrance.

"Templebreedy, one of the strongest in the kingdom" was Browne's reply. Cork Harbor, a magnificent natural harbor, had long been an important British naval base, and the ruins of older fortifications dotted the hills around it. Templebreedy was a new fortress, completed only three years before, and giant modern guns bristled in its battery.

"And do Redmond and his Gang want to take that place?" another voice asked.

"And why do you call them a 'Gang,' Sir?" a third person challenged.

John Redmond was an Irish Member of Parliament and a longtime campaigner for home rule, a form of self-governance for Ireland within the United Kingdom. The issue was highly topical as the Third Home Rule Bill supported by Redmond and his party was receiving its first reading in the British House of Commons that very day. And this time it looked as if home rule for Ireland might become a reality. Francis Browne, however, refrained from being drawn into a political discussion, since, with Cork Harbor in view, it was time for him to take his last luncheon on board. He carried his camera to lunch with him, and took the only surviving photograph of the *Titanic*'s first-class dining saloon in service. It is another less-than-perfect photograph, but in spite of its flaws it gives an intimate view of passengers sitting at tables set with white linen, silver, and upright menu cards, beneath the room's elaborately plastered ceiling.

While Frank Browne and the Odells had lunch, two tenders, the *Ireland* and the *America*, departed from the White Star jetty in Queenstown. The *Ireland* was the first to leave, carrying ten first- and second-class passengers along with some newspapermen going out for a look at the new liner. The tender steamed over to a quay a few hundred yards away to pick up 1,385 sacks of mail to be carried to New York. (The ship's mail service had earned it the designation RMS for Royal Mail Steamer.) Only three first-class passengers boarded at Queenstown: William Minahan, an Irish-American doctor from Fond-du-Lac, Wisconsin; his wife, Lillian; and his sister, Daisy. The Minahans had been visiting relatives in the "auld sod," and William had sent a postcard from Killarney to friends in Wisconsin, saying "It's a good place to come from but U.S.A is a better place to live."

The tender *America* followed slightly later, having been delayed by the late arrival of the train from Cork. It was heavily loaded with 113 third-class passengers, most of them Irish emigrants seeking a new life in the place for which their tender was named. Twenty-one-year-old Daniel Buckley, a farm laborer from Kingwilliamstown in County Cork, led a group of six friends, two of them teenaged girls aiming to become parlor maids. From County Mayo there was a similar group of fifteen, headed for Chicago. The night before they left home, dozens of their friends in Castlebar, County Mayo, had given them what was known as a "live-wake" with fiddle music and dancing. During the half-hour trip out of the harbor, a twenty-nine-year-old weaver from Athlone named Eugene Daly raised the spirits of all by playing his bagpipes, known as *uilleann*, or elbow pipes. One song that was greeted with applause was the nationalist anthem "A Nation Once Again," and many mouthed the words to the rousing chorus: "A Nation once again! A Nation once again,/ And Ireland, long a province, be/A Nation once again." With the news about the Home Rule Bill filling the newspapers that morning, the song seemed particularly timely.

As the tenders drew alongside the *Titanic*, passengers already on board crowded the decks to watch them being unloaded. Second-class passenger Lawrence Beesley, a thirty-four-year-old English schoolteacher making his first Atlantic crossing, wrote that "nothing could have given us a better idea of the length and bulk of the *Titanic* than to stand as far astern as possible and look over the side from the top deck, forwards and downwards to where the tenders rolled at her bows, the merest cockle-shells beside the majestic vessel that rose deck after deck above them." A number of "bumboat" vendors hawking Irish linen, lace, and other souvenirs had also come out with the tenders. This was a popular feature of any stop at Queenstown and many passengers were eagerly waiting to view their wares. John Jacob Astor was seen haggling with a shawl-clad woman before pulling out a wad of U.S. bills to purchase a lace jacket for Madeleine. Up on the boat deck a small incident occurred when a stoker with a coal-blackened face poked his head up through the fourth funnel. Shrieks were heard from several startled women who hadn't realized that this funnel was a dummy, used only for ventilation shafts from the galleys. The stoker had simply climbed up an interior ladder, likely to get

A woman watches from the boat deck as departing passengers board
the tenders for Queenstown.

a breath of fresh Irish air, but this innocent occurrence would later be recalled as yet another "ill omen" for the maiden voyage.

As the *Titanic* prepared to raise anchor at around one thirty, Francis Browne headed down to board the *Ireland* with the Odell family. With him was his brother William, a Catholic priest, who had come out on the tender to have a look at the *Titanic*. At the gangway, Browne greeted Purser McElroy and one of the postal clerks, saying, "Goodbye, I will give you copies of my photos when you come again [to Queenstown]. Pleasant voyage." From the tender, Francis continued to snap photos, taking the last shot of Captain Smith as he looked over the side from the starboard wing bridge. On the *Ireland*, Browne spotted a fellow photographer he knew, Thomas Barker, who had been taking pictures on board for the *Cork Examiner*. Barker's photographs along with Browne's and twelve by Kate Odell today comprise most of the photographic archive documenting the *Titanic*'s short life. Over the next two days, the *Cork Examiner* ran two stories about the *Titanic*, extolling both her splendid public rooms and also her safety features, noting: "Nothing is left to chance, every mechanical device that could be conceived has been employed to secure further immunity from risk either by sinking or by fire."

As the returning tender passed Roche's Point to enter the harbor, Queenstown came clearly into view, despite a blue haze that had descended. The town had originally been called Cove as in "The Cove of Cork" but was named Queenstown in 1849 to commemorate a visit by Queen Victoria. (After Irish independence, it would be renamed Cobh in 1922.) At the top of the town stood St. Colman's Cathedral, where Browne's uncle was bishop and where, following the *Titanic* disaster, as Francis Browne wrote, "we gathered ... to pray for those who had departed and for those on whom the hand of sorrow had fallen so heavily."

Among the fortifications that dotted the hills around the harbor were stone Martello towers, similar to the one made famous by James Joyce in the opening chapter of *Ulysses*. The young Joyce had been a classmate of Francis Browne's at Belevedere College and also at the Royal University in Dublin, and a character named "Mr Browne, the Jesuit" makes several appearances in Joyce's last novel, *Finnegan's Wake*. As the

Titanic began to make its departure, Francis Browne took a shot of the liner in profile with a flock of gulls swarming around its bow. Not far from where Browne stood, a twenty-four-year-old stowaway, John Coffey, a stoker from Queenstown, lay hidden under a pile of mailbags. "I'm going down to this tender to see my mother," he'd told another stoker before disappearing. While Coffey headed homeward, other young Irish men and women were finding their tiny berths in the *Titanic*'s lower decks. Single men were mostly berthed in communal cabins below the bow, while single women were housed in the stern. There was less of a scramble than there had been in Cherbourg since, as one of the stewards noted, "at least this lot spoke English."

As the *Titanic* steamed away from Queenstown, schoolteacher Lawrence Beesley noticed how a little house on the left side of the harbor entrance continued to gleam white in the distance. He also observed the gulls who followed them and marveled at their ability to soar alongside the ship while barely moving their wings. Before long, the lighthouse on the Old Head of Kinsale, fourteen nautical miles away, was spotted and the *Titanic* then turned outward as it continued to follow the shoreline along Ireland's southern coast. Years later, people in whitewashed cottages along the shore would remember looking up to see the huge new liner pass by, and recall what a splendid sight she was. At around four o'clock the white column of the Fastnet Lighthouse, planted on a small rocky outcrop off Ireland's southern tip, came into view. From there, the ship turned westward to head out across the open Atlantic. As the Irish coastline retreated in the distance, Eugene Daly once again hoisted his pipes, walked to the stern railing, and saluted his homeland with a mournful dirge called "Erin's Lament." Seagulls wheeled over the *Titanic*'s wake as the distant hills grew dark in the lowering sun and became ever smaller, until they finally disappeared in the offshore mist.

Passengers take the air on the second-class boat deck promenade.

FELLOW TRAVELERS

At the end of the afternoon a good number of the *Titanic*'s passengers were still out on deck. Margaret Brown described this time of day as one when "all take their exercise before descending to the dining hall ... the women in luxurious furs and the men in heavy overcoats ... and partly disguised in steamer caps." The air was chilly but there was little wind and the sea was remarkably calm—like a "silver lake" as one described it. A few passengers were walking their dogs, John Jacob Astor quite possibly among them. Although Madeleine Astor was mostly keeping to her cabin, Colonel Astor was often seen walking Kitty on the boat deck. It is thought that the *Titanic*'s kennels were located there, behind a door just aft of the fourth funnel. Kitty, however, was frequently to be found in the Astors' stateroom; they wanted to keep her near since she had recently gotten lost during their trip up the Nile, as Madeleine's sister Katherine Force later related:

> She [Kitty] wandered away from Colonel Astor's side one day at a landing and [he] was greatly distressed by the loss of the dog. He spent a great deal of time looking for her, and when he had to give up and start up the Nile again he employed scores of natives to look for her, promising a handsome reward for her return. Nothing was heard of Kitty until on the return trip [downriver] when, on passing another *dahabea* [boat], Colonel Astor spotted Kitty making herself at home on board. The Astor boat was stopped and Kitty found her master with joyous barks. After that, a closer

watch was kept of Kitty on board the *Titanic*. She slept in Colonel Astor's room [and he] took frequent walks and romped with Kitty a great deal.

Frank Millet and Archie Butt, too, often opted for a walk on the boat deck at day's end. On running into Astor on deck, both men would have greeted him, since they were social acquaintances, although the colonel was not a man for easy conversation. Astor's military rank was a result of his outfitting a 102-man artillery regiment called the Astor Battery at the outbreal of the Spanish-American War. He had accompanied the regiment to Cuba in June of 1898 and had observed from a safe distance as his distant cousin, Teddy Roosevelt, and his Rough Riders made their famous charge up San Juan Hill. He spent only a month in Cuba but it was enough to earn him the honorific that became his chosen mode of address. The colonel did not accompany the Astor Battery when they were sent to the Philippines in 1899, but Frank Millet did, traveling across the Pacific with the regiment and treporting on the war for *Harper's Weekly*. He later published his dispatches in book form as *The Expedition to the Philippines*.

In early February of 1910 Archie Butt had been seated near Colonel Astor at a dinner-dance in the New York mansion of Cornelius Vanderbilt III. It was a thrill for Archie to be invited to this function, since, as he noted to Clara, it marked "the first time a member of the Butt family has actually penetrated into the heart of the Four Hundred." Archie was told that Astor had been placed at the head table under the watchful eye of the hostess for fear he might be "cut" by some of the guests due to his recent divorce from Ava. A society woman whispered to Archie that, while she did not object to John Jacob Astor's morals, "she thought [he] looked like an ape," and Archie wrote, "I had to agree with her."

Much of the resentment toward the Astors in New York was driven by the fact that they were, in effect, the city's biggest slumlords. The first John Jacob Astor, a butcher's son from Baden who landed in New York in 1784, had left behind on his death in 1848 the largest fortune in the United States. Astor began as a fur trader but cashed in his fur company in the 1830s to buy up large parcels of New York real estate. "If I could

This 1898 magazine cartoon is captioned "A New Factor in
Modern Warfare: The Jack-Ass(tor) Battery."

live all over again," he once said, "I would buy every square inch of Manhattan." He very nearly succeeded—his son William would be known as
"the landlord of New York" for his vast holdings in the city. The Astors
preferred to lease out their land to others who would then return the
improved real estate once the lease was up. This also spared the family
the unpleasant business of collecting rents from the tenements that occupied many of their properties.

Astor-owned hotels like the Waldorf-Astoria and the St. Regis put an
elegant gloss on the hard fact that three-quarters of the family's income
came from rents derived from New York's poorest neighborhoods. In
this, the Astors and the White Star Line had something in common;

the *Olympic* and the *Titanic* would never have been built without the lucrative transatlantic immigrant trade to fill their lower decks. The accommodations the *Titanic* offered its poorer passengers, however, bore no resemblance to the squalid disease-ridden warrens that stood on Astor-owned properties. Descriptions of these by the crusading writer and photographer Jacob Riis in the 1890s had caused Colonel Astor to unload some of the worst of his holdings by 1900.

FRANK MILLET HAD likely spent most of April 11 immersed in paper-work—shipboard days were good for that. He had a lecture on period costumes to give in early May, a progress report to write on the Amer-ican Academy building on the Janiculum Hill, and he had to prepare for the pending Fine Arts Commission meeting regarding the Lincoln Memorial. Architect Daniel Burnham, the chairman of the commission, needed Millet's persuasive gifts to keep the politicians who made up the Lincoln Memorial Commission from making a hash of their plans. Burnham, who headed a large Chicago architecture firm that had designed such Gilded Age landmarks as New York's Flatiron Building and Washington's Union Station, had become fast friends with Frank during the construction of the World's Columbian Exhibition in 1892–93. Burnham was the man responsible for conjuring up a city of grand boulevards, canals, and classical facades from some scrubby acres of Chi-cago waterfront, and Frank Millet's unfailing good humor and gift for managing people under impossible deadlines had made him Burnham's closest lieutenant.

As the fair was about to open in May of 1893, Burnham asked Mil-let to become his director of functions and dream up events to boost attendance. Frank soon devised a host of parades, special days, and fire-works displays, but his most outrageous success was a gala evening called the Midway Ball. For this event, Turkish belly dancers and African and South Sea Island women from the Midway's replica villages were invited to a formal dance attended by directors of the fair and other leading citizens of Chicago. The newspapers described men in white tie and tails "swinging black Amazons with bushy hair and teeth necklaces" around

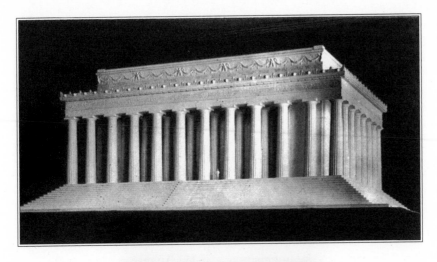

Daniel Burnham and a model of Henry
Bacon's design for the Lincoln Memorial

the dance floor. For the late-night buffet, Frank devised a menu with dishes like "Roast Missionary à la Dahomey" and "Boiled Camel Humps à la Cairo Street." To the *Chicago Tribune* the ball was "the strangest gathering since the destruction of the Tower of Babel."

Nineteen years after the Chicago exposition, Burnham and Millet were comrades-in-arms once again, on a project they knew was of great historic significance. Both had been young men when Lincoln was assassinated and had clear memories of the deep national grief that had ensued. For a memorial to the martyred president, Burnham had long supported a site overlooking the Potomac; he wanted the monument to be set apart from other structures and to extend the Mall, aligned to the Capitol and the Washington Monument. But Joseph Cannon, the gruff and influential former Speaker of the House known as "Uncle Joe," was determined to keep the memorial away from "that God-damned swamp" by the river. He favored a site across the Potomac in Arlington, Virginia, and thought that Southern members of Congress would support him. Burnham soon dispatched Frank Millet to seek out key Southern representatives and seed the notion that it would never do for the memorial to the "conquerer" to be placed on the land of the "conquered"—Arlington, after all, belonged to the sacred South.

Burnham had also asked Millet to write a report containing the Fine Arts Commission's recommendations, and by August 10, 1911, the Memorial Commission had accepted its main points and had agreed to hire architect Henry Bacon of New York to draw up a preliminary design. Only a few weeks later, however, Joe Cannon persuaded the commission to engage architect John Russell Pope to create a competing design for two sites other than the one by the Potomac. By December both Bacon and Pope had models ready for display. Bacon's Doric temple design had many symbolic elements and featured a statue of Lincoln inside with two chambers on either side carved with words from his Gettysburg and Second Inaugural Addresses. The design from John Russell Pope seemed rather pedestrian by comparison—a statue of Lincoln surrounded by a double row of columns—and the proposed sites for it were not particularly distinguished.

Frank Millet returned from Rome for the decisive meeting on February 3, 1912, when the Potomac Park site had finally won the day. But "Uncle Joe" and some of his cronies were still dissatisfied and angling to change the design. So Millet no doubt took time on the *Titanic* to gird himself for his next encounter with the fractious members of the Lincoln Memorial Commission.

Daniel Burnham would not be present at that meeting. On Saturday, April 13, the architect was leaving for Europe with his wife and daughter and son-in-law for a grand tour that would run into the summer. The ship he had chosen was the *Olympic*, and after dinner on Sunday night he would think of his old friend Millet, traveling in near-identical sur-roundings in the opposite direction. Burnham would summon a steward and write out a Marconi message to Frank Millet on the *Titanic*. He would not receive a reply.

AT 6 P.M. on Thursday, April 11, the sound of the *Titanic*'s bugler was heard on deck, indicating it was time for passengers to dress for dinner. The dress code had been waived on the first night at Cherbourg but from then onward "full dress was always *en règle*" as the Washington aristocrat and amateur historian Archibald Gracie noted approvingly. For Gracie and the other first-class men, this simply meant donning white tie and tails or a tuxedo, a standard part of any traveling wardrobe. Archie Butt had slightly more sartorial choice since his seven trunks were packed with both his regular and dress uniforms along with civilian evening wear. (At the White House, Archie often changed clothes six times a day.) For this first formal evening he may have simply chosen his regular uni-form or even civilian mufti, reserving a show of gold lace for later in the voyage. Most of the women, too, had a different gown packed in tissue paper for each night of the crossing but were saving their most splendid apparel for Sunday or Monday night.

The beauty of the women on board "was a subject both of obser-vation and admiration" according to Archibald Gracie. This display of loveliness, however, took considerable effort, making the "dressing hour" a stressful time for ladies' maids. The array of undergarments alone would baffle a modern woman, beginning with the corsets that most upper-class women still wore. The formidable whalebone devices of the Victorian era were a thing of the past, as were the padded S-curve corsets that had pushed the bosom forward and the derrière backward in the style so favored by King Edward VII. After 1907 a longer, slimmer look was in fashion and corsets had elastic gusset inserts that were supposed to make them less constricting.

But in 1912 a rebellion against the long reign of the corset was begin-ning. American debutantes had adoped a "park your corset" fad that year, where the constricting undergarments were shucked and left in dressing rooms at dances and parties. Lucile, Lady Duff Gordon, had introduced a corsetless gown in her spring 1912 collection, and in the current issue of the fashion magazine *Dress*, which some first-class ladies had probably brought on board, it was noted: "Quite as important as the more frivolous bits of underdress is the brassiere for the woman who wants to look pretty and be comfortable."

Yet the brassiere would not find wide acceptance till after World War I, by which time the corset had finally had its day. On this spring evening in 1912, therefore, only a few of the younger, more fashion-forward women on board, such as Edith Rosenbaum or Madeleine Astor, would have dared to shed their corsets for a brassiere and chemise. Most of the first-class women were helped into their corsets by their lady's maids, after which they stepped into the various layers of knickers and petticoats that followed. The elegant rustle of undergarments was part of the allure of a well-dressed lady in 1912, and each evening this sound was heard on the *Titanic*'s grand staircase during the procession down to dinner.

At 7:00 the ship's bugler, a twenty-six-year-old steward named Peter Fletcher, reappeared to summon passengers to dinner with a jaunty little tune called "The Roast Beef of Old England." By then, many passengers had already gathered in the wicker chairs of the Palm Room. On the second evening at sea there was a convivial, settled air on board, with table companionships well established and stewards addressing their clientele by name. Contrary to popular belief, there was no "captain's table" where E. J. Smith would entertain a favored selection of passengers each night. Smith normally took his meals at a table for six in the dining saloon or in his cabin, served by his valet or "tiger" as the captain's attendant was known.

Entertaining duties largely fell to Chief Purser Hugh McElroy, whose Irish wit and genial table talk made him well suited to the task. Passengers dining alone were usually assigned to the purser's table, and McElroy would then invite two additional passengers to round out the company each evening. W. T. Stead was asked to join McElroy's table one night, as was his dining companion Frederic K. Seward, who later recalled that all present were "almost spell-bound by the humor, and beauty, and breadth of vision of Stead's conversation." At one point on the voyage Seward was taken aside by an English passenger who whispered in his ear regarding Stead, "My dear fellow, you know that he was a pro-Boer?" Opposition to the Boer War in South Africa had indeed been one of Stead's contentious causes—in 1899 he had penned a pamphlet entitled "Shall I Slay My Brother Boer?"

It is not known whether W. T. Stead and Frank Millet spent time together on the *Titanic*, though the pairing of two such celebrated raconteurs would have made for a lively colloquy. The ubiquitous Mark Twain was a friend in common—Stead had met him aboard ship in 1894 while returning from his first visit to America. (By coincidence, Stead's ship on this crossing had been the *New York*, the same liner that had swung into the *Titanic*'s path while she was leaving Southampton.) During a storm at sea, Stead had kept Twain distracted by recounting one of his celebrated ghost stories. The two men had corresponded afterward, and exchanges of opinion between them had appeared in the *Review of Reviews*, the monthly journal Stead founded in 1890 after leaving the *Pall Mall Gazette*. On the same crossing, Stead had also met and befriended one of Millet's closest friends, Charles Francis Adams, a Back Bay aristocrat and descendant of the two Adams presidents, and brother of the Washington writer and diarist Henry Adams.

Given these connections, it's likely that Frank Millet at least greeted W. T. Stead on the *Titanic*, though he may have been wary of the old newsman's reputation for spooks and séances. Millet might also have taken a dim view of *If Christ Came to Chicago*, the book Stead wrote after his trip to the 1893 exposition. Stead had been fascinated by Chicago and had spent several months there interviewing criminals, gamblers, corrupt politicians, and prostitutes and then describing the city's underbelly from a viewpoint leavened with his unique brand of Christianity. When published in late 1894, *If Christ Came to Chicago* caused a considerable stir. It opened with an illustration of Christ casting out the moneychangers in front of the White City's central Court of Honor, and in its back pages was a color-coded foldout chart of Chicago's red-light district, locating all the brothels, saloons, and pawnbrokers to be found there. By unintentionally providing a handy guide to Sin

Archibald Gracie

City, the book became an instant bestseller.

As Millet, Archie Butt, and Clarence Moore passed through the dining saloon that Thursday evening, a likely table to have received friendly greetings was the one occupied by Colonel Archibald Gracie IV and his two companions, Edward Austin Kent, a Buffalo architect, and a New York clubman named James Clinch Smith. The affable Gracie was the most outgoing of the three and had the polished manners of a man from an old and distinguished family. His great-grandfather, Archibald Gracie I, was a Scottish-born shipping magnate who in 1799 had built a large Federal-style home in Manhattan overlooking the East River that is now known as Gracie Mansion, the official residence of the mayor of New York.

By the time Archibald Gracie IV was born in 1859, the family was living in Mobile, Alabama, where his grandfather had established a cotton brokerage business. When the Civil War broke out, Gracie's father, Archibald Gracie III, enlisted in an Alabama regiment, eventually becoming a Confederate brigadier general before being killed during the siege of Petersburg, Virginia, in 1864. Losing him at the age of five had left Archibald Gracie IV with a great curiosity regarding his father's life and Civil War service. With him on the *Titanic* were copies of *The Truth About Chickamauga*, his 462-page account of the 1863 battle in which his father had served. Like many Civil War battles, Chickamauga was a bloodbath, second only in carnage to Gettysburg—a victory for the Confederate side though a Pyrrhic one. Researching Chickamauga had exhausted Gracie. As he would later write in *The Truth About the Titanic*, "It was to gain a much needed rest after seven years of work thereon, and in order to get it off my mind, that I had taken this trip across the ocean and back. As a counter-irritant, my experience was a dose which was highly efficacious."

This richly ponderous writing style, along with Gracie's habit of pushing his Chickamauga book on other passengers, has caused him to be characterized as the club bore amid the clublike décor of the *Titanic*'s smoking room. Kindly old Isidor Straus, a co-owner of Macy's department store in New York, had accepted a copy of Gracie's book and then returned it a few days later expressing "intense interest" in having read it. Since even the most dedicated of Civil War buffs find Gracie's detailed descriptions of troop movements at Chickamauga to be daunting, Straus was undoubtedly merely being polite.

Frank Millet and Archie Butt were both quick-witted enough to nimbly rebuff being saddled with Gracie's book. Frank had clear memories of the Civil War; he had been seventeen when his father, Dr. Asa Millet, serving the Union cause as a surgeon, invited him to assist at an emergency field hospital in May of 1864. Exposure to the grisly realities of battle did not deter Frank from enlisting two months later as a drummer boy in the Sixtieth Regiment of the Massachusetts Volunteer Militia. His service was uneventful except for one occasion when he was called to drum out an alarm following the escape of forty Confederate prisoners from the camp where he was stationed.

Three of Archie Butt's uncles had been officers in the Confederate Army, and he had grown up in Augusta, Georgia, amid the hardships of postwar Reconstruction. Archie would make this era the setting for his 1899 novella *Both Sides of the Shield,* a story with a Chickamauga connection. The narrator of the novella is Palmer, a young newspaper reporter, as Archie had once been, who is sent south by a Boston newspaper to write accounts of postwar life in the former Confederacy. On the train, Palmer meets a courtly Southern colonel named Turpin who invites him to The Pines, a decaying plantation which the colonel's family is struggling to maintain. Palmer meets Turpin's strapping son, Bud, and his daughter, Miss Ellen, who is the mainstay of the household. He is invited to stay with the Turpins and eventually files a series of stories describing a diminished-but-proud Southern family's life in a post-slavery world. Palmer falls in love with Ellen, but when she discovers that he is the author of newspaper articles that she believes have ridiculed her family, he is banished from The Pines.

Palmer quits the newspaper and becomes a wanderer, haunted by memories of Miss Ellen. When war with Spain is declared, he enlists in the army and is stationed in a camp at Chickamauga, Tennessee. There he meets Bud Turpin, now an army officer, and tells him of his continuing devotion to Ellen. When typhoid fever sweeps through the camp, Palmer is stricken and Bud writes to his sister of Palmer's love for her. Miss Ellen comes to Chickamauga, Palmer's fever breaks, and all is forgiven. He is released from the army and taken back to The Pines by Miss Ellen, who tells him that he must resume his life as a writer.

The story conveys Archie's sentimental attachment to the lost world of the old South but is perhaps most interesting for something else it reveals about its author. In portraying a man with a hidden secret who finds redemption on the hallowed soil of Chickamauga through the love of a Southern woman not unlike his mother, Archie may well be describing his deepest wishes for himself. When it was published in *Lippincott's Monthly Magazine* in March of 1905, *Both Sides of the Shield* was much admired by Theodore Roosevelt, and it is said to be one of the reasons why Archie was selected as his White House aide.

After finishing their second dinner on the *Titanic*, Archie and his table companions would once again have taken coffee at one of the small tables in the Palm Room where the orchestra continued to play. Archibald Gracie recorded that he "invariably circulated around during these delightful evenings, chatting with those I knew, and with those whose acquaintance I had made during the voyage." In *The Night Lives On* Walter Lord imagines people "wincing at [Gracie's] approach, but putting up with him anyway, for he was kind, courtly and certainly meant well."

Gracie was also prone to name-dropping and informs us that after leaving the Palm Room, "the men of my coterie would always go to the smoking room, and . . . join in conversation with some of the well-known men whom we met there." He then names Archie Butt, Clarence Moore, and Frank Millet as three of the celebrated men whom he saw regularly. Gracie claims to have discussed politics with Major Butt, though Archie had written to President Taft from the *Berlin* that he liked to "haul in" the onboard political discussions and likely did so again with Gracie. The topic of the day was Theodore Roosevelt's run against Taft for the Republican nomination. Roosevelt had lost to Taft in the New York primary on March 26 but had won handily in Illinois on April 9, just two days ago, and was expected to take Pennsylvania that coming Saturday. Discussions of this may have fueled Archie's anxiety as he prepared for his return to the fray in Washington.

Gracie also mentions Arthur Ryerson as another of the prominent men who frequented the smoking room. Ryerson was encouraged to escape the grief-laden atmosphere of his stateroom by John B. Thayer, a neighbor from Haverford, Pennsylvania. Thayer was a second vice president of the Pennsylvania Railroad and was returning from a European tour with his wife, Marian, and seventeen-year-old son, Jack, who had been at boarding school in England. Marian Thayer was a friend of Emily Ryerson's and was looking in on her frequently as she kept to her room during the voyage.

John B. Thayer and Arthur Ryerson both knew George Widener, the last of the "well-known men" on Gracie's list, though he was far from the least in terms of social standing. Widener was the son of the Philadelphia streetcar magnate P.A.B. Widener, who had built one of the very grandest of all the Main Line estates, Lynnewood Hall—a 110-room palace built in French neoclassical style and set on three hundred acres that included formal gardens, a polo field, and a lake. George Widener managed several of the family companies and lived at Lynnewood Hall with his wife, Eleanor, and two sons and a daughter. Their eldest son, twenty-seven-year-old Harry Widener, was traveling with them and had a stateroom next to their C-deck suite. Since leaving Harvard five years before, Harry had devoted himself to acquiring rare books, and his collection already included an early folio of Shakespeare and a Gutenberg Bible. A recent book-buying foray in London had turned up a rare copy of Sir Francis Bacon's *Essaies* that he was proudly carrying home with him on the *Titanic*. Before leaving for Southampton, Harry had dropped into a London book dealer to show off his prized acquisition and jokingly remarked, "If I am shipwrecked you will know that this will be on me."

In the smoking room, Archibald Gracie and the other regulars soon settled into their club chairs, and decks of cards began to be shuffled. As cigar smoke wafted upward to create a misty glow around the cut-glass globes of the filigreed brass chandeliers, several of those at cards cast appraising glances around the room, since their purpose there was business rather than pleasure. Professional cardsharps had become enough of a problem on the transatlantic liners for White Star to post a special warning message opposite the first page of the passenger booklet. In the politest of terms, the message stated that "certain persons, believed to be Professional Gamblers, are in the habit of traveling to and fro in Atlantic Steamships," and warned that games of chance would afford these individuals "special opportunities for taking unfair advantage of others."

Fleecing the unwary was clearly lucrative, since it has been estimated that roughly sixteen "sportsmen," as the gamblers were known, had booked passage on White Star liners in early April of 1912 and that three of them had made it onto the *Titanic*. George Brereton of Los Angeles is listed as "George Brayton" on the passenger list, though he was most often known as George "Boy" Bradley. On the *Titanic*'s last night, Brereton would join up with two other cardsharps, Harry "Kid" Homer and Charles "Harry" Romaine, in an attempt to hustle two passengers in a game of bridge whist.

It's often written that Jay Yates, a notorious American cardsharp and con man who used the pseudonym "J. H. Rogers," was also on the *Titanic*. A haunting note that he reportedly thrust into the hands of a woman in a lifeboat reads, "If saved, inform my sister, Mrs. J. F. Adams of Findlay, Ohio. Lost, J. H. Rogers." But Yates was never on board and the note was a hoax—written to make the police think he was dead, since he was wanted for postal theft. Yates had hired a woman to pose as a survivor and drop the letter off at a newspaper office. The newspaper ran it, but the ruse failed and the police remained on Yates's trail.

The small tables used for cards in the smoking room had a raised lip around the edges to prevent glasses from sliding off in choppy seas. But on this night the glasses barely quivered as the liner moved smoothly forward through a remarkably calm north Atlantic. The ship was making excellent time and it looked as if the miles it was covering might exceed that posted by the *Olympic* on the first day of its maiden voyage. As J. Bruce Ismay retired to his suite for the night, he had every reason to be pleased with the performance of White Star's newest liner.

The first-class lounge was a regular haunt for Archibald Gracie
and his friend James Clinch Smith (above).

PRIVATE LIVES

The designers of the *Olympic* and the *Titanic* were fully aware of what décor appealed to the tastes of their wealthiest clientele. In America's Gilded Age palaces the opulence of France's *ancien régime* was the style most often simulated. As a result, the first-class lounge on A deck, the showiest of the *Titanic*'s public rooms, had been designed to emulate Versailles—though with some English coziness added in the patterned carpeting and comfortably upholstered sofas with large green pillows. The walls were paneled in oak with carved rococo detailing, although the use of gilding was restrained, reserved for some details on the plastered ceiling, a gilt ormolu wall clock, and the statuette of the Artemis of Versailles on the marble mantelpiece. At the far end of the room stood a mahogany, glass-fronted bookcase that held the ship's library, and from its shelves Archibald Gracie had already selected *The Old Dominion*, a novel set in colonial Virginia, for some relaxing shipboard reading. On Friday, April 12, and the calm sea days that followed, Gracie, like many of his shipmates, was often to be found in the lounge, reading, taking tea, and chatting with acquaintances.

Joining him there on occasion was his oldest friend on board, James Clinch Smith, a man of "quiet modesty" in the words of another acquaintance, though he was also known to possess a dry wit. Like Gracie, Jim Smith, as he was known, came from an old American family and was a direct descendant of the founder of Smithtown in northeastern Long Island. He had grown up there as one of the seven children of Judge J. Lawrence Smith and his wife, the former Sarah Clinch. An aunt of his mother's was the widow of department store magnate Alexander T. Stewart, and at thirty-four, Jim had come into $3 million from "Aunt Cornelia's" estate. He also inherited the Smith homestead, a white colonial farmhouse to which many additions had been made over the years. In 1897 Jim had commissioned his brother-in-law, the celebrated architect Stanford White, to enhance and harmonize the look of it. White had married Jim's youngest sister, Bessie, in 1884 and with her share of Aunt Cornelia's money had acquired a farm at nearby St. James which he soon transformed into a country estate he named Box Hill.

Smith himself would not marry until he was thirty-nine. His bride was the outgoing Bertha Barnes of Chicago, and for a time they were a popular couple in New York and Newport society. Bertha was an accomplished amateur musician and composer, and in 1904 she persuaded her husband that they should move to Paris. Once there, Bertha soon became well known in musical circles—particularly after she launched a popular all-female orchestra. Her husband was less at home in Paris and regularly boarded the liners to return to New York and the world he knew. This took a toll on the marriage and after a few years they were essentially living apart. In January of 1912, however, Bertha asked Jim to come to Paris and during that visit the couple were reconciled and Bertha agreed to come back to America and the Smithtown homestead. In April a family friend received a letter from Paris with the message "Jim sails today on the great *Titanic* for New York to get ready the old home for Bertha, who follows in October."

For someone who simply wanted the quiet life of a Long Island squire, fate had a way of finding Smith in the wrong place at the wrong time. Six years before boarding the *Titanic*, he had been a witness to the very public murder of his brother-in-law, Stanford White, and had been required to give testimony at the most sensational murder trial of the new century. On the night of June 25, 1906, he was sitting alone at a table in the roof garden restaurant atop Madison Square Garden, a massive Moorish-style complex designed by his brother-in-law. Below him was the giant amphitheater he knew well from attending the annual New York Horse Show; it could hold fourteen thousand people, and Stanford White had once had it flooded to create a Venetian spectacle. Looming

The roof garden
restaurant (top) at
Madison Square Garden
(left) was designed by
Stanford White (above) as
a venue for musical shows.

above Smith's table, illuminated against the night sky, stood the building's thirty-two-storey tower, topped by Saint-Gaudens's golden statue of
a naked Diana drawing her bow. For the roof garden, White had created
a partly outdoor restaurant decorated with trellises, potted palms, and

Japanese lanterns that were laid out around a stage where light cabaret was performed on summer evenings.

For lack of anything better to do on this hot June night, Jim was attending the premiere performance of a musical revue entitled *Mamzelle Champagne*. Not long after the show began, a man in evening dress and a long overcoat appeared at his table and asked if he could join him. His face was familiar and after he sat down Jim realized that he was Harry Thaw, the eccentric young millionaire from Pittsburgh whom people said was a cocaine addict or mad or both. Thaw offered Jim a cigar and began chatting about Wall Street and investments. The talk soon turned to travel and Jim mentioned that he was going abroad next week on the *Deutschland*. Thaw replied that he thought the *Deutschland* broke down too much and said he preferred the *Amerika*. Jim responded that he knew the captain of the *Deutschland* and that he was always very nice to Jim's wife.

"Where's your wife?" Thaw asked.

"She's in Paris."

"Are you very much married?"

Jim asked what he meant by that.

Thaw pressed on, asking if he was "above meeting a very nice girl" and offered to fix him up with a "buxom brunette."

Jim answered icily and turned away to watch the stage. So far *Mamzelle Champagne* didn't have much fizz and there was distracted chatter at nearby tables. Thaw tried to restart the conversation but Smith was unresponsive so he eventually stood up and left. As the show limped onward, the pretty actress in the title role popped out of a giant champagne bottle, but even that generated only meager applause. Later, there was a mild stir as Stanford White passed through the crowd to take his usual table—he was a large, imposing figure and a famous one in New York. Everyone knew the man who had designed the Washington Square Arch, the Colony Club, the Villard Houses, and many other city landmarks. Onstage the lead tenor was singing "If I Could Love a Thousand Girls" while twenty girls from the chorus pranced about him. The architect beamed up at the chorus girls, his teeth flashing from beneath his outsized mustache.

Suddenly there was a gunshot, followed by another and another. Someone laughed, thinking it was part of the show, but then came a crash followed by a loud scream. Stanford White's body lay on the floor beside his toppled table, a pool of blood spreading across the white table-cloth twisted underneath him. Harry Thaw stood over him holding his revolver in the air. "I did it because he ruined my wife!" he turned and shouted. "He had it coming to him. He took advantage of the girl and then deserted her!"

A New York City fireman had the presence of mind to relieve Thaw of his weapon which he meekly handed over. As the eerily placid gunman was escorted to the elevator, his young wife, Evelyn Nesbit Thaw, rushed forward and called out in disbelief, "Oh Harry, what have you done?"

Panicked Roof Garden patrons began streaming toward the exits and Jim Smith joined them. When he walked past the body he was unaware that the murder victim was his brother-in-law since White's face was partially blown away and blackened by powder burns. Smith would soon learn the truth and by morning the murder was front-page news. With each edition came new revelations about White's hidden life, accompanied by alluring photographs of the kittenish Evelyn Nesbit Thaw, whom White had reportedly known as a teenaged chorus girl before her marriage to Thaw. Newspaper circulations skyrocketed—never before had wealth, sex, and celebrity come together in quite such a perfect storm. To avoid curious crowds, White's funeral was moved from Manhattan to Smithtown, and Jim Smith was one of the mourners who accompanied the body on the funeral train from New York to Long Island and then to the small clapboard Episcopal church in St. James.

By the time Harry Thaw's trial began on January 23, 1907, Stanford White's name had become notorious. Thaw's tenacious widowed mother had hired a publicist to plant stories about White's seductions of young girls and had even sponsored three plays depicting a thinly disguised White as a predatory monster. The strategy worked; *Vanity Fair* head-lined one story STANFORD WHITE, VOLUPTUARY AND PERVERT, DIES THE DEATH OF A DOG. The man who had once personified the energy and ingenuity of the Gilded Age was decried from pulpits as a symbol of its excess and moral depravity.

At the trial, Jim Smith was a key prosecution witness and his description of Thaw's lucid manner just prior to the shooting cast serious doubt on the defense's claim of temporary insanity. Yet it was Evelyn Nesbit Thaw's testimony that excited by far the greatest interest. Taking the stand in a demure blue suit with a white Peter Pan collar, she was described by one reporter as the "the most exquisitely lovely human being I have ever looked at." It was this remarkable loveliness that had made Evelyn a sought-after model for artists and photographers when she was only fourteen. It had then won her a spot in the chorus of the musical *Floradora*. Both Stanford White and Harry Thaw had left gifts and messages for her at the stage door, but it was White who had first taken the prize, thus igniting Thaw's obsessive hatred.

Over a series of days in court, Evelyn would describe how White had won her over with his charm and attentiveness and had become a generous benefactor to her and her widowed mother and brother. She also described the architect's studio hideaway on Twenty-fourth Street, exotically decorated with statuary, silken kimonos, a polar bear rug, a

Evelyn Nesbit

mirrored room, and most famously, a red velvet swing on which Evelyn would soar upward to kick at paper Japanese parasols. The most sensational part of Evelyn's testimony was her description of how White had drugged her and taken her virginity when she was only sixteen. When this testimony was published, it caused a public outcry reminiscent of W. T. Stead's "Maiden Tribute." The White House was inundated with letters and telegrams demanding that President Roosevelt stop the newspapers from publishing such pornographic material, and in Congress a motion was introduced recommending that all publications containing "the revolting details of this case" be banned from the U.S. mail system.

After four months, the trial ended with a deadlocked jury. The second trial began on June 6, 1908, and moved more quickly, concluding in less than four weeks. In his closing statement, the prosecutor reminded the jurors of how rationally Thaw had behaved at James Clinch Smith's table only minutes before the murder. The jury, however, took just twenty-four hours to decide that Harry Thaw was not guilty on account of insanity. Thaw was taken to a state institution for the criminally insane where he was given comfortable accommodations until his release in 1915. Evelyn Nesbit pursued a slowly dwindling career as a vaudeville performer and silent film actress, and her later life was marked by alcoholism, morphine addiction, and suicide attempts. "Stanny White was killed," she once plaintively commented, "but my fate was worse. I lived."

In *The Vanderbilt Era*, Louis Auchincloss compares the fury stirred up by the White-Thaw scandal to that caused by the trials of Oscar Wilde a decade before. "There was surely a note of the philistine in it. 'So that's what these artist fellows are really up to!' " There are other similarities, too, between the writer who symbolized "the Yellow Nineties" and the architect who was the tastemaker for the Gilded Age. Both men were stalked by privileged, unbalanced, self-righteous pursuers, both were vilified for their sexual nonconformism, and both subscribed to the Bohemian credo that artists were not bound by the same rules as ordinary mortals. This view was embraced for a time by Frank Millet, as demonstrated in his unabashed love letters to Charles Warren Stoddard.

Frank Millet and Stanford White had, in fact, been part of the same Bohemian circles as young men. They had met in 1876 during the decoration of Trinity Church, the monumental Romanesque structure in Boston's Copley Square designed by H. H. Richardson. White, who had apprenticed with Richardson, persuaded the architect to bring in young artists to help complete John LaFarge's interior decorations. Millet and the other artists White befriended during the work on Trinity Church became the nucleus of the Tile Club, which formed in New York the following autumn. The club was established with the intention of making handcrafted decorative tiles in earnest William Morris–inspired fashion, but it quickly evolved into an artist's social club, with the exuberant "Stanny" as its chief fun-maker. For one gathering, Millet and Saint-Gaudens assisted White in the creation of a Roman-style dining room draped in creamy white fabric and decorated with tiger skins and brass objects. As the toga-clad Tilers reclined on couches, they were entertained by "the Hellion," an artist's model with the kind of sex appeal that, according to Frank, "would seduce Saint Anthony." Millet claimed to have never before attended a greater "semi-respectable spree."

Stanford White's "sprees" would become more extravagant and less respectable as his fame and wealth grew. A convivial clubman and designer of some of Manhattan's most elite clubhouses, he would also partake in the secret revels of the Sewer Club and the sexual liaisons that took place in a rented space called the Morgue. He also became the ultimate sugar daddy for a stream of young chorus girls—Evelyn Nesbit was not the only girl on the red velvet swing—and he would lavish money on gifts, clothes, and even their dental work. By the turn of the century, in the words of the architect's great-granddaughter, Suzannah Lessard, "his compulsions [had] acquired a cyclonic velocity." In 1906 White's red hair and outsized mustache had turned gray, and he looked twenty years older than a man of fifty-two. Unknown to him, he also had a degenerative liver disease and incipient tuberculosis that would likely have killed him within a year.

The notoriety that still clouded Stanford White's name in 1912 would have discouraged Frank Millet from recounting any "Stanny." stories to White's quietly reserved brother-in-law on the *Titanic*. John Jacob Astor, too, had known the famous architect but had fallen out with him in 1903 over the building of a sports pavilion for his Ferncliff estate near Rhinebeck. With Ava Astor's encouragement, plans for the complex had expanded to encompass an indoor marble pool, tennis court, library, billiard room, and guest quarters. Astor had never imagined anything so large, and soon he and the architect were not on speaking terms. White said he understood why the "Jackass" label had been applied to Astor. The Trianon-style building was eventually finished in 1904, and over a century later it provided the backdrop for the wedding of presidential daughter Chelsea Clinton. The Stanford White scandal also helped fuel the disapproval that greeted Astor's engagement to Madeleine Force in 1911. Photographs of a tall, mustached, middle-aged man squiring a teenaged girl summoned memories of the salacious stories that had filled the newspapers only a few years before.

AT NOON ON Friday, April 12, the ship's mileage for its first sea day was posted outside the Purser's Office. Since leaving Queenstown, the *Titanic* had covered 484 nautical miles, besting the *Olympic's* first-day tally of 428 miles. Interest in this was keenest among those taking part in the betting pool on the ship's run. According to Norris Williams, "practically the only excitement during the day's progress on the ocean is the posting of the day's run with the thrill that goes to the lucky winner." The pool was organized by Purser McElroy but run by a committee of passengers who would select twenty numbers centered around the expected next day's mileage. An auction was held after dinner in the smoking room where the numbers could be bid on by committee members and non-members alike, with members receiving a rebate of 50 percent on their winning bids for any of the twenty numbers. Norris Williams claimed that on Thursday evening the pool for Friday's tally had run up into four figures and that there were some smaller informal pools as well. The purser would keep roughly 10 percent of the pool winnings for donation to a seaman's charity. Many passengers would check the noon mileage tally each day on their way down to luncheon since the purser's notice board was near the grand staircase, one deck above the dining saloon.

The luncheon bill of fare for April 12 included Melton Mowbray Pie, Boiled Chicken with Bacon, and Lamb with Mint Sauce—the kind of English fare that would have been familiar to Frank Millet from his years in Broadway. After lunching with Archie Butt and Clarence Moore, he would likely have repaired to his cabin to tackle more paperwork. Archie Butt, too, may have done some letter writing that afternoon, perhaps penning a note to his sister-in-law Clara to keep up his epistolary diary. Although he had written several letters to President Taft during his time in Europe, he had not sent any accounts of his travels to Clara, and there was much to describe, from his audience at the Vatican to the time spent in Chester with his brother and his sixteen-year-old niece Arrington, to whom he was devoted.

W. T. Stead also found the *Titanic* a good place to work and was busily correcting the proofs of an autobiographical sketch he was preparing for publication. "The ship is as firm as a rock, and the sea is like a millpond," he had written to his wife from Queenstown. "If it lasts, I shall be able to work better here than at home, for there are no telephones to worry me, and no callers." Although Friday's weather was showery, the calm seas had lasted and the ship continued on its smooth and steady course to New York. By Friday afternoon, most of the ship's passengers had been lulled into the out-of-time tranquillity that often accompanied a calm ocean crossing amid comfortable surroundings. There were no organized shipboard activities and most passengers spent their time reading or chatting in the public rooms, taking walks on deck, being served hot bouillon while sitting well wrapped on deck chairs, or perhaps playing a game of deck quoits. Daisy Spedden, the mother of the boy whom Francis Browne had photographed spinning a top on deck the day before, recorded in her diary that she had taken young Douglas to the boat deck once again on Friday to play ball.

For those wishing more strenuous exercise, there was the gymnasium, with its enthusiastic instructor, T. W. McCawley, described by passenger Helen Churchill Candee as a "powerful five-feet-five of white flannels" who "bounded about the place" urging passengers to try out the gym's various exercise machines. Archie Butt had ridden the mechanical horses and camel in the gymnasium of the *Berlin* on his way over, so he may well have done the same on the *Titanic*, as he still needed to build up the stamina he had lost during his illness.

The British ritual of afternoon tea was observed on White Star liners and many of the *Titanic*'s American passengers took tea with a pastry or some biscuits at four o'clock even though this was not something they were accustomed to doing at home. The Palm Room was a popular place to do this since the orchestra played there from four to five each day. So was the Café Parisien, which had been created on the starboard side of B deck, and was a room not found on the *Olympic*. Ivy-covered trellises and café tables with wicker chairs provided a Continental atmosphere where elegant sandwiches and a selection of pastries were served from the circular, tiered buffet. "The Parisian café is quite a novelty and looks very real," an English passenger wrote to his wife, "it will no doubt become popular amongst rich Americans."

Not long after teatime ended came the bugle call indicating that passengers should begin to dress for dinner. By this time the staff of the Café Parisien had cleared away the teacups and cake plates, and the tables in the A La Carte Restaurant next door were already set with artfully folded linen napkins standing upright beside gold-rimmed Crown Derby china created expressly for the room. The restaurant and the adjoining café were run as a private concession managed by Luigi Gatti, a successful London restaurateur. The restaurant was known to passengers as "the Ritz Restaurant" because it so closely resembled the dining concessions operated by the Ritz-Carlton hotels on the Hamburg-Amerika liners. White Star had even copied the Ritz's signature rococo styling in the restaurant's gilded boiseries and fluted walnut columns. In this elegant ambience, for an added fee, passengers could dine on more deluxe fare than that offered in the dining saloon. In the early evening, a piano, violin, and cello trio would begin playing in the restaurant's reception room for the diners who would soon gather in the silk-cushioned chairs set around the white-paneled walls. The music drifted past the nearby aft grand staircase into the stateroom corridors, and the strains of a waltz or an operatic tune no doubt wafted into cabin B-82, where Benjamin Guggenheim was dressing for dinner with the aid of his valet.

At forty-six, Ben Guggenheim had graying hair but was still handsome in a soft-faced, dreamy-eyed way. Women usually found his warm smile and wealthy air to be attractive, and he, in return, had always had a keen interest in them. Ben was not the only one of Meyer Guggenheim's seven sons to have extramarital liaisons, but according to a nephew, "of all the brothers, he was the most extravagant in his amorous divagations, even

Benjamin Guggenheim

introducing them into his own home." One such "divagation" involved an attractive nurse who was moved into the family's Manhattan mansion, supposedly to give Ben massages for his neuralgia. This took place when his daughter Marguerite, known as "Peggy," later a celebrated art collector, was around five or six. She would later write that she adored her handsome father but remembered being punished at the age of seven for blurting out, "Papa, you must have a mistress as you stay out so many nights."

Ben's marriage in 1894 to Florette Seligman had been described by the *New York Times* as "one of the handsomest weddings of the season," uniting the "Silver Prince" of the wealthy mining family with a daughter of one of the city's most prominent banking clans. The Seligmans were an old New York Jewish family and are said to have regarded "the Googs" as arrivistes. The Guggenheim fortune was indeed quite new, with the lion's share of it having been made during the last decade when the family moved from lace importing to acquiring mines and building smelters. In 1885, at the age of twenty, Ben had been sent out to Leadville, Colorado—the same town where Margaret Brown's husband had made his fortune—to work as a bookkeeper in a family-owned mine. He then advanced to the job of managing a smelter at Pueblo, Colorado, which he did with some success, and the family soon began to focus on smelting as a core business. In 1901, however, a dissatisfied Ben resigned from M. Guggenheim & Sons to live on his investment income. This would prove to be a shortsighted decision since he would miss out on the family's highly profitable expansion into mining in Africa and South America, and it would leave his three daughters far less wealthy than their cousins.

Ben, however, was now free to cultivate his own interests, which included travel, art collecting, and philandering. Florette threatened divorce but the Guggenheims prevailed on her to remain married for the sake of their girls: Benita, born in 1895; Peggy, born in 1898; and Barbara Hazel (called Hazel), born in 1903. Florette, however, was far from a doting mother and relied on servants to care for the girls; Hazel remembered that her mother never read her a book or told her a story. Peggy would recall that Florette spent endless hours playing bridge and taking tea with other "Our Crowd" ladies. (Excluded from the Four Hundred, New York's elite Jewish families had formed their own "crowd.") Ben, meanwhile, spent more and more time in Paris, where he had a business, the International Steam Pump Company. Despite such lucrative contracts as the building of the elevators for the Eiffel Tower, the company required constant infusions of Guggenheim's capital.

By April of 1912, Ben had been in Paris for over eight months and was returning home for Hazel's ninth birthday. Traveling with him on the *Titanic* was his newest mistress, a petite twenty-four-year-old blond cabaret singer known as Ninette, but whose full name was Léontine Pauline Aubart. She is listed on the passenger list as "Mrs. N. Aubert [*sic*] and maid" though she was likely unmarried. Ninette occupied stateroom B-35, a discreet distance away from Ben's cabin though on the same deck. Her ticket was booked without a meal provision, which meant that she intended to take all her meals in the A La Carte Restaurant. Ben likely thought that this would be a less conspicuous place for them to dine than the dining saloon. There were always people one knew on board during a crossing—this time it was Isidor and Ida Straus, whose nephew, Roger, was married to Ben's niece, Gladys. Ben had helped ensure that Ninette would be expensively gowned for each evening's dinner, and the claim for lost luggage that she later sent to the White Star Line lists four trunks containing twenty-four dresses, twenty-four pairs of shoes, an array of lingerie, seven hats (two with plumes), long gloves, several jeweled bags, theater glasses, and a tiara.

Remarkably, there was another millionaire on board the *Titanic* who had also fallen for a twenty-four-year-old Paris cabaret singer and had also purchased a cabin so she could travel with him. The passenger in cabin C-90 was listed as "Mrs B. de Villiers," but her real name was

Berthe Mayné, though she sometimes used the stage name Bella Vielly. Berthe was actually Belgian, and it was in Brussels that she had met twenty-four-year-old Quigg Baxter, from Montreal. Quigg was sturdily built, handsome despite having lost an eye in a hockey game, quite rich, and besotted with her. He also spoke perfect French, though with an *accent Canadien*, since that was his mother's first language.

Quigg's mother, Hélène Baxter, was from an old Quebecois family that dated back to the time of Champlain. In 1882 she had married Quigg's father, James Baxter, nicknamed "Diamond Jim," who was of Ontario Irish stock but was busily making a fortune in Montreal as a diamond trader and banker. He eventually opened his own bank and built a twenty-eight-store retail development known as the Baxter Block. Diamond Jim was a bit of a rogue, and in 1900 he was sentenced to five years in prison for embezzlement. He died shortly after his release, and it was believed that by then most of his wealth was gone. But Baxter had cash squirreled away in Swiss bank accounts and in some investments in France and Belgium. The widowed Hélène soon made a habit of departing for Europe each fall to escape the Montreal winter and to keep an eye on her money. In November of 1911, she had sold the Baxter Block and sailed for Paris, taking her twenty-seven-year-old married daughter, Suzette, and younger son, Quigg, with her. For the trip home in April she had reserved one of the more elegant B-deck suites on the *Titanic*, unaware that Quigg had booked another cabin one deck down for his Belgian girlfriend. Whether he planned to marry Berthe in Montreal is unknown; the match would likely not have received *Maman*'s blessing— a Belgian newspaper had described the singer as being "well-known in Brussels in circles of pleasure."

For the first few days of the voyage, nausea had kept Hélène Baxter confined to her cabin, which allowed her son more time to spend with Berthe. On the evening of Friday, April 12, Quigg may also have chosen the Ritz Restaurant as the place for them to dine. But whether Ben Guggenheim and Quigg Baxter ever spoke or the two curiously similar couples even acknowledged each other on the *Titanic* is unknown.

AT 7:45 P.M. on that Friday evening a wireless message was received from the captain of the French liner *La Touraine* saying that they had "crossed [a] thick ice-field" and had then seen "another ice-field and two icebergs" and giving the positions of the ice and that of a derelict ship they had spotted. Captain Smith sent his thanks and compliments back and commented on the fine weather. While adding this information to the map in the chart room, Fourth Officer Boxhall remarked to the captain that *La Touraine*'s positions were of no use to them since French ships always took a more northerly course. "They are out of our way," he noted as the ship's helmsman guided the new liner onward through the calm, dark sea.

Daisy Spedden (at right) took her son's nursemaid, Elizabeth Burns (left),
for a Turkish bath on Saturday morning.

SHIPBOARD COTERIES

I took a Turkish bath this morning," Daisy Spedden recorded in her diary entry for April 13. "It was my <u>first</u> and will be my <u>last</u>, I hope, for I never disliked anything in my life so before, though I enjoyed the final plunge in the pool." Daisy had taken "Miss B," her son's nursemaid, Elizabeth Burns, for what was probably her first steam bath as well—Turkish baths had been popular in Britain since the 1860s but were less common in the United States. Installing them on ships was a White Star innovation, the first having been introduced on the *Adriatic* in 1907. For their *Olympic*-class liners, White Star had decided that the baths would be a showpiece amenity and had decorated them in a style hailed in *The Shipbuilder* as evoking "something of the grandeur of the mysterious East."

At the entrance to the bath complex on F deck, Daisy and Miss Burns were given a complete set of towels and directed to the small changing rooms at the far end of the cooling room. Upon entering this room, the nurse and even her more-traveled employer were no doubt momentarily dazzled by the décor, which, from its gilded ceiling hung with bronze Arab lamps to its intricate tilework and fretted "Cairo" screens, was pure *Arabian Nights* fantasy. Once they were swathed and turbaned in white toweling, the first stop for most bathers was the elaborate weighing chair, a canvas seat encased in a gilded wooden bench with brass scales that printed out a ticket of one's weight. From there, they proceeded to the temperate room for fifteen minutes or so of moderate dry heat, before advancing to the hot room, which was maintained at around two hundred degrees Fahrenheit. Daisy Spedden apparently soon fled the hot room to recline on one of the gilt-edged loungers in the cooling room, possibly taking a glass of water from the lion's head faucet on the wall.

After a cooling shower or plunge in the pool, bathers then went into one of the two "shampoing" rooms for a full body wash in showers with an encircling spray. Each of these rooms also had a long marble slab where patrons could receive a horizontal shower massage from an invention called a "blade douche," an overhead pipe fitted with adjustable nozzles. The adjoining swimming pool in which Daisy Spedden took her plunge was filled with seawater warmed by heated salt water piped down from a tank on the boat deck. When finished, Daisy and Miss Burns likely returned to their cabins on E deck before heading to the dining saloon for luncheon—and the erasure of any weight loss shown on their post-bath weigh-in tickets.

Much of the talk at luncheon, once again, was of the miles the ship had covered; today's posted tally was 519 nautical miles, besting yesterday's mileage and pleasing those who had guessed as much in the betting pool. It was also the subject of an after-luncheon conversation between J. Bruce Ismay and Captain Smith that was overheard by a passenger named Elizabeth Lines. Mrs. Lines was yet another American in Paris; she had taken up residence there some years ago with her husband, a doctor and former medical director of the New York Life Insurance Company. With her sixteen-year-old daughter, Mary, Mrs. Lines was making the crossing to New York to attend her son's graduation from Dartmouth College. After luncheon, as had become her custom, she took her coffee alone in the Palm Room, finding a table in a quiet corner. Before long, Captain Smith and Bruce Ismay sat down together on a nearby settee. Mrs. Lines recognized Ismay from when they had both lived in New York some years before and confirmed his identity with her table steward. She also noted that the White Star director was doing most of the talking while the captain merely nodded his assent. Ismay compared the *Titanic*'s mileage to the *Olympic*'s and expressed great satisfaction with the new liner's performance. He repeated several times that he was certain they would make an even better run of it tomorrow as more boilers were lit. Finally, he smacked his hand down on the arm of the wicker settee and said emphatically, "We will beat the *Olympic* and get in to New York on Tuesday!"

Mrs. Lines's recollection of this conversation has been disputed by historians who feel that Ismay has been made a scapegoat for the sinking. They point out that arriving in New York on Tuesday night could have caused docking problems and would have disrupted passengers' arrival plans, not to mention the ceremonious harbor welcome for the maiden crossing. Moreover, Captain Smith himself had said to the press after the *Olympic*'s maiden voyage, "There will be no attempt to bring her in on Tuesday. She was built for a Wednesday ship." Yet the New York arrival time was not measured by when the liner docked but by when it passed the Ambrose Lightship, a navigation beacon moored off Sandy Hook, New Jersey, where it marked the main channel into New York harbor. On her maiden voyage the *Olympic* had passed the Ambrose Lightship at 2:24 a.m. on Wednesday, June 21, 1911. Ismay knew that to beat the *Olympic*'s maiden crossing record and "arrive on Tuesday," the *Titanic* had simply to pass the Ambrose Lightship before midnight and best her sister's time by only two and a half hours. On her second westbound crossing, the *Olympic* had, in fact, reached the lightship at 10:08 p.m. on Tuesday, July 18. With the *Titanic* already achieving average speeds of just under twenty-two knots over the last two days, she was well on her way to making the Tuesday arrival that Ismay had so enthusiastically predicted.

DAISY SPEDDEN SPENT most of Saturday afternoon playing cards with Jim Smith in the lounge. Smith and the Speddens moved in similar circles in New York society and even had a few relatives in common. Yet Daisy and Frederic Spedden were not drawn into the shipboard clique that Smith and his tablemates Archibald Gracie and Edward Kent had become part of by Saturday. To Walter Lord, this circle of seven people was "one of those groups that sometimes happen on an Atlantic voyage, when the chemistry is just right and the members are inseparable." Archibald Gracie dubbed them "our coterie." The queen bee of "our coterie" was the Washington socialite and writer Helen Churchill Hungerford Candee. She was one of the "unprotected ladies" on board whom Colonel Gracie, adhering to a rather quaint practice, had offered to "safeguard." In "Sealed Orders," her account of the voyage published in *Collier's Weekly*, Mrs. Candee would dub Gracie "the talkative man," and she soon found that she had more in common with "the sensitive man," the Buffalo architect Edward Kent, who shared her interest in antiques and interior decoration. The tall, genteel Kent, fifty-eight, a lifelong bachelor, was remembered by the writer Mabel Dodge Luhan as a man "with a leaning toward beauty and lovely colors."

But it was another member of the coterie, a "cosmopolitan Englishman" named Hugh Woolner, who would kindle stronger feelings in Mrs. Candee. Woolner was eight years her junior and at six-foot-three towered above her small, stylishly dressed form. He was the son of an eminent Victorian sculptor and had been sent to the best schools and to Cambridge, where he had been on the varsity rowing team. Woolner's upper-class manners were impeccable but his business dealings were less so. After his father's death in 1892, he had used his inheritance to found a brokerage firm that ran into trouble during the South African war. In attempting to refloat his sinking fortunes, Woolner engaged in a number of illegal practices that resulted in his being barred from the London Stock Exchange. By 1907 he was bankrupt and also a widower, his American wife having died the year before, leaving him with a nine-year-old daughter. Woolner decided to put his daughter in the care of his American in-laws and seek opportunities in the western U.S. states, and by 1910 he had raised enough capital to discharge his British bankruptcy debt, permitting him to once again call himself a company director.

Unaware of Woolner's checkered business reputation and flattered by his attentions, Helen Candee allowed the suave Englishman to accompany her on long walks around the *Titanic*'s decks, as she describes in "Sealed Orders": " 'Let us wander over the ship and see it all,' said she of the cabin de luxe to him of the bachelor's cabin. So they mounted the hurricane deck and gazed across to the other world of the second class and wondered at its luxury, and further across to the waves and wondered at their clemency." In an unpublished memoir, Helen also pictures "the Two," as she calls herself and Woolner, standing together at the prow of the ship. "As her bow cut into the waves, throwing tons of water to right and left in playful intent," she wrote, "her indifference to mankind was significant. How grand she was, how superb, how titanic." This depiction prefigures the famous pose of the lovers in James Cameron's cinematic epic, but since the ship's forecastle deck was off-limits to passengers, it may be also be a fanciful one.

Hugh Woolner was not the first charming rogue to have won Helen's attentions. In her mid-twenties, she had fallen for Edward W. Candee, a wealthy businessman from Norwalk, Connecticut. Her marriage to him produced a daughter and a son, but Candee proved to be an abusive drunk who eventually abandoned his wife and children. Helen could have turned to her family for help—the Churchill Hungerfords were a comfortably off and socially prominent clan—but she chose instead to generate her own income by becoming a journalist. Articles with her byline soon appeared in the *Ladies' Home Journal, Harper's Bazaar,* and other women's magazines, and in 1900 she produced a self-help book, *How Women May Earn a Living,* that became a bestseller. The next year she published her only novel, *An Oklahoma Romance,* which was praised by reviewers for its authentic descriptions of the western territory, though whether the passionate love affair it depicts is also authentic is unknown. Helen had spent several years in Guthrie, Oklahoma, in the mid 1890s to facilitate a divorce from Candee. To both seek a divorce and move to a frontier town was highly unconventional for a woman of her background, but Helen had an independence of mind that was well ahead of her time.

By 1904, Helen and her children were living in Washington, D.C., and within a few years the *Washington Times* would describe her as "a member of the city's most exclusive smart set" who had "attained a reputation as a brilliant hostess" and at whose Rhode Island Avenue mansion "some of the world's most prominent persons have visited." This style of living was made possible by an inheritance she had come into after her mother's death, but Helen continued to earn money through her writing and by advising some of Washington's leading ladies on how to decorate their homes. Among her clients was Mathilde Townsend Gerry, Archie Butt's lost love, as well as both of the first ladies Archie served, Edith Roosevelt and Nellie Taft. Helen had grown up with antiques—a chair owned by *Mayflower* elder William Brewster was a family heirloom— and her advocacy for their use was featured in her 1906 book *Decorative Styles and Periods*. Horses had also been part of her childhood in the Connecticut countryside, and in Washington she rode with Clarence Moore and his wife at the Chevy Chase Hunt Club. Helen was an active campaigner for women's voting rights and would lead a contingent of smartly dressed equestriennes in the historic Woman Suffrage Parade in Washington on March 3, 1913.

Although fully committed to the cause of female suffrage, Helen declared that, unlike some of the more severe supporters of votes for women, she had no interest in "dressing like the matron in an asylum." The social columns often commented on the elegant attire of the "lovely Mrs. Churchill Candee," who was fond of black velvet and ermine and the large feathered hats then so much in fashion. An equally chic but more modest hat crowned her head as she sat reading on the *Titanic*'s enclosed promenade deck, where she usually reserved two steamer chairs, "one for myself and the other for callers, or for self protection." Returning there after luncheon one day, Mrs. Candee found all six of her "coterie" waiting by her chairs. In addition to Gracie's trio and Hugh Woolner, her other admirers were two acquaintances that Woolner had made on board. One was Mauritz Håkan Björnström-Steffansson, the twenty-eight-year-old son of a Swedish pulp baron who was pursuing technical studies in Washington, and the other was a jolly, rotund Irish engineer named Edward Colley, who had a home in Victoria, British Columbia.

"We are here to amuse you," one of them announced. "All of us here have the same thought, which is that you must never be alone." Her solicitous admirers were well aware that Mrs. Candee was returning to

Helen Candee was frequently to be found
reading in a steamer chair on the enclosed
A-deck promenade.

America to be at the bedside of her injured son, Harold. Archie Butt
and Frank Millet, two Washington acquaintances, may also have stopped
at her steamer chair to offer some polite words of concern during their
daily walks around the decks. Ella White's companion, Marie Young, frequently spotted them out walking together and later described how the
"two famous men passed many times every day in a vigorous constitu-
tional, one [Archie] talking always—as rapidly as he walked—the other
a good and smiling listener."

Marie Young had been a music teacher to the Roosevelt children in
Washington and knew who both Archie and Frank were, though she
was not an acquaintance. On her regular visits to the galleys on D deck,

where she went to check on "the fancy French poultry we were bringing home," Marie also enjoyed seeing some of the workings of the ship. She would later describe "the cooks before their great cauldrons of porcelain and the bakers turning out the huge loaves of bread, a hamper of which was later brought up on deck, to supply the life boats." She had asked the ship's carpenter to have crates built for the hens and roosters, and when she paid him with gold coins, he thanked her by saying, "It is such good luck to receive gold on a first voyage." Meanwhile, the hens laid eggs busily, and Marie relayed each day's count to Ella White, who remained cabin-bound in their C-deck stateroom, recovering from her fall while boarding.

Another passenger who was keeping to his cabin was Hugo Ross, the ailing member of the Canadian "Three Musketeers" who had been brought aboard in Southampton on a stretcher. His companions Thomson Beattie and Thomas McCaffry would often look in on his A-deck stateroom, as would another old friend, Major Arthur Peuchen, a Toronto millionaire, militia officer, and yachtsman. Ross had crewed for Peuchen on his sixty-five-foot yacht, the *Vreda*, while a student at the University of Toronto, and had often joined him in post-race celebrations on the veranda of the Royal Canadian Yacht Club overlooking Lake Ontario. Peuchen had no doubt invited Ross to visit "Woodlands," his estate on Lake Simcoe north of the city, where boating was combined with rounds of tennis, golf, and croquet on the grassy acreage that surrounded the high-gabled red-brick house. All of this, along with a substantial home at 599 Jarvis, then Toronto's grandest street, was made possible by Peuchen's development of an innovative method for extracting acetone (a chemical once primarily used in making explosives) from wood. His Standard Chemical Company owned large tracts of timber in Alberta and factories in Ontario and Quebec, which shipped crude alcohols to refineries in England, Germany, and France. Peuchen's wide-ranging business interests made him a frequent transatlantic traveler; the *Titanic*'s first crossing would be his fortieth, and he was aiming to be home for his fifty-third birthday on April 18.

Peuchen was one of thirty Canadians traveling in first class, and they

Major Arthur Peuchen

comprise a fascinating sampling of the young dominion's business elite. If America's Gilded Age plutocracy was a small world, then Canada's was a village. Major Peuchen knew most of the prominent Canadians on board, and he was to his shipboard circle what Colonel Gracie was to "our coterie." The similarities between the two men continue even further: both were born in 1859; both were comfortably off and owed their military titles to fashionable militia regiments; both were similarly mustached (though Peuchen also sported a small goatee)—and both were expansive, often garrulous, men.

Though he had booked only a modest cabin on C deck, Arthur Peuchen was enjoying the *Titanic*'s comforts and would later declare, "The *Titanic* was a good boat, luxuriously fitted up—I was pleased with her. But when I heard that our captain was Captain Smith, I said, 'Surely we are not going to have that man.' " Peuchen thought Smith was rather too much the society captain. Opining about captains and ships was a common conversational gambit among the well traveled, and Peuchen no doubt pontificated about Captain Smith to his table companions, Harry Markland Molson, a member of the famous brewing family and director of the Molson's Bank in Montreal, and Hudson J. C. Allison, who at thirty has already made a killing in Montreal real estate and stocks. Allison was traveling with his young wife, Bess, their two infant children, and four servants they had recently hired in England. Molson, the wealthiest Canadian on board, was a director of one of Peuchen's companies and had been persuaded by him in London to travel on the *Titanic* rather than wait for the *Lusitania.*

A quiet, unassuming man with a clipped beard and mustache, Molson was still a bachelor at fifty-five—though not of the confirmed variety: his nickname "Merry Larkwand" (a play on "Harry Markland") had been earned by his reputation as a playboy. In *The Molson Saga*, family chronicler Shirley E. Woods writes that Harry had for some years maintained an intimate relationship with Florence Morris, the attractive wife of one of his cousins. Florence's husband seemingly acquiesced to the affair—his wife would often cruise alone with Molson on his yacht or stay with him at his summer house—and the ménage à trois was no secret in Montreal society. Before departing for England, Molson had changed his will, leaving one of his houses and a substantial sum of cash to Florence, "to be unseizable and entirely her own property."

If the bespectacled "Hud" Allison and his wife had heard rumors of Molson's mistress, they would have chosen to ignore them, since they were a quiet and conservative young couple, actively involved in church work at Montreal's Douglas Methodist Church. While in England, they had arranged for their baby son, Trevor, to be baptized at a church in Epworth where Methodism's founder John Wesley had once preached. In London, Hudson Allison had attended a directors' meeting of the British Lumber Corporation, and it was perhaps there that he had encountered Peuchen and agreed to share a table with him on the *Titanic* during the crossing home.

While in his early twenties, Hudson Allison had spent two years in Winnipeg, where he had gotten to know some of the other Canadians now traveling in Peuchen's shipboard coterie—Thomson Beattie of the "Musketeers," for one, as well as the real-estate magnate Mark Fortune and his family. Mark Fortune had arrived in Winnipeg in 1871 when it was little more than a fur-trading outpost and he was a young man from rural Ontario sporting a name and an ambition worthy of a Horatio Alger story. He had shrewdly acquired a thousand acres of land through which Portage Avenue, the burgeoning city's main street, would eventually pass, an investment that would earn him a fortune to match his name. By 1911 Fortune had also made his mark as a city councilor and had built a grand pseudo-Tudor mansion in the city's poshest neighborhood. The following year he decided to take his wife, Mary; nineteen-year-old son, Charles; and three of his daughters, Ethel, twenty-eight, Alice, twenty-four, and Mabel, twenty-three; on a grand tour of Europe.

On the crossing from New York in January aboard the *Franconia*, Alice Fortune had found an admirer in William Sloper, an affable young banker's son from New Britain, Connecticut, who found her to be "a very pretty girl and an excellent dancing partner." Yet the twenty-eight-year-old Sloper was not about to tie himself down to just one girl on this trip of a lifetime. As he recalled in a memoir, there was also the "vivacious, good-looking niece" of a Connecticut couple who caught his fancy, along with "two attractive sisters from Chicago" whom he agreed to join for a few weeks on the Riviera in the spring. But before that there was a Mediterranean cruise to enjoy, followed by an excursion down the Nile. The first stop in Egypt for most tourists was Shepheard's Hotel in Cairo, and when Sloper arrived there in February, he found that the Fortune family was already staying there. He joined them for drinks on the terrace one afternoon, and Alice Fortune soon noticed a small Indian man in a maroon fez waving his hands at them through the terrace balustrades and sent Sloper to fetch him. The Indian proved to be a fortune-teller who, while gazing at Alice's palm, proclaimed, "You are in danger every time you travel on the sea, for I see you adrift on the ocean in an open boat. You will lose everything but your life. You will be saved but others will be lost." This doleful prediction was immediately dismissed with a laugh, and the little fakir was quickly paid and dispatched.

Sloper soon left Cairo on a Nile steamer with the Connecticut couple and their vivacious niece, while the Fortunes and "the Three Musketeers" set off on their own river excursion. They would not see each other again until Sunday, April 7, in London, when Sloper spotted the Fortunes taking tea in the Palm Court of the Carlton Hotel on Pall Mall. "When are you going home?" was Alice's first question after he had joined them. Sloper replied that he had just booked a ticket on the *Mauretania* for Saturday. Alice suggested he try and change his ticket to the *Titanic*, which was sailing on Wednesday, and assured him there would be at least twenty people he knew from the *Franconia* on board. She also agreed to join him the following night for dinner and the theater. When Sloper called on her at the Carlton on Monday evening, he proudly announced that he had booked a stateroom on the *Titanic*. "You have forgotten that I am a dangerous person to travel with," Alice replied playfully, reminding him of the fortune-teller's prediction in Cairo. Sloper was merely amused at this and on Wednesday morning he met the Fortunes at Waterloo Station to board the Boat Train for Southampton.

BY FOUR O'CLOCK on Saturday, Daisy Spedden had finished her last hand of cards with Jim Smith and decided to have a tea tray brought to her in the lounge. After tea, she chatted with Malvina Cornell, the wife of a New York judge, and her sister Caroline Brown, whose husband was a partner in the Boston publishing firm of Little, Brown. A third sister, fifty-three-year-old Charlotte Appleton, was also on board, as the three women were returning from the funeral in England of an elder sister who had married a British diplomat. Archibald Gracie's wife was a friend of "the Lamson sisters," as these women had once been known, and on meeting them while boarding in Southampton, Gracie had volunteered to be their male "protector" on board, the same quaintly gallant service he had offered to Mrs. Candee. He later met a fourth and younger member of this all-female coterie, thirty-six-year-old Edith Corse Evans, a relation by marriage to Malvina Cornell, who boarded in Cherbourg. "How little did I know of the responsibility I took upon myself for their safety," Gracie would later write regarding these four women.

In the late afternoon, the decks began to fill up once again with passengers taking their pre-dinner exercise. Norris Williams and his father had walked on the boat deck that afternoon in their fur coats, and Norris recalled that the main topic of conversation among those they met was "the speed of the boat and how she would prove by far the most popular boat on the ocean." As the sun headed toward the Atlantic horizon for another end-of-day display, Steward Fletcher put his bugle to his lips to signal that it was time for passengers to dress for what would be the *Titanic*'s penultimate dinner.

Lucile, Lady Duff Gordon, and her husband, Sir Cosmo Duff Gordon,
seen fishing at his Aberdeenshire estate.

DESIGNING WOMAN

While Helen Candee, Edith Rosenbaum, and Ninette Aubart contemplated which of their Paris-designed gowns they would don for Saturday's dinner, some of the other first-class ladies were selecting dresses created by the most fashionable English couturiere, Lucile, Lady Duff Gordon. That the designer of their exquisitely finished Lucile gowns was actually on board was not something many of them realized, since she was traveling under an assumed name. On the passenger list a "Mr. and Mrs. Morgan" appear as the residents of portside cabins A-16 and A-20 when, in fact, these rooms were occupied by Sir Cosmo and Lady Duff Gordon.

The "Morgan" pseudonym was likely employed to allow the Duff Gordons a quiet crossing, free from a flurry of shipboard invitations that would have required Lucile to spend her time charming the wealthy ladies who formed so much of her clientele. And for her husband, a reserved Scottish baronet, seven days of making small talk with ostentatious Americans would have been a week of purgatory. Sir Cosmo particularly detested the New York reporters who would be waiting at the pier to pester his wife with impertinent questions if they knew that she was on board. Lucile did not travel often with her husband, but this trip required his steady business hand as she was about to negotiate the lease for larger premises for the New York branch of Lucile Ltd. It was business that had first brought them together—Cosmo had invested in her fledgling fashion house in 1895—but he had soon become captivated by the small, spirited woman behind the enterprise. His mother, however, was adamantly opposed to a "scandalous union" with a divorcée, so they were not married until after her death in 1900.

Like Helen Candee, Lucile had made an unfortunate first marriage. At the age of twenty-one she had married James Stuart Wallace, a wine merchant who was twenty years her senior. Wallace soon displayed an excessive fondness for the product he sold and was serially unfaithful, giving Lucile what she called the worst six years she ever knew. After he abandoned her for a music hall dancer, she was determined to divorce him, an action that at the time was both expensive and stigmatizing for a woman. Left with a young daughter and no source of income, Lucy (as she was familiarly known) realized she must find work, though options for genteel women were limited. But soon she had an idea. "One morning when I was making a little dress for [daughter] Esmé," she wrote, "I had a flash of inspiration. Whatever I could or could not do, I could make clothes. I would be a dressmaker."

Lucy could indeed make clothes—for most of her life it had been a necessity. Much of her childhood had been spent in Canada, in what was then the backwoods town of Guelph, Ontario. Her father, Douglas Sutherland, an engineer from Nova Scotia, had met her mother, Elinor Saunders, the daughter of the local magistrate, while working there in 1859 on the construction of the Grand Trunk railway line. Shortly after their marriage in 1861, engineering work took Sutherland first to New York, then to Brazil, and finally to Italy. His wife went with him but stayed in lodgings in London while he was working in Italy, and it was there that Lucy was born in June of 1863. The following year another daughter, Elinor, was born in October of 1864, but only five months later Douglas Sutherland fell ill with typhoid and died. His wife was forced to return to Canada with her two small girls and live with her family at a farm called Summerhill on the outskirts of Guelph.

The household at Summerhill was dominated by Lucy's grandmother, a formidable Victorian matriarch in black bombazine who was determined to instill genteel manners in her granddaughters. Life could be rather drab in the gray limestone house on the hill, particularly during the long winter months, but each year was brightened by the arrival of *le tonneau bienvenue*, a barrel sent from Paris by the family's French relatives. The

Lucy Sutherland, aged ten

two girls shivered with anticipation as the top of the barrel was pried off to reveal brightly colored dresses, silk stockings, ribboned bonnets, frothy lace petticoats, corsets, and even gloves and wigs. Most important for Lucy, there were bolts of cloth, the scraps from which she used to create outfits for her handmade dolls.

Before he died, Douglas Sutherland had made his wife promise that his daughters would be raised and educated in England. The only man in Guelph who could help the young widow fulfill this vow was a dour sixty-three-year-old Scotsman named David Kennedy, who had retired to a nearby farm. In October of 1871, Elinor Sutherland became engaged to Kennedy and a few months later, the two girls and their mother and new stepfather sailed for England. It wasn't long before both sisters developed an intense dislike for Kennedy, whom Elinor described as a "crotchety, cranky invalid." They settled in Jersey, a Channel island just off the coast of Normandy, where the living was cheap and the mild climate suited the poor constitution of their stepfather. Kennedy's miserliness meant that the girls were indifferently educated by a succession of underpaid governesses and tutors. Luckily, they found much to fire their imaginations in the library of the handsome

Georgian house that Kennedy had managed to rent quite inexpensively. It also had some first-class paintings on the walls, a Gainsborough, a Lawrence, and a Lely among them, and Lucy soon began sketching costumes inspired by the clothes she saw in the portraits and in books. Her sister Elinor's romantic nature was stirred by the stories of kings and queens she devoured in the library.

Social life in Jersey revolved around Government House, the residence of the lieutenant governor, and Lucy and Elinor soon befriended the governor's daughter. One day when Lucy was eleven, the girls became consumed with excitement when they heard that Lillie Langtry would soon be dining at Government House. Lillie was a local girl, a daughter of the dean of Jersey, who had married and gone to London, where her beauty caught the eye of painters such as John Everett Millais. In the one good black dress she owned, Lillie had also drawn the gaze of the Prince of Wales and soon became his mistress. This granted her entrée to his exclusive Marlborough House set, and before long she was the most celebrated beauty of the age; women imitated her unique style—from her simple coif to her habit of wearing only black or white.

On the night that the "Jersey Lily" was to appear at Government House, Lucy and Elinor hid under a dressing table in the cloakroom, peering through peepholes they had cut in its calico-and-muslin cover. Once Lillie Langtry entered the room, however, the girls' excitement gave them away and the famous beauty pulled them out from beneath their hideaway. Years later, Elinor could still describe the details of Lillie's "white-corded silk dress with a tight bodice and a puffed-up bustle at the back." The "Jersey Lily," too, would remember in her memoir "the two pretty red-headed girls" peeping from under the dressing table.

The next day, the girls spied Mrs. Langtry walking in the town wearing black velvet and furs. Lucy drew a sketch of her that inspired a gown she would make for one of the first balls she attended at Government House. "It was in black velvet," she remembered, "which fell in soft folds to the feet, and there was a little tight bodice finished with a deep belt." While wearing this same black frock at another dance, Lucy met a handsome young army captain who became her first love. Just when it seemed as if marriage to him might be a possibility, however, a lovers' quarrel

Lillie Langtry

erupted. Ignoring her mother's advice, the ever-volatile Lucy packed her bags and went to stay with relatives in England. "I decided that there was only one thing to be done," she later wrote. "I must let him [the army captain] see that I did not care. So to this end I married the next man who asked me, and he happened to be James Stuart Wallace."

After her marriage to Wallace ended in divorce in 1893, Lucy was practically penniless and living in her now-widowed mother's flat near Berkeley Square. Not long after she had her epiphany about becoming a dressmaker, a friend who moved in society circles came to call and mentioned that she needed a new tea gown for an upcoming country house party. Tea gowns, or "teagies" as they were known, were worn without corsets at teatime—a time of day when gentlemen called on their mistresses—and they were filmy, pretty creations designed with just a hint of the boudoir. Lucy set to work creating a tea gown with soft, accordion-pleated folds inspired by one she remembered seeing in a play. At the country house party it drew a host of admiring comments, and before long every woman who had seen it wanted Lucy to make a tea gown for her. Soon she had to hire an assistant to help her fill the demand.

Most fashionable women in 1890s London bought their clothes in Paris, from couturiers like Worth or Doucet, or perhaps took a design from a magazine to their favorite "little dressmaker" to be copied. Lucile could have remained yet another of London's many "little dressmakers" had she not come up with the idea of creating original designs that were not copies of Paris originals. When society women discovered they could have dresses made that would never be seen on anyone else, Lucy's order books quickly filled up. The finishing touches in Lucile's frocks were much admired as well—tiny buttons, frills of lace and ribbon, and delicate silk flowers that became a kind of Lucile signature. By 1893 Lucy had hired four assistants and opened a shop in Old Burlington Street. At Royal Ascot the following June, the society columns noted that frocks by Lucile were much in evidence.

But even more comment would by caused by Lucile's creation of a room at Old Burlington Street where undergarments—hitherto known as "unmentionables"—were displayed. And instead of the plain white cambric underwear that proper women were supposed to wear, Lucy's taffeta-hung Rose Room offered pastel knickers and pale pink lingerie. "In those days virtue was too often expressed by dowdiness," she recalled. "I loosed upon a startled London, a London of flannel underclothes, woolen stockings, and voluminous petticoats, a cascade of chiffons, of draperies as lovely as those of ancient Greece." According to her memoir, "Half the women flocked to see them though they had not the courage to buy them at first. Those cunning little lace motifs . . . those saucy velvet bows . . . might surely be the weapons of the woman who was 'not quite nice.' " To the aristocratic set surrounding the Prince of Wales, being "nice" was an utterly déclassé notion, and when Lucile's cobweblike creations were adopted by women such as the Countess of Warwick, one of the prince's favorites, others in society soon followed.

"Daisy" Warwick was a friend of Lucy's sister, Elinor, who in 1892 had married Clayton Glyn, a bluff Essex squire with an estate not far from the Warwicks' imposing Easton Lodge. Elinor had devoted most of her twenties to finding a wealthy mate from a "good" English family. With no dowry to bring to a marriage, she had had to rely on the allure of her striking looks—bright red hair, green eyes, and perfect pale skin—all complemented by eye-catching clothes made by her sister. After her marriage, however, Elinor was unhappily surprised to learn that Clayton's means were more modest than they seemed. Yet this didn't deter her from dressing in style as she and her husband mixed with "the *crème de la crème* of English aristocracy" at Easton Lodge house parties.

As a divorceé, Lucy was not invited to country house gatherings and preferred, in any case, the company of "café society" as London's haute Bohemia was then called. Yet in this milieu, Lucy did not lack for admirers. One was the artist Philip Burne-Jones, son of the pre-Raphaelite painter Edward Burne-Jones; another was the distinguished throat surgeon Sir Morell Mackenzie, who hosted Thursday evening gatherings of notables from the artistic world. At one of Mackenzie's salons, Lucy met Oscar Wilde, whom she thought was "the oddest creature I had ever seen," wearing black velvet knee breeches and a sunflower in his buttonhole.

Another theatrical figure, the actress Ellen Terry, would make a far greater impression. Lucy became one of the actress's female acolytes, and Terry consoled and encouraged her in the aftermath of her divorce. She also introduced Lucy to friends in the theatrical world which led to her being asked to design costumes for plays. At the time, clothes worn on the stage tended to be made of stiff brocades and velvets, but by using lighter fabrics and creating clothes that could have been worn offstage as well as on, Lucy brought a new realism to theatrical design. Cecil Beaton would recall her costumes as "masterpieces of intricate workmanship" and claim that her influence was enormous. Many years after seeing a "Snow Princess" dress Lucile created for the actress Lily Elsie to wear in

The Merry Widow, Beaton would use it as the inspiration for the white ball gown he designed for Audrey Hepburn in the film of *My Fair Lady.*

Lucy introduced some of the effects she learned in the theater into the world of fashion retailing. When Lucile Ltd. moved to a town house on fashionable Hanover Square in 1897, she decorated the rooms with gray silk wall coverings and installed gilt chairs and couches where customers could sip tea while choosing clothes. And instead of wax dummies displaying her frocks, Lucile had living mannequins, girls she carefully groomed into her own lovely creations with names like "Hebe," "Dolores," and "Gamela." Although some of the Paris couture houses already had "mannequin parades" where models would walk about the showrooms, it is Lucile who can be credited with creating the first real fashion shows.

Shortly after she had moved to larger quarters on Hanover Square in the spring of 1904, Lucy sent out engraved invitations to her first staged fashion "parade," "keeping the illusion that I was inviting my friends to some afternoon party." She realized that "on this parade of mine I would stand or fall and as the day grew near I was terribly anxious." On April 28, however, a good number of Lucile's friends and faithful clients turned up at Hanover Street to find the premises decorated with three thousand handmade silk roses. In the carpeted showroom, Ellen Terry ushered attendees to their seats before a stage that was "all hung with misty olive chiffon curtains . . . which created the effect I wanted." Heads turned when Lillie Langtry took her seat alongside aristocratic luminaries like Princess Alice of Albany and the Duchess of Westminster. Also in attendance was one of Lucy's friends, the always "vivid and amusing" Margot Asquith, whose husband, Herbert Asquith, would later become Britain's prime minister.

As the lights dimmed, a string orchestra began playing, and then the first of the models appeared. "I shall never forget the long-drawn breath of admiration which rippled round the room as the curtains parted," Lucy later wrote, "and the first of my glorious girls stepped upon the stage, pausing to show herself a moment before floating along the room to a burst of applause." The next day the newspapers raved about Lucile's "gallery of exquisite creations," and Lucy herself wrote, "There was never such a triumph for me as that afternoon. Orders flowed in by the dozen, so that saleswomen could hardly cope with them." Within months she was putting on as many as three shows a day, and in the spring of the following year, she began hosting parades of outdoor wear in the garden at Hanover Square, sometimes with models accompanied by pedigreed dogs on jeweled leashes, each "matched" to the model's dress. One newspaper dubbed Lucile's unique style as "Lady Duff and Her Stuff" since by then Madame Lucile had become equally well known as Lady Cosmo Duff Gordon—though it had very nearly turned out otherwise.

By the time Cosmo's mother died in early 1900, he had almost missed his chance with Lucy. That spring she had gone to Monte Carlo with her mother for a holiday during which a titled (and married) Irish landowner began being very attentive to her. When Lucy and her mother moved on to Venice, the Irish baron followed, and rumors soon reached London that he was planning to divorce his wife in favor of Lucy. On catching wind of this, a furious Cosmo sent a telegram to her hotel saying, "If you are going to marry anyone it is going to be me." He then rushed to Venice, had a noisy confrontation with his rival in the hotel lobby, and persuaded Lucy to marry him instead.

On May 24, 1900, they were married at the British Consulate in Venice, and on the honeymoon that followed Lucy would write that they were both very much in love. It would not be long, however, before she would be complaining that Cosmo was "most extraordinarily dull to be with." She found visits to his Scottish estate at Maryculter in Aberdeenshire to be "deadly, *deadly* dull," since he was a keen sportsman and she was not. At house parties, Cosmo's idea of good fun was to have some of the guests don fencing masks while he shot at them with wax bullets. Cosmo himself had lost an eye in a shooting accident but this did not lessen his expertise as a fencer, and he would lead the British fencing team to a silver medal in the 1906 Olympics. He was also tall (six-three) and quite presentably handsome behind his handlebar mustache, and his title unquestionably raised Lucy's status.

Her husband's baronetcy notwithstanding, as a divorcée, Lucy could not take part in the society ritual of being presented at court. Her sister, Elinor, however, *was* presented at Buckingham Palace in May of 1896, a fact that Lucy would always bitterly resent, though she designed a lovely white satin court dress for her sister to wear along with the requisite white ostrich plumes. By then Elinor was four years into her marriage to Clayton Glyn and had a daughter, Margot, who was almost three. But the romance with Glyn had evaporated; in the style of many men of his class, he had begun being unfaithful after only two years of married life.

While recovering from the difficult birth of her second daughter, Elinor began penning a comic novel entitled *The Visits of Elizabeth*, which satirized some of the manners and mores she had observed at country house parties. Her friend Daisy Warwick found the manuscript highly amusing and used her connections to have it serialized in a London newspaper. The excerpts were published anonymously, but after they became a much-talked-about success, Elinor couldn't resist stepping forward to take the credit. When *The Visits of Elizabeth* was published in book form in 1901, the career of Elinor Glyn, novelist, was launched. Several more novels followed, but it was the publication of a steamy love story in 1907 called *Three Weeks* that would make her both famous—and notorious. The story of a three-week affair between a handsome young Englishman and an exotic older woman (the queen of an unnamed Balkan kingdom), the novel was based on Elinor's own short-lived but passionate attachment to a young Guards officer named Alistair Innes Kerr, a son of

Elinor Glyn

the Duke of Roxburghe. Friends who read the manuscript urged her not to publish it, but she needed the advance money, as Glyn's finances were rapidly proceeding from precarious to calamitous. The book was a runaway bestseller—it would eventually sell more than five million copies and be widely translated internationally. But it was a *succès de scandale*—the novel was condemned as unfit for the young and was banned in Boston and, for a time, in Canada. Though tame by modern standards, *Three Weeks* shocked not just because it described adultery and an out-of-wedlock birth, but because it was the story of a brief affair that was initiated, controlled, and finally ended by the female. This contravened all the sexual power conventions of the day, but by so doing Elinor launched a new publishing genre—the erotic romance novel.

The key seduction scene in *Three Weeks* takes place on a couch draped in a tiger skin, which prompted an anonymous bit of doggerel that would forever dog Elinor:

> *Would you like to sin*
> *With Elinor Glyn*
> *On a tiger skin?*
> *Or would you prefer*
> *To err*
> *With her*
> *On some other fur?*

Along with the undulations on tiger skins, clothes are ubiquitous in *Three Weeks,* and many of the shimmering garments described are unmistakably Lucile in style. Lucy would return the compliment by naming a provocative new frock "the Elinor Glyn."

For her first American publicity tour, Elinor packed several trunks of Lucile-designed clothes, and on arrival in New York harbor on October 5, 1907, she was garbed entirely in purple, including a hat with trailing purple chiffon veiling—all evoking the heroine of her book. The press was captivated, and soon invitations from leading hostesses began arriving at her suite in the Plaza. When Lucy heard of Elinor's success, she decided to come over in December to scout prospects for a New York branch of Lucile Ltd. While staying with her newly famous sister at the Plaza, she wrote home to Cosmo: "I'm sure we can make a fortune here, if we can find the money. There are such opportunities of wearing good clothes here." Lucy returned to London in January while Elinor stayed on in New York, relieved to no longer have to share the spotlight with her sister.

During her New York stay with Elinor, Lucy had noted the value of publicity in making a splash in America. "The one thing that counts," she would write, "is self-advertisement of the most blatant sort." For the New York branch of Lucile Ltd., she found a brownstone on West 36th Street and in late 1909 asked her friend, the pioneering interior designer Elsie de Wolfe, to decorate it in the style of her shop on Hanover Square. Elsie also hired a publicist who generated such a flurry of articles with headlines like LADY DUFF GORDON, FIRST ENGLISH SWELL TO TRADE IN NEW YORK that one newspaperman waggishly dubbed Lucile "Lady Muff Boredom."

Yet the press went into raptures when Lucy arrived on the *Lusitania* in early March of 1910 with four of her statuesque models and a new collection of what she called "dream dresses." This was a variant on her theme of "personality frocks" or "emotional gowns" where each dress was given a name to reflect its "personality," whether it be "When Passion's Thrall Is O'er," "The Sighing Sound of Lips Unsatisfied," or "Red Mouth of a Venomous Flower." In a crasser mode she dubbed part of her American collection "Money Dresses," and, in case anyone missed the point, explained in her advertising copy, "because it takes so much to buy them." Such blatancy seems to have discouraged very few, since on opening day orders were taken for over a thousand gowns, none of them costing less then $300 (the equivalent of $6,000 today).

Her fashion shows were so mobbed that lineups of elegant ladies stretched down West 36th Street and Lucile came up with a plan to sell tickets and donate the proceeds to the Actors Fund. Sitting on a divan next to Lucy at the first New York fashion show was her good friend Anne Morgan, daughter of J. P. Morgan and a principal investor in her New York venture. "Ours was a new playhouse for rich American women," one of Lucile's employees would recall. "Never had we seen such extravagance, or seen so little importance attached to the price of clothes." Lucile's American clients would range from Gertrude Vanderbilt Whitney and Alice Roosevelt Longworth to the dancer Irene Castle and the stars of the Ziegfeld Follies. Madeleine Force and her mother would also visit the 36th Street salon to shop for a Lucile trousseau before her 1911 wedding to John Jacob Astor.

Having conquered New York, Lucile's next pinnacle was Paris. The Parisian designers looked askance at the English invader, but after the opening of her new salon on April 4, 1911, Lucy had the satisfaction of reading in a French newspaper, "The dramatic performance with which Lady Duff Gordon startled Paris today will be copied by every self-respecting couturier here before long." Even French *Vogue* would eventually succumb, noting: "We are so accustomed to having everything of value come out of Paris, that we are amazed to find an Englishwoman making some of the greatest contributions to fashion anyone ever made." For the girl from the Canadian backwoods who had been thrilled to receive a barrel of cast-off clothes from Paris each year, this must have been a very sweet victory indeed.

The following April she was required in New York to sign the lease for her new shop. "As business called me over in a great hurry," she recalled, "I booked passage on the first available boat. The boat was the *Titanic*." On the platform at the Gare St. Lazare a group of her shopgirls and mannequins showed up to give her a surprise send-off, pressing a basket of lily-of-the-valley into her arms. Usually, a contingent of employees would have traveled with her: "The designer was accustomed to traveling grandly," writes her biographer Randy Bryan Bigham, "complete with an armful of Pekinese and an entourage of beautiful models dressed in her latest fashions." This time, no doubt in deference to Cosmo, she had brought along only her personal assistant, Laura Mabel Francatelli, familiarly known as either "Mabel" or "Franks."

Lucy would later claim that she had felt some anxiety about making the crossing on a new ship, but once settled in her *Titanic* stateroom, she relaxed. "Everything aboard this lovely ship reassured me, from Captain Smith with his kindly, bearded face and genial manner . . . to my merry

Irish stewardess with her soft brogue." Lucile was also delighted with her "pretty little cabin, with its electric heater and pink curtains" that made it "a pleasure to go to bed." When Lucile did retire for the night, however, it was not with Cosmo, who had his own cabin across the corridor. The relationship that had begun as business now appeared to be mostly about business; in a drama in which she held center stage he had become a supporting player. In photographs, Lucy usually stands apart from Cosmo, staring out at the camera while he casts a puzzled but adoring gaze in her direction.

"One can only amuse oneself when one has a nice young man," Lucy had once observed, and she indeed cultivated a constant stream of young male admirers. Cosmo was fairly complaisant about this since most of them were homosexual; a granddaughter remembers that Lucile was "regularly surrounded by queer gentlemen who were designers in their turn, picked up pins and did her bidding." Edward Molyneux, whom Lucy called "Toni," was just one of the protégés who would later become a celebrated designer in his own right. Among her female friends, lesbians were particularly prominent: her closest friends in New York were Elsie de Wolfe and her partner, the theatrical agent Bessie Marbury, as well as Anne Morgan and her lover Ann Harriman Vanderbilt, and in Paris she was friendly with the lesbian novelist Natalie Barney and her circle. Lucy admired these independent, forthright women, and according to Randy Bryan Bigham, "a sexual ambiguity on Lucy's part is possible."

DURING THE *TITANIC*'S "dressing hour" on Saturday, April 13, Charlotte Cardeza, our lady of the fourteen trunks, may have instructed her maid to select her rose-colored Lucile evening dress from the eleven gowns she had with her. Mrs. Cardeza also owned one of Lucile's exquisite satin petticoats trimmed with lace and flowers and would list it on her liability claim with a value of $300 ($6,000 today). Marian Thayer, the wife of the Pennsylvania Railroad vice president John Thayer, may also have worn a Lucile gown that evening since she was both a client and a friend of Lucy's. But no passenger was a better exemplar of the Lucile look than the designer herself. *Vogue* noted that her personal style was very simple though "smart to the last degree." Black remained a favorite color, recalling the hand-sewn dress she had worn to her first Government House ball.

On that Saturday evening, therefore, one can imagine Lucile in a black evening gown, accented by the pearl earrings she often favored, taking Cosmo's arm as they descended the grand staircase to the dining saloon on D deck. As they stepped onto the blue-and-red-carpeted expanse of the Palm Room, they were greeted by what she described as "the hum of voices, the lilt of a German waltz—the unheeding sounds of a small world bent on pleasure." But what she calls in her next sentence the "disaster swift and overwhelming" was now only one night away.

The church service was held in front of a carved oak sideboard (top, at center) in the first-class dining saloon. The piano installed there was reserved for Sunday services.

A CALM SUNDAY

Time like an ever rolling stream
Bears all its sons away

The old English hymn "O God Our Help in Ages Past" received a full-voiced rendition at divine service on Sunday morning, since "quite one-half" of the 329 first-class passengers, as noted by Margaret Brown, were in attendance. It was held at 10:30 in the center section of the dining saloon, where a large and elaborately carved oak sideboard with a piano set into it provided a fittingly ecclesiastical-looking backdrop. Captain Smith no doubt cut an impressive figure as he stood before it in his gold-trimmed blue uniform reading from the White Star Line prayer book. It is generally assumed that the captain conducted the service since it was the first of a maiden voyage and there was nothing urgent requiring his presence on the bridge. A message from the Cunard liner *Caronia* had been received in the Marconi Room at 9 a.m. warning of "bergs, growlers and field ice," but its estimated position lay well ahead of the ship's course.

Archibald Gracie was impressed by the reading of the "Prayer for Those at Sea" that morning, and also by the words to "O God Our Help in Ages Past." W. T. Stead admired the old Isaac Watts hymn as well, and had included it in a collection of songs of worship he had compiled in 1897 entitled *Hymns That Have Helped.* For the book, Stead had asked prominent people to name their favorite hymns, and "O God Our Help" had been selected by the future prime minister Herbert Asquith, while the future King Edward VII had chosen "Nearer My God to Thee," a hymn that would become forever associated with the *Titanic.* Archie Butt had asked Theodore Roosevelt to name his favorite hymn after church during his visit to Sagamore Hill in July of 1908. Archie described to his mother how the president and first family members had mentioned several hymns, and then, with eerie foreshadowing, he wrote, "At my funeral I should like to have sung 'Nearer My God to Thee' . . . it appeals to the sentimental side of me."

Even in worship, the distinction of classes was observed on the *Titanic*; assistant purser Reginald Barker conducted the service for second-class passengers in their dining saloon, and a Catholic mass was held in the second-class lounge by Father Thomas Byles, followed by one for those in third class. (There was no Sabbath observance for the significant number of Jews on board, though kosher food was available in all classes.) The first-class church service ended shortly after eleven, and Daisy Spedden, an accomplished pianist, stayed on to play the piano while the dining saloon stewards rearranged the chairs and prepared the tables for Sunday luncheon. At noon, the day's mileage was posted and this again became a principal topic of lunchtime conversation with many noting that today's tally of 546 nautical miles was the best so far. A pink-cheeked Archibald Gracie likely recounted to his tablemates Edward Kent and Jim Smith how he had arisen early that morning for a game of squash with the ship's racket professional and followed it with a dip in the pool. Over the past four days he had enjoyed the ship's lavish meals and comforts "as if I were in a summer palace on the seashore," but now felt in need of some exercise and had made an appointment with the ship's racket profes-sional to play squash again the next morning.

Archie Butt, Frank Millet, and Clarence Moore were back at their reg-ular table for Sunday luncheon, and that afternoon Archie and Moore took a walk on deck despite the chilly weather, which kept many passengers indoors. After luncheon, Archibald Gracie repaired to his usual haunt, the lounge, and returned his finished copy of *Old Dominion* to the library steward. Once again he chatted with Isidor and Ida Straus, who told him that they were sending a wireless message to their son and his wife who were traveling to Europe on board the German liner *Amerika*. The can-ister containing the Strauses' message would have joined many others in the wire basket in the Marconi Room since the wireless equipment had been out of commission for most of the night and the two operators were now working furiously to clear the backlog. At 1:40 p.m. they paused for an incoming message from the White Star steamer *Baltic*, which notified them that "the Greek steamer *Athinai* reports passing icebergs and large quantity of field ice." This message was quickly forwarded to Captain Smith, who, instead of giving it to the officers on watch, put it in his pocket. He soon ran into Bruce Ismay chatting on the windowed A-deck promenade with George and Eleanor Widener and passed the message to him. Ismay gave it a brief glance and then pocketed it.

Around this time, cards were being dealt for a poker game hosted by Charlotte Cardeza's son, Thomas, on the private deck of their deluxe B-deck suite. Among those present was a New York theatrical producer named Henry B. Harris, who had invited his wife René to sit in as the eighth "man" at the table. During an earlier poker session, there had

been suspicions that one of the players was a professional gambler, and rather than bar him from the next game, it was thought easier to simply let him see that the table was full. When the suspected cardsharp was later pointed out to René, she "thought he was a minister of the gospel, he looked so virtuous."

René also recalled that stakes were a dollar a chip and that she was ahead by $90 when the bugle signaling the dressing hour ended their card play. If any of the more conservative matrons on board had spied the petite René playing poker (and very likely puffing on a cigarette) while surrounded by seven men, there would have been some raised eyebrows. Yet this would not have troubled René in the slightest—it was her brash and outspoken nature that had attracted the more reserved Henry—"my boy," as she

René and Henry B. Harris

called him—in the first place. And for René, the *Titanic* so far had been "one big party" with "a spirit of camaraderie unlike any I had experienced on previous trips." She and Henry had bonded with Jacques Futrelle, the mystery writer whom Francis Browne had photographed on the first day, and with his wife, May. The Harrises already knew the Futrelles, probably from when Jacques had worked in the theater some years before, and were pleased to discover that their cabin was just across the corridor. Other acquaintances on board included John and Madeleine Astor.

The high life would once have seemed an unlikely prospect for Irene (René) Wallach, the seventh of nine children born to a large Jewish family in Washington, D.C. Her father owned a jewelry store located beside the Willard Hotel but died when she was six, leaving her mother with five children to support. The family took in boarders to help make ends meet, and several of them were secretaries on Capitol Hill. One suggested to the teenaged René that she take a stenographic and typewriting course, which she did, and by nineteen she had landed a job as secretary to a Tennessee congressman. She also studied law at night school, and after three years moved to New York to take a clerical position with a Manhattan law firm. After only a few months in her new job, however, René found she "couldn't do a damn thing" as she sat at her desk with a dreamy smile on her face. The cause of the smile was a theatrical promoter named Henry Harris who had been wooing her with flowers, dinners, and carriage rides in Central Park. The romance had begun unpromisingly when Henry had stroked the back of her neck while sitting behind her at a music hall matinee. René had rebuffed him for being "fresh," and when the lights went up she had turned around to rebuke "Mr. Freshy" but then quickly realized, "I knew I couldn't hate him. He had the softest eyes and the loveliest smile I ever saw."

On October 22, 1899, Henry Burkhardt Harris, thirty-two, and Irene Wallach, twenty-three, were married. René gave up her legal ambitions and transferred her considerable energies to Henry B. Harris Enterprises, the company her husband set up in 1901. She helped out at the office, read scripts, attended rehearsals, and even played a small part in one production. The couple took an apartment at the Wellington Hotel where René befriended Evelyn Nesbit, who was living there with the support of

Stanford White. René found the sixteen-year-old Nesbit to be "childlike and lovable" and would often play Ping-Pong with her in the lounge. She was aware of the famous architect's interest in Evelyn but never believed any romance was involved until the story made the headlines. Another famous acquaintance was Lillie Langtry, who became a friend when Henry acted as her U.S. manager in 1902. Still beautiful in her fifties, Lillie was a big draw when she brought plays to Broadway and would later even tour in a one-acter on the vaudeville circuit. According to René, Lillie spoke openly of her affair with King Edward VII when he was Prince of Wales, and on a 1906 visit to London she introduced the Harrises to the king at Epsom Downs, where they were invited to watch the races from the royal box.

The early years of the new century were good ones for Harris Enterprises. In 1903, Harry (as Henry B. was known) and a partner built the lavish Hudson Theater, which featured a one-hundred-foot lobby, the largest on Broadway, crowned by a backlit Tiffany stained-glass ceiling. The playhouse opened with Ethel Barrymore starring in the comedy *Cousin Kate*. The Hudson would also present the first exotic, Eastern-styled performances of dancer Ruth St. Denis, one of the pioneers of modern dance and a teacher of Martha Graham. Within two years, Harry was able to buy out his partner and own the Hudson outright, and he would soon acquire another theater, which he named the Harris after his father, who was also a theatrical producer. As the money rolled in, the couple moved to a swankier apartment on Central Park West, with windows overlooking the park, where René would sometimes enjoy a morning canter wearing the smartest of riding togs. "Life was all play for me and I had but to enjoy myself" is how she would recall these heady years of champagne and first nights. Yet René was much more than a pampered wife. "If anything happens to me, she could pick up the reins," Harry would often say of her in words that would prove to be prophetic.

One of Harry's few missteps was the opening of the Folies Bergère Theater in 1911, a New York incarnation of the famed Paris nightspot. "Harry lost $430,000 in nine months," René recalled of the venture. Even though it introduced Mae West to Broadway and premiered such

ragtime tunes as "Oh You Beautiful Doll" and "Alexander's Ragtime
Band," Harry was forced to turn the cabaret back into a conventional
theater named the Fulton. In search of a moneymaker, he backed a musical comedy that had been a success in London, called *The Quaker Girl*.
It proved to be a hit in New York as well, starring one of Harry's dis-
coveries, the winsome Ina Claire, as the girl whose simple Quaker garb
becomes all the rage in Paris. Novelist F. Scott Fitzgerald recalled being
smitten by Ina Claire when he saw the show as a teenager. It was a lavish
production with beautiful gowns designed by Lucile, another acquaintance who would greet Harry on the *Titanic*.

In December of 1911, Harry had decided to sail with René to Europe
for a working holiday during which he would scout out foreign plays that
might help recoup his Folies Bergère losses. Their four-month hiatus from
Broadway would include some shopping in Paris for René as well as side
trips to Italy, Egypt, and Morocco, before they made their way to London,
where business awaited. From London, Harry sent a letter to his office saying that he hadn't seen any plays that would work on the New York stage.
But he told the *London Standard* that he had signed a contract to produce
his first motion picture, a movie version of the play *The Miracle*. Before
boarding the *Titanic*, he also sent a telegram to Ruth St. Denis assuring
her that he would fund a dance recital for her on his return.

WHILE THE POKER chips were piling up beside René Harris on the Car-
dezas' wicker table that Sunday afternoon, "the Two," as Helen Candee
called herself and Hugh Woolner, were braving the cold on the boat deck.
To warm up they stepped into the gymnasium, where the ever-eager
instructor, T. W. McCawley, put Helen on the mechanical horse and then
sat down on a rowing machine and suggested Woolner take the other one
and try to "beat him with a Cambridge stroke." After an hour on what
Helen called the "toys in this wonderful retreat," "the Two" went back
onto the boat deck to find that it was still sunny but getting colder and
that even the loungers on the A-deck promenade had been abandoned.
There were more people walking on the enclosed promenade, however,
and when a beautiful young woman passed by, Helen accused Woolner of

"flirting with the prettiest girl," to which he could only reply sheepishly, "Man is omnivorous." ("The prettiest girl" was almost certainly Dorothy Gibson, a twenty-two-year-old illustrator's model and silent-film actress who was returning with her mother from a European vacation.)

In a quick recovery, Woolner interjected, "One of the women I most admire is this one," noting Ida Straus walking arm in arm with her husband. "They have just finished a Marconi chat with their son, whose east-bound ship is talking to ours," he added. The Strauses had indeed received a reply that afternoon from the Marconigram they had sent to the *Amerika*, an indication that operators Phillips and Bride had caught up with their message backlog. The *Titanic's* Marconi Room had also received and relayed a wireless message that the *Amerika* had sent to the U.S. Hydrographic Office in Washington, D.C., reporting "two large icebergs" in the same area as those already noted by the *Caronia* and the *Athinai.* Since this message concerned navigation, it should have been sent to the bridge, but it was not.

As the sun drew lower in the sky, Marian Thayer went to the B-deck cabin of her grieving friend Emily Ryerson to persuade her to come and see what promised to be a beautiful sunset. Until now, Mrs. Ryerson had not left her cabin except for some walks with her husband after dark when they were less likely to meet anyone. After strolling for about an hour, the two women settled into steamer chairs on the A-deck promenade, where J. Bruce Ismay unexpectedly joined them.

J. Bruce Ismay

"I hope you are comfortable and all right," he said to Emily Ryerson as he seated himself on the next chair. She thanked him for providing an added stateroom and steward for her family, though she was in no mood for conversation and wished he would leave.

"We are in among the icebergs," Ismay suddenly announced, in what Mrs. Ryerson called "his brusque manner." He pulled out the message from the *Baltic* given to him earlier by the captain and held it up for her to see. "We are not going very fast, twenty or twenty-one knots," he continued, "but we are going to start up some new boilers this evening."

Mrs. Ryerson noticed a reference to the *Deutschland* (a German oil tanker) in the Marconigram and asked what that meant.

"It is the *Deutschland* wanting a tow, not under control," Ismay replied.

When she inquired what he was going to do about this, Ismay answered that they were not going to do anything about it but instead would get into New York early and surprise everybody. When the two women's husbands arrived, Ismay departed. Back in their stateroom, Emily Ryerson discussed with her husband what they would do if they arrived in New York on Tuesday night rather than Wednesday morning.

The message from the *Baltic* remained in Ismay's pocket until Captain Smith ran into him in the smoking room at around seven-ten and asked for it back so he could post it in the chart room. The captain was already fully aware that ice lay ahead, and for this reason he had delayed the ship's turning of "the corner," the point at which it changed course to steam due west for the Nantucket Lightship, from 5:00 to 5:50 p.m. This set the *Titanic* on a course ten miles south of the normal shipping route. When Second Officer Lightoller came on duty at 6 p.m., he asked Sixth Officer James Moody to calculate what time they would reach the ice. Moody soon reported that it would be around eleven o'clock that evening.

With poignant symbolism, the *Titanic*'s final sunset was indeed its most beautiful. When Edith Rosenbaum went on deck that evening she noticed a group of men looking over the side toward the stern, admiring the reflection of the sunset on the water that was being thrown up from the propeller in "a wide blood-red band from the ship's side to the horizon." She had been feeling the cold that afternoon in her cabin and soon noticed how frigid it had become out on deck

By then "the Two" were seated snugly amid green cushions by the glowing fireplace in the lounge, where they were served tea and toast. It reminded Helen Candee of settling down before a home fire after a frosty afternoon ride over the fields. The Strauses came in and sat nearby and, on seeing Colonel Gracie in the room, told him of receiving a message in reply from the *Amerika*. When the bugle sounded at 6 p.m., the lounge began to clear as passengers returned to their staterooms to dress for dinner. One deck below, the Cardeza poker party broke up and the Harrises walked to the grand staircase to go down to their C-deck stateroom. Suddenly, René slipped on a greasy spot left by a dropped tea cake and, in her words, "took a header down six or seven steps" and landed "in a heap at the foot of the stairs." Several men, including Harry, rushed to her aid and lifted her up. "I knew that I was all right," she recalled, "except for my right arm. I couldn't bear to have it touched."

She insisted on walking to her stateroom, where Harry called for the ship's doctor, William O'Loughlin. The "little doctor," as René called him, pronounced the arm broken and began to prepare a cast where her arm would be held straight out. But René wanted a second opinion. She had heard that there was a New York orthopedic surgeon on board and, with apologies to Dr. O'Loughlin, asked if he could be consulted. Very soon the burly, bewhiskered figure of Dr. Henry Frauenthal, a specialist in joint diseases, arrived at their cabin door. He recommended that her arm be set with its elbow bent and the palm resting on her shoulder. After this was completed, bed rest was recommended, but René was determined to keep their dinner date with the Futrelles in the Ritz Restaurant. "Although I was suffering torture," she recounted, "I knew I would feel it no less if I stayed in my room ... so I struggled into my dinner dress—a sleeveless one, of course." Meanwhile news of René's accident had spread. "Before I left my room," she recalled, "I had a dozen or more sympathetic messages."

The evening gown that René struggled into was likely one that she had recently purchased in Paris. Her friend and table companion May Futrelle later recalled "how fondly" the women wore their newly acquired Parisian finery that evening. And René's tumble on the stairs may also have been fashion-related—the narrow, tapered "pencil" skirts then so much in style hampered movement and could have contributed to her becoming, quite literally, a fashion victim. Most constricting of all was the ankle-cinched "hobble" skirt championed by designer Paul Poiret, which had been much in vogue in 1910–11. In reaction, Lucile Duff Gordon had designed some of her "pencil" skirts with slits (discreetly covered with fabric) to allow for freer movement. But tapered skirts were for day wear only, and for this Sunday dinner, the most gala so far, the ladies in first class were selecting their showiest evening gowns. Helen Candee observed the women in the Palm Room "shining in pale satins and cling-ing gauze" before dinner and spotted "the prettiest girl" in a "glittering frock of dancing length with silver fringe around her dainty white satin feet." (Dorothy Gibson would later include just such a pair of white satin slippers in her lost luggage claim.) During the dressing hour, jewelry cases had been retrieved from the purser's safe, and May Futrelle recalled how jewels flashed from the gowns of the women at dinner.

Eleanor Widener would probably have donned her famous multi-strand pearl necklace (valued at $250,000), since she and her husband and son Harry were hosting a dinner for Captain Smith in the Ritz Res-taurant at seven-thirty that evening. They had invited their Philadelphia Main Line neighbors—the Thayers from Haverford and William Carter and his wife Lucile from Bryn Mawr. "Billy" Carter, thirty-six, was a keen horseman and polo player, and during the winter he and his family rented Rotherby Manor in Leicestershire so that he could take part in the many fox hunts held near Melton Mowbray. The Carters were returning to "Gwedna," a large colonial-style mansion in Bryn Mawr, with their two children, three servants, two dogs, and a 25-horsepower Renault that was crated and stored in the forward hold. The ninth guest invited to the Wideners' table was Archie Butt, who could be relied on to keep the con-versation lively with witty stories and Washington gossip. For the evening, Archie likely selected his dress uniform, the same one he had worn for his audience with the pope, considering a show of gold lace to be appropriate for dining with the captain and the cream of Philadelphia society. Elea-nor Widener would have conferred earlier with the restaurant's manager, Signor Luigi Gatti, regarding the menu and placement for her guests in the elegant room, which, with its gilded Louis XVI décor, was remarkably similar in style to her own dining room at Lynnewood Hall.

As many of the passengers dressed for dinner, they noticed that the rhythm of the ship's engines had increased, an indication that extra boil-ers had been lit and that an even better mileage tally might be posted at noon tomorrow. At 7:15 Seaman Samuel Hemming, one of the ship's lamp trimmers, arrived on the bridge to report to First Officer Murdoch that all the ship's navigation lights had been lit. Murdoch was then acting as officer of the watch since Lightoller had gone to the officer's mess for dinner. As Hemming was leaving, Murdoch called him back and asked him to close the fore scuttle hatch on the forecastle deck since there was a glow coming from it. "I want everything dark before the bridge," Murdoch ordered in his Scottish-accented voice. With ice ahead, any ambient light could interfere with the lookouts' ability to see clearly. The steamship *Californian* had advised at 6:30 p.m. that it had seen three large bergs five miles to the southwest, but this message wasn't received by the *Titanic*'s Marconi Room. Junior operator Harold Bride was then writing up the day's accounts and letting the equipment cool down after a very busy day. An hour later, when the transmitter was operating again, he intercepted the same message being sent from the *Californian* to the *Antillian* and delivered it to the bridge. By then Second Officer Lightoller had returned from dinner, and on his arrival, Murdoch had remarked on how the temperature had gone down four degrees, to thirty-nine degrees Fahrenheit, in the half hour that he had been gone. Within an hour it would drop to just above freezing.

The passengers, too, were aware of the plunging temperatures, and according to Margaret Brown, some of the women wore warm wraps over their evening dresses to dinner. There was much discussion that evening of the ship's increased speed and the possibility of arriving earlier in New York. There was also talk that icebergs lay ahead. Yet, remarkably, there was no thought of any pending danger. As May Futrelle later wrote:

In the elegantly furnished drawing room [lounge], no premonitory shadow of death was present to cast a cold fear over the gaiety of the evening. It was a brilliant scene, women beautifully gowned, laughing and talking—the odor of flowers—ridiculous to think of danger. Why, it was just like being at some beautiful summer resort. There was not one chance in a million of an accident happening.

Eleanor Widener had reserved a table for nine in the Ritz Restaurant
for a dinner in honor of Captain Smith.

THE LAST EVENING

René Harris was hailed like a wounded hero as she entered the Ritz Restaurant on Harry's arm. Bruce Ismay and Dr. O'Loughlin stood up to greet her from their table by the entrance, George and Eleanor Widener left their dinner guests to do the same, and the Duff Gordons were graciously sympathetic as the Harrises passed by them. Shortly after they had sat down with the Futrelles, Captain Smith, too, stopped by to compliment René on her spirit. "It made me feel that a broken arm was an asset," she later noted.

The Widener dinner party had gathered at seven-thirty in the restaurant's reception room and was soon seated at a long table that extended into an alcove not far from the entrance. Mahala Douglas, who dined on the other side of the alcove with her husband, noticed through an opening in the carved paneling that the captain was seated at the head of the table, with Eleanor Widener to his right and Archie Butt on his left. She also remembered that the tables were decorated with pink roses and white daisies and that the food was superb: "caviar, lobster, quail from Egypt, plover's eggs, and hothouse grapes and fresh peaches." Mahala Dutton Douglas was the second wife of Walter Douglas, a Quaker Oats heir and mill owner from Cedar Rapids, Iowa, who possessed a net worth equal to that of most of the millionaires at the Wideners' table. Widowed in 1899, Douglas had married Mahala in 1906 and had recently retired at the age of fifty to enjoy life with her in a French Renaissance mansion they had built on Lake Minnetonka near Minneapolis. The couple were returning from a five-month

European tour in search of furnishings for the lakeside home that they had dubbed Walden.

Mahala had an artistic temperament and a flair for writing, and she would later describe how the evening passed quietly to the strains of Puccini and Tchaikovsky from the string trio outside in the reception room. She also maintained that "any claims of excessive gaiety" from the Widener table were "absolutely unfounded." Eleanor Widener confirmed that the captain consumed no alcohol at dinner (as White Star regulations forbade), and Marian Thayer claimed that she heard no discussion at the table of icebergs being in the neighborhood since "Mr. Widener, Major Butt and I were engrossed in other subjects during the entire time of the dinner." It seems, however, that it was mainly Archie Butt who engrossed Marian Thayer that night. In an emotive letter sent to President Taft one week after the disaster, she wrote:

> From the moment we met we never moved from each other for the rest of the evening. Never before have I come in such close contact immediately with anyone. He felt the same & we both marveled at the time at the strangeness of such a thing, for we both realized it while actually opening our innermost thoughts to each other. He told me much about his mother and their letters. . . . He spoke with deep enthusiasm of leaving his mark and memorial of truth to the world with those letters which should be published after he had gone.

In case such instant intimacy could be misconstrued, Marian added: "He said I was just like his mother and opened his heart to me & it was as though we had known each other well for years." She even goes on to suggest a past-life connection, a still-exotic notion for the time:

> It was the strangest sensation and felt as tho' a veil was blown aside for those few hours eliminating distance between two who had known each other always <u>well</u> long, long before and had just found each other again—I believe it. Otherwise we could not have met just then and talked as we did.

Marian Thayer and Archie Butt

Observing this intent discussion from across the table, Eleanor Widener may have been less than thrilled that one of her prized guests was being monopolized. She had likely expected Archie to regale them with Washington anecdotes rather than leave her to engage the captain in dinner conversation. Yet she was evidently not marooned with the captain for long, since Marian Thayer reported that the meal was served very quickly and that at eight-thirty the party went out into the reception room for coffee, with Captain Smith departing by eight-forty-five. That an elaborate multi-coursed dinner should be completed in an hour seems surprising, and other guests in the restaurant that evening claimed that the Widener party actually lasted longer. Yet Marian Thayer's timeline agrees with that of Second Officer Lightoller, who stated that the captain arrived on the bridge at eight-fifty-five. Smith's first words to Lightoller were about how cold it had become. Lightoller replied that it was only one degree above freezing and said that he had advised the ship's carpenter to make sure that the liner's water supply didn't freeze.

"There is not much wind," the captain then observed.

"No, it is a flat calm as a matter of fact," Lightoller replied, and Smith repeated, "Yes, a flat calm."

"It is a pity there is not a breeze," Lightoller said, meaning that there would be no waves breaking on the icebergs to make for easier sighting. "In any case," he continued, "there will be a certain amount of reflected light from the bergs." The captain agreed, noting that even with the blue side toward them, the white outline of the icebergs would still be visible. But he added that if it became at all hazy, they would have to slow down, and as he left the bridge at 9:20, said to Lightoller, "If in the slightest degree doubtful, let me know."

Back in the restaurant's reception room, the rest of the Wideners' guests were just finishing their coffee. Archie Butt, it seems, continued to be absorbed in conversation with Marian Thayer, and it was perhaps here, away from the table, that he confided to her that he "did not know how he was going to stand the rushing life he was returning to." From the descriptions in Archie's letters to Clara, "the rushing life" is an apt term for the fevered existence he led in Washington, where long days at the White House were followed by evenings of dinners, receptions, and cotillions. Marian Thayer goes on to describe to President Taft how Archie had agreed to meet her the following afternoon for a session where she would teach him "a method of control of the nerves through which I had just been with a noted Swiss doctor." To acknowledge that one had been receiving treatment of this kind was a remarkably candid confession to make in 1912, particularly to the president of the United States. Mrs. Thayer then tells Taft that she thought "it would be a very wonderful thing for him [Archie] if he could just get hold of it [the nerve control technique] for he was very nervous . . . and we were going to work so hard over it the rest of the time on board."

"Nervous" was then a general term for mental distress and what afflicted Archie might today be diagnosed as an anxiety disorder or even depression. By making himself indispensable, and always available, to the president and to social Washington, Archie's "rushing life" had brought him to the brink of nervous collapse. And despite his time away, he still suffered from black moods, as his cousin and her husband in London had observed. Archie knew that the pace during the coming fall election would be blistering, but he felt unable to leave his post. Doing so, he claimed, would seem disloyal and look as if he were abandoning Taft for Roosevelt. It was this quandary and his anxiety about returning home that kept him talking seriously with Marian Thayer for some time after the dinner.

May Futrelle

A jollier mood prevailed at the Harrises' table, where May Futrelle recalled that her husband and Henry Harris discussed the latest American plays and "everybody was so merry. We were all filled with the joy of living." There was an equally festive air two decks below in the Palm Room, where "our coterie" had assembled after dinner and the orchestra was playing requests. Helen Candee suggested a little Puccini while Hugh Woolner wanted to hear some Dvořák. Helen noticed that "the prettiest girl" asked for dance music and "clicked her satin heels and swayed her adolescent arms to the rhythm." When the orchestra began packing up their instruments at nine-fifteen, Helen and her admirers were in no mood to end the party and so decided to walk up the grand staircase to the Café Parisien. As they sat down at a table for seven, Mrs. Candee saw that the only other occupied table was "made gay by the party of a president's aid [sic]," indicating that by then Archie had put on a more social face and was entertaining a few of the guests he had neglected at dinner.

"But how cold it is, how arctic!" said Helen as she drew close her scarf around her neck.

"Something hot, then," Woolner suggested to the waiter, who took orders for Scotch and lemon, hot whiskey and water, and warm lemonade. But the cold didn't put a chill on their mood, as Helen recalled:

> How gay they were, these six. The talkative man [Gracie] told stories, the sensitive man [Kent] glowed and laughed, the two modest Irishmen [Colley and probably Smith] forgot to be suppressed, the facile Norseman [Björnström-Steffansson] cracked American jokes, the cosmopolitan Englishman [Woolner] expanded, and the lady felt divinely flattered to be in such company.

Inside the restaurant, the Harrises and Futrelles lingered over dinner, as did Walter and Mahala Douglas. Another table was occupied by the Minahans, the Irish-American doctor from Wisconsin and his wife and sister who had boarded in Queenstown. The Duff Gordons had already left, with Lucile donning the squirrel coat she had worn to dinner on account of the cold. She and Cosmo had gone up one deck to the lounge, where they sat with a young New York couple named Edgar and Leila Meyer, who had also dined in the restaurant that evening. Lucile was aware that twenty-five-year-old Leila was the daughter of Andrew Saks, the owner of Saks Fifth Avenue, who had died while dining at Sherry's on April 8. The Meyers had received a telegram in Paris the next day and had quickly booked passage home on the *Titanic* for the tenth. While chatting with them, Lucile brought out her autograph book, which was a "confessions" book, a then-popular novelty with pages where friends could write in appropriate comments about themselves under such headings as "Likes," "Abominations," and even "Madnesses." Edgar Meyer, who was twenty-eight, took Lucile's book, and when he came to "Madnesses," laughed and wrote, "I have only one—to live"—a sad irony given that only hours remained to him.

Upon leaving the restaurant, the Harrises decided to stop in the smoking room for an after-dinner cigarette while the Futrelles opted for a walk on deck since Jacques had a slight headache. René was likely the only woman to "infest" the smoking room that night—to use Frank Millet's term. Frank himself was there, enjoying a round of cards with Clarence Moore. There had been only the two of them at their table in the dining saloon that evening since Archie was dining upstairs. The meal had been the most gala of the voyage so far, with a menu card featuring "Oysters à la Russe," "Filets Mignons Lili," "Calvados-Glazed Roast Duckling," and "Chocolate Painted Eclairs" among its eleven courses. Arrangements of hothouse grapes and other fresh fruits decorated the tables, and two-year-old Loraine Allison had been brought to the table her parents shared with Arthur Peuchen and Harry Molson so she could see how beautiful it was.

Baskets of fruit had adorned the tables in the second-class dining saloon as well, and after dinner a group of about a hundred passengers

Clarence Moore (left) and Frank Millet were among those in the
first-class smoking room on Sunday night.

had taken part in a hymn sing around the piano. In third class the main
meal, as usual, had been served at midday followed by a hearty English
savory tea in the late afternoon. Afterward, in the spartanly furnished
third-class "general room," an informal party had begun with music

provided by the upright piano and the passengers' own instruments. It's unlikely there was much dancing, however, given that the room's large double-backed benches left little open floor space and it was, after all, the Sabbath. At one point a rat was sighted and several young men chased it to squeals from the women. At ten o'clock the stewards turned out the lights in the general room and the "smoke room" next door, and passengers dispersed to their berths in the bow and stern, while a few may have sought dark spaces on the well deck for romantic encounters.

At this time on the bridge, Second Officer Lightoller was preparing to turn over the watch to First Officer Murdoch. Lightoller recapped for Murdoch his earlier conversation with the captain and also told him that he had sent orders up to the crow's nest for the lookouts to keep a sharp eye for small pieces of ice and low-lying bergs known as "growlers." This message had just been passed on to lookouts Fred Fleet and Reginald Lee, who were beginning their two-hour shift. That the crow's nest binoculars still had not been found did not seem to be of pressing concern. And another ice warning message that came into the Marconi Room at about nine-forty may not have struck operator Jack Phillips as being terribly pressing either. He had already delivered several ice messages to the bridge, and this one from the *Mesaba*, describing "heavy pack ice and great number large icebergs, also field ice," likely didn't seem very different from the others. He may have set it aside, as he had just made contact with the wireless station at Cape Race, Newfoundland, and was busily transmitting passenger messages. Second Officer Lightoller would later claim that this all-important message, indicating that not just random icebergs but a huge ice field lay directly ahead of the *Titanic*, went undelivered. As Lightoller left the bridge, he mentioned to Murdoch that he estimated they should reach the ice at around eleven o'clock.

Norris Williams and his father had been out walking on deck after dinner, but even in their fur coats they found it too chilly and so went inside to the smoking room. There they joined a group of men that included John B. Thayer and Archie Butt, and very soon the cold weather and the possibility of icebergs ahead came up for discussion. Charles Williams then related the story of how he had been aboard a ship in 1879 called the *Arizona* when it had struck an iceberg. The collision knocked a hole in the *Arizona*'s forward bow but the crew and passengers had taken bales of cotton from the ship's cargo hold and plugged the leaking bulkhead so that the ship was able make it into St. John's, Newfoundland, thirty-six hours later.

At around the same time, another shipwreck anecdote was being related at a table in the Palm Room to John and Marian Thayer's teenaged son, Jack. With his parents dining upstairs at the Wideners' party, Jack had eaten alone in the dining saloon and then gone into the Palm Room. As he searched for a free table, a young American named Milton Long waved him over. The two struck up a conversation and the twenty-nine-year-old Long, a judge's son from Springfield, Massachusetts, began regaling Thayer with stories of his travels. One of the most impressive of his adventures had occurred in Alaska, where he was on board a small steamer that ran aground on an offshore reef. As the ship was tipping over, Long managed to jump onto some shoals and then made his way from one rock to another until he reached shore with only wet feet.

W. T. Stead was in storytelling mode that evening as well, and his table companion, Frederic Seward, recalled how over cigars in the smoking room Stead told the tale "of a mummy case in the British Museum which, he said, had had amazing adventures, but which punished with great calamities any person who wrote its story. He told of one person after another who . . . had come to grief after writing the story, and added that, although he knew it, he would never write it. He did not say whether ill-luck attached to the mere telling of it." This tale later became attached to the *Titanic* story, and the notion that a mummy with a curse on it was traveling on board her became one of the many enduring myths about the sinking. Stead had also predicted a sea disaster remarkably similar to the one he was about to experience, in an 1886 article entitled "How the Mail Steamer Went Down in Mid-Atlantic," which concluded with the statement "This is exactly what *might* take place and what *will* take place if the liners are sent to sea short of boats."

Sometime after ten o'clock, Walter and Mahala Douglas rose from their table in the now almost-empty restaurant. On the way down to their stateroom on C deck they noticed a strong vibration on the staircase and remarked to each other that the ship was going faster than it ever had. As he sat reading on the bunk in his second-class D-deck cabin, Lawrence Beesley noticed that the "dancing motion" in his mattress caused by vibrations from the engines was more pronounced than usual. The indomitable René Harris had by then persuaded Harry to move on from the smoking room to the first-class lounge, where they, too, sat down with Edgar and Leila Meyer. The Duff Gordons by then had gone—Cosmo had retired to bed in his cabin, while Lucile and her assistant, Franks, sat chatting in front of the electric heater in her room across the hall. An electric fire was also burning in the fireplace of the lounge but it was not providing enough heat to dispel a chill in the room and Harry was soon urging René to go to their stateroom. "I must have looked pretty fagged—I felt it," she recalled, "so at about ten thirty we turned in." In the Café Parisien, Mrs. Candee, too, was feeling the cold, and soon retired to her cabin, possibly escorted by the gentlemanly Edward Kent. The Irish engineer Edward Colley also called it a night while the four other men stayed at the table, finishing what Woolner called their "hot grog."

By eleven, the lounge was mostly empty except for a foursome absorbed in a lively game of bridge. One of the players was William Sloper, the young Connecticut banker who had been persuaded to take the *Titanic* by Alice Fortune. He had spent considerable time with Alice during the first four days of the voyage but had not seen her at all that day. After dinner, he had been writing thank-you letters to his London friends at a desk in the lounge when what he described as "a very pretty young woman" approached and asked him if he would join her group to make a fourth for bridge. Although Sloper was not very proficient at bridge, he wasn't about to turn down an invitation from Dorothy Gibson, the prettiest girl on board. Dorothy's distinctive beauty had also caught the attention of the illustrator Harrison Fisher, who had put her face on the covers of *Cosmopolitan* and the *Saturday Evening Post*, as well as on countless picture postcards. This had led to some appearances in motion pictures, and in July of 1911 Dorothy was hired as the first leading lady for the American branch of Éclair, a French cinema company making films in Fort Lee, New Jersey. By March of 1912 she had completed a string of silent one-reelers and, in need of a rest, decided to take a holiday in Europe with her mother. After only a few weeks abroad, however, she had been called back to Fort Lee by the head of Éclair to start work on two new films.

When Sloper joined Dorothy, she and her mother were sitting with W. T. Stead's tablemate, Frederic Seward, whom Dorothy knew because they attended the same church in New York. Seward asked the library steward to set up a bridge table for them in the center of the room near the fireplace. After a few hours, the four were so involved in their game that they were oblivious to the nearly empty room and to the pacing library steward, who was eager to turn out the lights. Edith Rosenbaum, who had been writing letters at one of the desks in the lounge, realized it was time to go and gave the steward some envelopes to post for her and took two books from

Dorothy Gibson in a Harrison Fisher illustration

the bookcase. Finally at eleven-thirty, the steward asked the bridge players to finish the game so he could close the room. As the group walked toward the grand staircase, Dorothy Gibson announced to William Sloper that she wanted to take a walk around the deck before bedtime. He suggested they both go below and put on warmer clothes and meet on the A-deck staircase landing. He quickly went down one flight to his cabin, put on a Shetland wool V-necked sweater under his suit, donned his winter-weight overcoat, and went up the staircase to wait for Dorothy. A map of the north Atlantic was on the wall nearby, so he began to study it while he waited.

After eleven, the smoking rooms in first and second class were usually the only two public rooms that were kept open. When the café closed, the remaining men from "our coterie" made their way up to the first-class smoking room. Archibald Gracie joined a table where Charles Melville Hays, the stocky, grizzle-bearded president of Canada's Grand Trunk Railway, was holding forth with a cigar in hand. Gracie overheard Hays make a pronouncement that "the White Star, the Cunard, and the Hamburg-American lines are now devoting their attention to a struggle for supremacy in obtaining the most luxurious appointments for their ships, but the time will soon come when the greatest and most appalling of all disasters at sea will be the result." In recalling this, Gracie would write that "the pleasure and comfort which all of us enjoyed upon this floating palace" seemed "an ominous feature to many of us . . . who felt it almost too good to last without some terrible retribution inflicted by the hand of an angry omnipotence." It is unlikely that Charles Hays believed that luxurious accommodations would lead to God's retribution, since he was embarked on the building of a string of luxury railway hotels and was returning home for the opening of the first of them, the Château Laurier in Ottawa, on April 26. A bust of the former Canadian prime minister, Wilfrid Laurier, for whom the hotel was named, was to be unveiled, and accompanying the Hays party was its sculptor, Paul Romaine Chevré. With his drooping mustache Chevré looked every inch the Left Bank *artiste* as he sat at a nearby table enveloped in *tabac noir* smoke and absorbed in auction bridge with two other Frenchmen and one American.

Archie Butt was by then playing bridge whist with Clarence Moore, and two men from the dinner party, Harry Widener and William Carter. Bridge whist was also the game of choice for the three professional gamblers who were setting up an American oil company executive as their next victim. Earlier René Harris had pointed out one of the suspected cardsharps to May Futrelle, who had noted his cold, calculating smile. At a smaller table, Frank Millet was playing cards with a New York stockbroker and yachting enthusiast named Frederick Hoyt, who was returning from a combined business trip and vacation in England with his wife. Arthur Peuchen sat chatting and smoking with two of "the Three Musketeers," Thomson Beattie and Thomas McCaffry, and an Englishman who was headed for Canada. At around eleven-twenty Peuchen bade them good night and headed down to his room on C deck. In cabin C-83, the Harrises were not yet in bed as the pain in René's arm was quite intense, and she had refused to take the morphine the doctor had left. Harry had cut a sleeve out of a pair of pajamas for her, helped her into a bathrobe, and then wrapped her in a blanket on a chair. He sat opposite while they played a game of double Canfield.

Up in the crow's nest the two lookouts were into the second hour of their watch. A slight haze had emerged on the horizon which Fred Fleet had pointed out to Reginald Lee, but neither of them thought it was important enough to report to the bridge. The stars were still twinkling overhead and the sea remained a flat calm. At about ten-thirty the freighter *Californian* had steamed into the ice field that lay ahead of the *Titanic*'s course and had decided to stop there for the night. The captain asked the ship's wireless operator to notify ships in the area about the ice. Just before eleven, Jack Phillips was busily transmitting passenger messages when the *Californian*'s call blasted into his headset: "Say, old man, we are stopped and surrounded by ice." An exhausted Phillips angrily tapped back, "Keep out! Shut up! I am busy. I am working Cape Race." The *Californian*'s operator listened in as Phillips apologized to Cape Race for the interruption and asked for a repeat of the last message. Twenty-five minutes later the *Californian*'s wireless man could still hear Phillips sending messages to Newfoundland, so at 11:35 he took off his headset, turned off his equipment, and went to bed.

On the *Titanic*'s bridge Quartermaster Robert Hichens was at the ship's wheel, with Sixth Officer Moody standing beside him in the wheelhouse. All the lights on the bridge had been extinguished so that they could see clearly through the windows. The ship was now moving at twenty two and a half knots. Suddenly Fred Fleet spied a large, dark shape directly ahead. It could be only one thing. Reaching past Lee, he quickly rang the crow's nest bell three times. He then grabbed the telephone and heard it being picked up in the wheelhouse.

"Is someone there?" Fleet asked.

"Yes," replied Moody. "What do you see?"

"Iceberg right ahead!"

The iceberg struck the liner's starboard bow only thirty-seven seconds after
lookout Fred Fleet telephoned the bridge.

COLLISION AND AFTER

SUNDAY, APRIL 14, 1912, 11:40 P.M.

A blue-white cliff face suddenly loomed out of the darkness. The liner raced on, its prow aimed directly toward it. Fred Fleet braced for a crash. Then slowly, slowly, the ship began to turn. Would they miss it? He saw the tip of the bow slide past. But then came a shuddering jar on the starboard side. Large chunks of ice thudded into the well deck. Fleet heard a grating noise from deep below as the berg scraped along the starboard hull. Less than a minute had passed since he had first sighted it.

As he stood on the staircase landing, William Sloper felt the ship lurch slightly to starboard. It reminded him of a ferryboat striking the planks of a landing slip. Dorothy Gibson came hurrying up the stairs and they ran out onto the A-deck promenade. Peering over the side into the starlit darkness, they could just make out a large white shape disappearing behind the stern. In the smoking room, Hugh Woolner sensed a heavy grinding shock passing right under his feet. Several men headed for the door at the back of the room and he quickly followed. On reaching the afterdeck, Woolner heard excited talk in the night air. Over the clamor a loud voice called out, "An iceberg just passed astern!" Archie Butt soon appeared with the other men from his card game—William Carter, Harry Widener, and Clarence Moore—and just then the engines stopped. The unusual silence caused everyone to become quiet. Algernon Barkworth, a Yorkshire justice of the peace, spotted W. T. Stead, who told him "An iceberg has ground against the starboard side." Soon the words "iceberg" and "nothing to worry about" were passed along. The men nodded, shrugged, and returned to the smoking room and their card games. William Carter, however, left to go down to his cabin on B deck to check on his wife and two sleeping children. Hugh Woolner thought of Helen Candee and decided that he should look in on her. Frank Millet took Carter's place at Archie's table as the bridge whist resumed.

The collision was less noticeable to passengers in their staterooms. Many were in bed and sensed only a slight, grating jar. Ella White was about to turn out the light when it seemed as if the ship ran over a thousand marbles. Lucy Duff Gordon was awakened by an odd rumbling noise that sounded like a giant hand was playing bowls deep beneath her. Madeleine Astor thought there had been an accident in the kitchens. René Harris was still up playing cards with Harry and noticed that the dresses in her open closet were swaying. It wasn't until the engines stopped that René, like many other passengers, realized something might be amiss.

Captain Smith knew it immediately. "What have we struck?" he demanded as he hurried onto the bridge from his cabin behind the wheelhouse.

"An iceberg, sir," First Officer Murdoch replied. He explained how he had tried to maneuver around it but the berg had been too close.

"Close the watertight doors," the captain ordered.

"The watertight doors are closed, sir," Murdoch replied.

In Boiler Room 6 stoker Frederick Barrett had just been sprayed by a geyser of water that had shot through the hull about two feet away from him. When the light above the room's watertight door suddenly began flashing he had been forced to make a run for it and had jumped through the closing door followed by another man, while a third stoker scrambled up an emergency ladder. After climbing to a higher deck, Barrett looked down to Boiler Room 6 and saw that it was already eight feet deep in seawater.

In a small cabin deep in the forward bow, steerage passenger Daniel Buckley was awakened by a shuddering noise. He jumped down from his bunk and felt water under his bare feet. His three roommates from County Cork were still snoring in their bunks and protested groggily when he roused them. Buckley dressed and went out into the corridor. There he heard two crewmen shouting, "All up on deck unless you want to get drowned." As Buckley headed upward, the third-class corridors began to fill with steerage passengers carrying their belongings toward the stern.

As he lay reading on his bunk on D deck, Lawrence Beesley noticed that the dancing motion of his mattress had stopped. Slipping on a dressing gown and shoes, he went out into the corridor and up the staircase to the

Lawrence Beesley

boat deck. As he peered over the side at the calm black sea below, nothing seemed amiss, so he went into the second-class smoking room and asked some of the cardplayers if they knew what had happened. They told him that they had seen an iceberg pass by and gave estimates that it had been anywhere from sixty to a hundred feet high. One of them said, "I expect the iceberg has scratched off some of her new paint and the captain doesn't like to go on until she is painted up again." Another pointed to his glass of whiskey and quipped, "Just run along the deck and see if any ice has come aboard. I would like some for this." Amid the general laughter, Beesley returned to his cabin and resumed reading. But on hearing voices in the corridor, he donned a warm jacket and once again went up to the boat deck. There he saw that the ship was moving ahead slowly and noticed a little white foam breaking at the bow.

The fact that the *Titanic* slowly resumed her course after hitting the iceberg is not included in many accounts of the disaster but it was noted by several others on board besides Lawrence Beesley. Quartermaster Alfred Olliver later testified that Captain Smith gave the "Half Speed Ahead" order for the engines not long after the collision. The captain had by then sent Fourth Officer Boxhall below on a tour of inspection, so it seems likely that he thought the ship would have to limp in to New York or Halifax under its own steam and that they could proceed slowly in the meantime. By best estimates, the ship moved forward for about ten minutes and may have stopped when Chief Officer Wilde reported to Smith that the forepeak tank, a water ballast tank deep in the forward bow, was taking in seawater.

Bruce Ismay had awakened in his deluxe B-deck suite not long after the collision and lay in bed wondering why the ship had stopped. His first thought was that they had dropped a propeller blade. Stepping into the hallway in his pajamas, he asked a steward, "What has happened?" The steward replied that he did not know, so Ismay donned an overcoat and slippers and went up to the bridge.

"We have struck ice," Smith explained.

"Do you think the ship is seriously damaged?" Ismay asked.

"I am afraid she is," he replied.

Ismay returned to the grand staircase, where he met Chief Engineer Bell and asked him if he thought the damage was serious. Bell replied that it seemed to be so but that he thought the pumps would keep the ship afloat. Smith clearly believed this as well, since otherwise he would not have given the "Half Speed Ahead" order.

Just before midnight, Fourth Officer Boxhall returned to the bridge from his brief inspection down as far as F deck and told the captain he had seen nothing awry. Smith ordered him to find the ship's carpenter so he could "sound" the vessel. Boxhall was on the stairs to A deck when he met the carpenter coming up. "The ship is making water," he reported breathlessly. Boxhall asked him to report this to the captain and continued down the staircase until he met a mail clerk, who announced, "The mail hold is filling rapidly."

"You go and tell the captain and I will go down and see," Boxhall replied.

When the fourth officer entered the post office on G deck, the mail clerks were hastily pulling armfuls of envelopes out of the sorting racks. On looking down into the lower storage room, he saw mailbags floating in water. When Boxhall reported this to the bridge, the captain gave the order for the lifeboats to be uncovered and went below to see the damage for himself. The ship's designer, Thomas Andrews, was already making his own inspection tour of the lower decks. He went into the post office and soon dispatched a mail clerk to find the captain. The clerk hurried along the corridor and returned with Captain Smith and Purser McElroy.

After they had viewed the damage, Andrews was overheard saying to Smith, "Well, three have gone already, Captain." Andrews was undoubtedly referring to three of the ship's bulkheads that divided the ship into the watertight compartments that gave the *Titanic* its reputation for unsinkability. With only three compartments flooded, however, there was a chance that the pumps could stay ahead of it. The captain then returned to the bridge and gave the order for women and children to go up on deck with lifebelts. Thomas Andrews, meanwhile, continued his inspection.

At around twelve-twenty-five William Sloper saw Andrews racing up the staircase with a deeply worried look on his face. As the ship's designer passed by Dorothy Gibson, she put her hand on his arm and asked him what had happened. Andrews simply brushed past the prettiest girl and continued upward three stairs at a time. He had just discovered that two more watertight compartments had been breached. Andrews knew how serious this was. The bulkhead between the fifth and sixth compartments extended only as high as E deck. As the ship was pulled down at the bow, the water would spill over it into the next compartment, and then the next, until the ship inevitably sank. In all his planning at Harland and Wolff, he had never imagined a scenario such as this. Andrews informed the captain that the ship had only an hour left to live—an hour and a half at best. Smith immediately told Fourth Officer Boxhall to calculate the liner's position and take it to the Marconi Room so the call for assistance could be sent out. He also gave orders to muster the passengers and crew.

Only moments after Andrews had rushed by him and Dorothy Gibson, William Sloper heard a steward announce, "The captain says that all passengers will dress themselves warmly, bring their life preservers and go up to the top deck." He arranged to meet Dorothy and her mother shortly and returned to his cabin. Having pulled down his lifebelt from an overhead rack, he then went back into the hallway, and there a voice from a nearby cabin called out, "What has happened?" It was the sickly Hugo Ross, one of the trio of Canadian bachelors that Sloper had dubbed "the Three Musketeers" on the *Franconia*. He went into Ross's room and tried to reassure him by saying he didn't think the ship was in serious difficulties. Ross had already been told about the iceberg by Major Peuchen, who had visited him shortly after the collision.

At eleven-forty Peuchen had been preparing for bed when he felt the ship quiver from what he thought was a heavy wave. After going up to A deck and spying ice lying along the railing in the well deck, he had decided to inform Hugo Ross, who reportedly said to him, "It will take more than an iceberg to get me out of my bed." The major then knocked on Harry Molson's door but found him out. Peuchen soon saw another Canadian acquaintance, Charles Hays, walking with his son-in-law on C deck and asked him if he had seen the ice. Hays replied that he had not, so Peuchen took the two men up to the A-deck promenade to show it to them. There he noticed a change from his last visit. "Why, she is listing," he said to Hays. "She should not do that, the water is perfectly calm and the boat has stopped." The railroad president was dismissive. "You can't sink this boat," he replied. "No matter what we've struck, she is good for eight or ten hours."

Archibald Gracie was also on the promenade deck at around this time but did not sense any listing. He had awakened after the collision to the sound of steam being vented and had decided to investigate. Gracie went up first to the boat deck, which he found deserted, and then down to A deck, where he peered over the rail and saw nothing unusual. On returning to the staircase, he spotted Bruce Ismay hurrying upward with a crewman. Ismay was by then wearing a business suit, and Gracie thought he looked preoccupied but not alarmed. Gracie then ran into his friend James Clinch Smith and a few other passengers by the staircase landing on B deck. Smith opened his hand to reveal a piece of ice that was flat and slightly rounded, like a pocket watch, and wryly suggested that Gracie might want to take it home as a souvenir. He also told Gracie what he knew about the collision and reported that someone who had rushed out from the smoking room to see the berg claimed that it had towered above A deck. Gracie also heard about the postal clerks dragging mailbags out of the storage room. Soon there was a noticeable list in the floor of the staircase landing, and Gracie and Smith decided to go back to their staterooms and meet later.

Major Peuchen was standing near the A-deck staircase foyer at approximately twelve-twenty-five, when a group of grim-faced people came down from the boat deck, Thomson Beattie of "the Musketeers" among them. "The order is for lifebelts and boats," Beattie reported. Peuchen was taken aback. "Will you tell Hugo Ross?" he asked. Beattie replied that he would. Peuchen then returned to his cabin on C deck and began to change out of his evening clothes. After donning heavy under- wear, two pairs of socks, and a warm sweater, he put on his overcoat and a life preserver. As he left his small cabin, he glanced at a tin box that contained some jewelry and $217,000 worth of stocks and bonds. This was no time to bother with valuables, he decided, and stepped outside. The corridor was filled with passengers in lifejackets, and a few of the women were weeping. Some wore only dressing gowns or kimonos and were advised to go and dress more warmly. Peuchen, too, turned around and went back into his room. He retrieved his favorite pearl tiepin, pock- eted three oranges, and returned to the staircase.

No one had to tell Margaret Brown to dress warmly. After hearing about the order for lifebelts, she had pulled on several pairs of woolen stockings under a black velvet suit with white silk lapels, placed a silk cap on her head, and wrapped herself in sable furs. She found two lifebelts in her cabin and decided to carry both. Before leaving her stateroom, she retrieved the small turquoise tomb figure she had bought in Egypt for good luck and tucked it into her pocket. When she reached the staircase foyer on A deck, her traveling companion Emma Bucknell came toward her. "Didn't I tell you something was going to happen?" she whispered nervously, recalling their conversation on the *Nomadic*.

Edith Rosenbaum, who had had similar premonitions on the ten- der, was now surprisingly calm. She had gone up to the boat deck before midnight and seen the ice fragments in the well deck but when told that there was nothing to worry about, had returned to her cabin. As she was about to get back into bed, a crewman knocked on her door and announced that all passengers were required to put on lifebelts.

"What for?" Edith asked.

"That is an order," he replied and moved on.

Edith packed up her clothes and jewelry and tidied her room to leave it looking presentable. She locked all her trunks, closed the curtains, put on a warm fur coat, and left the cabin without taking her lifebelt. On meeting her room steward, Robert Wareham, she asked him if he thought there was really any danger or if the order for lifebelts was just following regulations. The steward replied that the orders were for life-belts and lifeboats but that he expected the ship would be towed to Hali-fax. Edith pulled out the keys to her trunks and gave them to Wareham, asking him to clear them at customs there for her.

"Well, if I were you, I would kiss those trunks good-bye," he replied.

"Do you think the boat is going to sink?" Edith asked, slightly startled.

"No one thinks anything, we hope," the steward responded more cir-cumspectly.

On her way to the lounge, Edith passed the open cabin door of a shipboard acquaintance named Robert Daniel, a young banker from an old Virginia family. Daniel had purchased a French bulldog in England named Gamin de Pycombe and Edith found it whimpering in the state-room. She tucked the dog under the bedcovers, patted its head, and left.

Norris Williams and his father had also decided to go up on deck after being awakened by the collision, and they, too, had observed the ship slowly gliding forward at half speed. After returning to their room to don their fur coats and lifebelts, they found a steward trying to open a jammed cabin door on C deck. Over objections from the steward, Norris put his shoulder to the door and broke it open—to the relief of the man inside. As he walked away, Norris heard the steward call out, "I will be forced to report you for having damaged company property!"

Sometime after twelve-thirty, steerage passenger Daniel Buck-ley watched as a man kicked at a locked iron gate at the top of a forward stairway. The gate had

Edith Rosenbaum

been unlocked earlier when Buckley had gone through it up to B deck. There he'd seen first-class passengers tying on their lifebelts and decided he'd better return for his. Pushing his way down through a stream of third-class passengers surging upward, Buckley arrived at the corridor to his cabin only to find it under water. As he climbed back up the stairway to B deck Buckley heard a commotion as a crewman pushed a man from steerage back down the stairs and locked the gate, barring the way to the first-class deck. The furious steerage passenger picked himself up, smashed through the locked gate, and raced off in pursuit of the crewman. He later told Buckley he would have thrown the sailor into the ocean if he had caught him.

Thomas Andrews, meanwhile, circulated along the first-class hallways making sure that the stewards were getting passengers out of their staterooms. He saw stewardess May Sloan, whom he knew from Belfast, knocking on doors and told her to make sure that all passengers put on their lifebelts, adding that she should find one for herself and get up on deck soon. His face, she thought, "had a look as though he were heart broken."

At around twelve-thirty-five, William Sloper rejoined his bridge companions, Dorothy Gibson, her mother, and Frederic Seward, on the A-deck staircase foyer. The foursome walked up to the boat deck past the elegant wall clock set into a carved relief of Honor and Glory crowning Time. On the chilly boat deck they were greeted by the deafening roar of steam being vented through pipes that ran up the sides of the three forward funnels. The noise made conversation impossible—it even made it difficult for operator Jack Phillips in the Marconi Room to hear replies to his calls for assistance.

Shortly after the collision, Captain Smith had walked to the wireless room and told operator Jack Phillips that the ship had struck an iceberg and to stand by in case the call for assistance was required. Seemingly unperturbed, Phillips continued sending his messages to Cape Race and casually told Harold Bride when he came on duty at midnight that the ship might have to go back to Belfast for repairs. When the captain returned at approximately twelve-twenty-five, Phillips came out of the sleeping quarters.

"You had better get assistance," Smith announced grimly.

"Do you want me to use a distress call?" Phillips asked.

"Yes, at once," the captain replied and left.

Phillips took the piece of paper with the *Titanic*'s position that Fourth Officer Boxhall had brought in earlier and began tapping out the distress signal *CQD*, repeating it six times followed by *MGY*, the *Titanic*'s call letters. Then he sent: *Have struck an iceberg. We are badly damaged, Titanic. Position 41°44'N, 50°24'W.*

About five minutes later the captain came back to the Marconi Room.

"What are you sending?" he asked.

"*CQD*," Phillips replied.

"Send *SOS*," Harold Bride interjected. "It's the new call, and it may be your last chance to send it." All three men laughed, and Phillips later began tapping out both *SOS* and *CQD*. Though *SOS* was indeed a new call, it was not, as is often claimed, the first time it had been used by a ship in distress.

While Phillips listened for replies, the first lifeboats on the starboard side were swung out. When Lifeboat 7 was flush with the deck, First Officer Murdoch and Fifth Officer Lowe called out for ladies to step forward. But very few complied. William Sloper and his bridge companions stood in a group of passengers who were huddled for warmth against the wall near the entrance door. As the crowd moved toward the lifeboat, most people balked and turned away. Murdoch called out that it was perfectly safe as the sea was quite calm. He added that once the damage had been assessed they would be brought on board again. Yet not many wanted to leave the warmth and security of the ship for a freezing excursion in a small open boat.

But Dorothy Gibson was not one of them. She was certain the *Titanic* was going to sink and kept repeating hysterically, "I'll never ride in my little gray car again!" William Sloper tried to calm the prettiest girl and helped her into the bow of Lifeboat 7, while Frederic Seward placed Dorothy's mother in a seat nearby. Dorothy clung to Sloper's hand and insisted that he come, too. After a nod from Murdoch, both Sloper and Seward stepped into the boat. Sloper later wrote that they then sat for ten minutes looking up at the uncertain faces of passengers standing on the deck.

Helen Bishop, the young newlywed from Dowagiac, Michigan, claimed that she and her husband, Dickinson, were pushed into Boat 7 after an officer took her arm and told her to be very quiet and to get in immediately. Helen had earlier left her lapdog Frou Frou in their room, even though the little dog had tugged at the hem of her dress while she was putting on her life preserver. Thinking it would be inappropriate to take her pet, Helen had closed the stateroom door to the sound of her tiny dog's high-pitched barks. But another young woman was not going anywhere without her Pomeranian. Twenty-four-year-old Margaret Hays of New York had taken her little dog along on a European tour she had just completed with a school friend and her mother. When the three women decided to dress and go up to the boat deck, Margaret wrapped her pet in a blanket and took it with her. Near the staircase on C deck they were greeted by Gilbert Tucker, a young magazine editor and writer from Albany, New York, who had developed a crush on Margaret. Tucker was holding three lifebelts which he proceeded to help Margaret and the two others to put on. When Jim Smith passed by and saw this, he quipped, "Oh, I suppose we ought to put a life preserver on the little doggie, too!" Tucker and the three women then proceeded to the boat deck, where all four, along with the little doggie, were permitted to enter Lifeboat 7.

"Any more ladies?" Murdoch called out through his megaphone. When none were forthcoming, the sculptor Paul Chevré and two of his French card-playing companions came forward and were allowed to get in. Lifeboat 7 now held over thirty people, roughly half of its capacity of sixty-five. At twelve-forty Murdoch instructed the crewmen to let out the ropes around the iron bitts on the deck and lower the first of the *Titanic*'s lifeboats down the side.

When the next boat forward, Lifeboat 5, was being swung out, Third Officer Herbert Pitman noted how easily the davits worked compared to the older ones he had used on other ships. Thirty-four-year-old "Bert" Pitman, a farmer's son from Somerset, had been working on ships since he was eighteen. The *Titanic*'s new Welin davits were indeed state-of-the-art and were actually equipped to carry more than the one boat each held. But outdated British Board of Trade regulations required a ship the size of the *Titanic,* which could accommodate 3,511 people, to have only sixteen lifeboats, for a maximum of 962 passengers. White Star had actually exceeded the regulations by including four Engelhardt boats with collapsible canvas sides, making room for a total of 1,178. Yet even if all of the *Titanic's* boats had been filled to capacity, there would only have been places for slightly more than half of the 2,209 on board. No one had imagined a situation where such a watertight ship would need to be wholly evacuated before help could arrive.

Pitman thought that lowering the lifeboats was mainly a precaution. He had therefore been surprised when a tall, mustached man had come up to him while he was uncovering Lifeboat 5 and announced ominously, "There is no time to waste." When the boat was ready for boarding, the tall man returned and told Pitman he should load it immediately with women and children. Pitman replied tartly that his orders came from the captain. After the man walked away, it dawned on the third officer that he might have just rebuffed J. Bruce Ismay. He scurried forward to the bridge and told Captain Smith that a man he suspected was Bruce Ismay had told him to get his boat away.

"Go ahead, carry on," Smith replied calmly.

"Come along, ladies," Pitman called out after returning to Lifeboat 5 and stepping into it. A number of men and women walked forward and climbed in. Bruce Ismay approached Karl Behr, who was standing nearby with Helen Newsom and her mother and stepfather and urged them to get in as well.

"Can the men come too?" asked Helen's mother, Sallie Beckwith.

"Of course Madam, every one of you," Ismay replied. Karl Behr then assisted the Beckwiths and Helen Newsom into the boat along with their friends, the Kimballs of Boston, before getting in himself. Henry and Annie Stengel, a middle-aged couple from Newark, New Jersey, also came forward. Henry put his wife into the boat but stood aside when Pitman said the boat was full. Dr. Henry Frauenthal, the New York orthopedist who had treated René Harris's arm earlier that evening, brought his wife Clara and put her in the lifeboat while he and his brother Isaac remained on the deck. Isaac had been Henry's best man at his wedding to Clara in Nice only two weeks before.

When Lifeboat 5 had nearly forty people in it, First Officer Murdoch approached and said to Pitman, "You go ahead in this boat and hang around the after gangway." Murdoch shook his hand and wished him good luck. When Pitman called out, "Lower away," Bruce Ismay picked up the order and began chanting, "Lower, away! Lower, away! Lower, away!" while waving one arm in circles.

"If you will get to hell out of that I shall be able to do something!" shouted Fifth Officer Lowe in indignant, Welsh-accented tones. "Do you want me to lower away quickly? You will have me drown the whole lot of them!" Like Pitman earlier, Lowe had no idea who this meddling person was.

As a chastened Ismay walked away, the lifeboat began its descent. Just then, Henry Frauenthal jumped down into it, followed quickly by his brother, Isaac. According to Annie Stengel, the large "Hebrew doctor" landed on her, knocking her unconscious and dislocating two of her ribs. As Boat 5 continued its descent, the first distress flare rocketed into the sky and burst above the forward funnel in a shower of stars accompanied by a loud bang. The noise alarmed many of the passengers standing on the boat deck.

"They wouldn't send those rockets unless it was the last," remarked Emily Ryerson to her husband. "Don't you hear the band playing?" he replied, trying to calm her. The ship's orchestra, which had begun playing earlier in the lounge, had now moved to the boat deck foyer and cheerful ragtime tunes drifted across the deck. The music was reassuring, and so was the sight of another ship's mast lights off the port side, making it seem as if rescue was at hand.

The lights of the *Californian* did indeed seem tantalizingly close. But the steamer was not responding to the *Titanic*'s *CQD* calls because its Marconi operator had turned off his equipment and gone to bed over an hour before, after being told to "Shut up" by Jack Phillips. Fourth Officer Boxhall had tried signaling the ship with a Morse lamp but had received no response. He was relieved when Quartermaster Rowe arrived carrying more distress rockets. Surely the ship would see these and come over. "Fire one, and then fire one every five or six minutes," Captain Smith ordered. Boxhall continued flashing with his lamp between rocket bursts.

Meanwhile, Frank Millet, Archie Butt, Clarence Moore, and an unknown fourth man continued their card game in the smoking room, seemingly oblivious to all that was going on. At twelve-thirty the smoking room steward had announced, "Gentleman, the accident looks serious. They are lowering away the boats for women and children." After that, even the professional gamblers had evacuated the room, but when Archibald Gracie looked in about ten minutes later, he saw Archie's table still at cards. To Gracie it seemed as if they "desired to show their entire indifference to the danger and that if I advised them as to how seriously I regarded it, they would laugh at me." At approximately twelve-forty-five, however, the four men were seen exiting the smoking room by their dining room steward, Fred Ray. It was perhaps then, when they saw passengers standing gathered in lifebelts and noticed the list in the floor, that Archie and Frank fully grasped how serious things had become. In the A-deck staircase foyer Marian Thayer noticed Archie walking toward the stairs with what she called "a strange unseeing look on his face." She caught hold of his coat and said, "Major Butt, Major Butt, where are you going? Come with me."

"I have something to do first but will come then," Archie replied distractedly, heading down to his stateroom.

"He has gone for his letters," Marian Thayer thought to herself.

At dinner Archie had spoken to her about how much he valued his letters, yet it was most likely the official communications for President Taft that were preoccupying him now. In his cabin he either destroyed these letters from the pope and several U.S. ambassadors or decided to tuck them into his tunic. At this time, Archie may have exchanged the dress uniform he had likely worn at dinner for his everyday army uniform. Frank Millet chose not to change out of his evening clothes but added a gray woolen vest that Lily had knitted for him, donned an overcoat, and then took down his lifebelt from the top of his cupboard.

Archie Butt was next seen standing calmly on the starboard boat deck while Lifeboat 3 was being lowered. In this boat were Daisy and Frederic Spedden; their young son, Douglas; his nurse, Elizabeth Burns; and Daisy's maid. Douglas lay asleep in Miss Burns's lap clutching his stuffed toy polar bear. "Miss B" had awakened him earlier and told him they were taking a trip "to see the stars." Nearby sat Henry Sleeper Harper cradling the little brown Pekingese, Sun Yat-sen. Harper had actually seen the iceberg scrape by his porthole and, over his wife Myra's objections, had insisted that they both dress and go on deck right away. The long wait to get into a lifeboat seemed endless for Harper, who had been in bed with tonsillitis for most of the voyage. He later described the delay as "rather like a stupid picnic where you don't know anybody and wonder how soon you can get away from such a boresome place." Yet the

Charles Hays

"boresome" wait saved Harper's life and that of his handsome Egyptian servant, Hammad Hassab, as well. Thomas Cardeza also got into the boat with his manservant, after his mother, Charlotte, had boarded with her maid. Clearly believing this to be a temporary measure, Mrs. Cardeza had left behind her jewel case and its fabulous contents.

Lifeboat 3 began its descent at twelve-fifty-five, carrying thirty-two people, seventeen of them men. The railroad president Charles Hays stood by with a cigar butt clenched in his teeth as his wife Clara, married daughter Orian Davidson, and his wife's French-Canadian maid disappeared from view. He had told Orian, "You and mother go ahead, the rest of us will wait here till morning." Orian was so reassured by her father's confidence that she didn't even think of kissing him or her husband, Thornton, good-bye. The boat began to descend very jerkily since the two crewmen at the ropes were having trouble coordinating the lowering. At one point Daisy Spedden was sure they would be tipped into the sea. "At last the ropes worked together, and we drew nearer and nearer the oily black water," recalled another passenger, Elizabeth Shutes. "The first wish on the part of all," she continued, "was to stay near the *Titanic*. We all felt so much safer near the ship. Surely such a vessel could not sink."

The lifeboats had to be lowered 60 feet down to the water.
Second Officer Lightoller supervised the lowering on the port side.

TO THE LIFEBOATS

As 1:00 a.m. approached, Second Officer Lightoller was feeling frustrated. None of the lifeboats on the port side had yet been launched, despite his best efforts. He had managed to get Lifeboat 4 swung out and lowered half an hour ago, even though Chief Officer Wilde had twice told him to wait. Both times Lightoller had jumped rank and gone directly to Captain Smith to get the go-ahead to proceed. The captain had also suggested that Lifeboat 4 be lowered to A deck since he thought it would be easier for the passengers to board from there. But a crewman had just shouted up that the A-deck windows were locked. (Smith may have forgotten that, unlike the *Olympic*, the *Titanic* had a glassed-in forward promenade.) Lightoller sent someone to unlock the windows and to recall the passengers who had been sent down there.

Meanwhile, he moved aft to prepare Lifeboats 6 and 8, ordering that the masts and sails be lifted out of them. Just then the roaring steam was silenced and Lightoller was slightly startled by the sound of his own voice. Arthur Peuchen overheard the order and, ever handy around boats, jumped in to help cut the lashings and lift the masts out onto the deck. After that the call went out for women and children to come forward. The "women and children only" order would be more strictly enforced here than on the starboard side where men were being allowed into boats. When a crowd of grimy stokers and firemen suddenly appeared carrying their dunnage bags, Chief Officer Wilde was spurred into action. "Down below, you men! Every one of you, down below!" he bellowed in a stern, Liverpool-accented voice. Major Peuchen was very impressed with Wilde's commanding manner as he drove the men right off the deck, and thought it "a splendid act."

Helen Candee, however, felt sympathy for the stokers whom she later described as a band of unknown heroes who had accepted their fate without protest. She was waiting by Lifeboat 6 with Hugh Woolner, who had been by her side ever since he had gone down to her cabin from the smoking room after the collision. "The Two" had then walked together on the boat deck, amid the roar of venting steam, and had noticed that the ship was listing to starboard. They went into the lounge to escape the cold and the noise, and there a young man came over to them with something in his hand. "Have some iceberg!" he said with a smile as he dropped a piece of ice into Helen's palm. The ice soon chilled Helen's fingers, so Woolner dashed it from her and rubbed her hand and then kept it clasped in his.

"Why are we so calm?" she asked him.

"We are Anglo-Saxons," he replied.

When the order for lifebelts was given, "the Two" returned to their rooms before proceeding together up to the boat deck accompanied by Woolner's young Swedish friend, Mauritz Björnström-Steffansson. On the staircase they met another member of their coterie, Edward Kent, who told Helen that he was on his way to find her. Mrs. Candee was touched by this and gave the architect two family mementos for safe-keeping—a little silver flask engraved with the Churchill crest and an ivory cameo of her mother.

As she waited by Boat 6, Helen felt nervous about having to climb into the lifeboat. When she finally clambered down into it, one of her expensively shod feet became wedged between two oars stowed along the gunwales. She lost her balance and twisted her ankle, fracturing it. Helen grimaced in pain but refused to let it show as she stoically covered herself with the steamer rug that Woolner passed down to her.

The young Montrealer Quigg Baxter soon appeared by Lifeboat 6 carrying his mother, Hélène, in his arms. He placed her in the boat and helped his sister 'Zette to a seat beside her. Then he fetched his girlfriend Berthe Mayné, who appeared in a long woolen motorcoat she had put on over her nightgown and slippers. On discovering that Quigg would not be going with her, the Belgian chanteuse became very agitated and refused to get into the boat. Margaret Brown intervened and tried to reassure her but Berthe kept insisting she had to go back to her cabin for her money and jewelry. Mrs. Brown persuaded her that boarding the boats was just a precaution and that passengers would soon be able to return to the ship. Quigg then assisted a pacified Berthe into the boat and introduced her to his puzzled mother and sister. He also pulled out a silver brandy flask, took a swig from it, and passed it to his mother who promptly scolded him about his drinking.

Margaret Brown soon spotted her friend Emma Bucknell sitting in the next boat aft, Lifeboat 8, and went over to speak to her. Mrs. Bucknell was accompanied by her Italian maid, Albina Bazzani. Ida Straus's English maid, Ellen Bird, was also in the boat, though her employer was not. Mrs. Straus had followed her maid toward the lifeboat but with one foot on the gunwales had suddenly stopped. She then turned and went back to her husband, saying, "We have been living together for many years, and where you go, I go."

"I am sure nobody would object to an old gentleman like you getting in," Hugh Woolner said to Isidor Straus. "There seems to be room in this boat."

"I will not go before the other men," Straus replied firmly. The elderly couple then walked down the deck together arm in arm.

The doughty Ella White had been helped into Boat 8 along with her maid and her companion, Marie Young. While waiting in the boat, Mrs. White gestured frequently with her "opera cane," a walking stick with an electric light in its handle. The bobbing light was causing Lightoller to see spots before his eyes, and he told someone to have her switch it off or he would "throw the damn thing overboard."

"Any more ladies?" Captain Smith called out for Boat 8. When none came forward, he instructed Thomas Jones, the seaman in charge, to row toward the light of the nearby ship, land the passengers, and come back for more. The boat began its descent at 1:00 a.m, with twenty-two women and three crewmen on board. Lightoller was relieved that it wasn't loaded to its capacity of sixty-five, because he feared the davits might not be able to stand the weight. He thought that more women could be boarded from the lower gangway doors and had sent two crewmen down to open them, but the men had never returned.

With Lifeboat 8 gone, Lightoller was keen to lower Lifeboat 6. When it began to be lowered at approximately one-ten, Margaret Brown claimed that a man took hold of her, saying "You are going, too!" and dropped her into the boat. As it descended, Hugh Woolner and Björnström-Steffansson waved to Mrs. Candee, calling out that they would help her back on board after the ship had steadied itself. When the boat had gone down a few decks, Quartermaster Hichens shouted up from the stern, "I can't manage this boat with only one seaman!"

Lightoller called out for another crewman but no one responded. Arthur Peuchen then stepped forward.

"May I be of assistance?" he asked.

"Are you a seaman?" Lightoller asked.

"I am a yachtsman and can handle a boat with an average man," replied the major.

Lightoller responded that if Peuchen was enough of a sailor to climb out on the davit and lower himself into the boat then he was welcome to do so. Captain Smith suggested to Peuchen that he go below, break a window, and climb in from there. The major did not think this was feasible and shouted to the crewmen in the boat to throw him the end of a loose rope that was hanging from the davit arm. As he later described it, "One hundred and ninety pounds is a good weight to come suddenly on the end of a slack rope, but my grip held." To swing out over a sixty-foot drop and then shinny down thirty feet into a boat in the dark is a considerable feat of derring-do—particularly for a man a few days shy of his fifty-third birthday. But it was to be Peuchen's finest moment of the night.

When the lifeboat arrived at the water, Quartermaster Hichens began to unhitch the pulleys from the boat and Peuchen asked if he could help. "Get down and put that plug in," Hichens ordered curtly. The plug was for a hole that allowed water to drain from the lifeboat when stored on deck. Peuchen scrabbled on his knees for the plug but could not find it in the dark. In frustration as water seeped in, he stood up and suggested that Hichens find it while he undid the pulleys. A furious Hichens came rushing back, saying "Hurry! This boat is going to founder!" Peuchen thought he meant the lifeboat but Hichens was referring to the *Titanic*.

Once the boat had been made ready, the quartermaster brusquely ordered Peuchen to sit and row beside the other crewman, who, as it happened, was lookout Frederick Fleet. Hichens had been the man at the ship's wheel when Fleet called in his fateful "iceberg right ahead" message. As he stood at the tiller of the lifeboat, a nervous and shivering Hichens urged Fleet and Peuchen to row away quickly from the liner, muttering dire predictions about the suction that would occur when it sank.

Fear of suction was also a concern in another lifeboat that was just then pulling away from the opposite side of the ship. Lady Duff Gordon heard one of the men in her boat say that the *Titanic* was so enormous that "none of us know what the suction may be if she's a goner." Later, Lucile couldn't swear that this was *exactly* what was said since the motion of the boat was making her feel nauseated. The couturiere lay against the starboard gunwale of Lifeboat 1 wrapped in her squirrel coat with a turquoise crepe scarf tied around her head. Yet she still felt chilled through since under her fur coat was only a lavender silk kimono she had put on over her nightdress. But at least her feet were snug in a pair of pink-velvet mules with pom-pom toes and ermine lining, custom-designed for her by the legendary Paris shoemaker Pietro Yantorny. Cosmo sat in front of Lucy in his Norfolk jacket while her secretary, Mabel Francatelli, was seated behind wearing a long woolen coat and sweater she had hastily put on over her nightgown.

Franks had come to Lucy's stateroom after midnight in a panic, claiming that she had seen water creeping along the corridor as she left her room on E deck. Cosmo had then arrived and taken them both up the staircase to the boat deck foyer. On hearing the call for ladies to board, the three of them had stepped out onto the starboard deck where crewmen soon tried to pull the two women toward the boats. But they had loudly protested—Lucy would not leave without Cosmo and Franks clung to her. After Lifeboat 3 departed, the crowd on the forward deck dispersed and Lucy suddenly noticed that a smaller emergency boat was being prepared for lowering.

"Shouldn't we try to get into that?" she asked Cosmo.

"We must wait for orders," he replied. But a few minutes later Cosmo went forward and asked First Officer Murdoch if they could get in.

"Yes, I wish you would," he responded.

The emergency boat was a cutter that was kept permanently swung out over the railing. This meant that the two women had to be hoisted over the railing and then, as Lucy put it, "plopped" into the boat. Soon Henry Stengel approached, having seen his wife, Annie, depart in Lifeboat 5. Murdoch suggested that he jump in as well, so the New Jersey leather manufacturer climbed the rail and rolled himself into the boat— causing Murdoch to break out laughing. "That is the funniest sight I've seen tonight," he chortled, making Stengel think that perhaps the situation wasn't as grave as he'd thought. Yet when another rocket shot up from the nearby starboard wing bridge, Lucy Duff Gordon became even more certain that the ship was in dire trouble.

Soon a New York businessman named Abraham Salomon came forward and Murdoch allowed him to join the small group in the boat. The first officer then put two seamen in to handle the oars and, seeing no more passengers on the deck, told five stokers and firemen who were standing nearby that they could jump in too. He put one of the *Titanic*'s lookouts, twenty-four-year-old George Symons, in charge and ordered him to row away from the ship and then to stand by in case they needed to be called back.

As the lifeboat was lowered past A deck it became snagged on a guy wire and Franks recalled how the boat shook while they were being cut free. On reaching the sea, Lookout Symons was surprised to see that the portholes on D deck were awash and that water was creeping toward the name *Titanic* painted on the bow. He then stood at the tiller as the crewmen rowed away from the ship. In a lifeboat that could have carried forty people there were only twelve, only five of whom were passengers, and only two of them women.

So far, none of the six lifeboats that had left the *Titanic* had been filled to capacity, and none had carried any second- or third-class passengers. Second-class passengers had been told to board from their own promenade area farther aft on the boat deck. Crowds of steerage passengers, meanwhile, were waiting patiently in the well decks, while others sat in the third-class general and smoking rooms, chatting and playing cards. The gates leading up from the aft well deck had been locked to prevent men from third class from going up to the boats. But a number of them had climbed onto the large round bases of the two cargo cranes and were clambering along the arms of the cranes into second class.

As the boats at the aft end of the boat deck began to be swung out, a group of passengers rattled at the locked gates on the stairs that led up from the well deck. A crewman came to the barrier, where Mary Murphy, twenty-five, her teenaged sister, Kate, and their two roommates, Katie Gilnagh, seventeen, and Kate Mullen, twenty-one, peered through.

"For God's sake man, let the girls past to the boats, at least!" shouted Jim Farrell, a farmworker from County Longford. The crewman opened the gate for the four Irish girls and then quickly shut it behind them. On reaching the boat deck, Mary Murphy and the three Kates got into Lifeboat 16, the farthest boat aft on the port side. At one-twenty they were lowered down the side with forty-three other women, all from second or third class, along with five crewmen and one baby. Five minutes later, the neighboring portside boat, number 14, began its descent with approximately forty on board. In charge was Fifth Officer Lowe, the volatile young Welsh officer who had bawled out Bruce Ismay by Boat 5 about forty minutes ago. Lowe was now worried that anyone jumping into the heavily loaded boat might cause it to buckle. As the lifeboat descended with Lowe in the stern, he spotted what he later described as "a lot of Italians, Latin people, all along the ship's rails . . . and they were all glaring, more or less like wild beasts, ready to spring." Lowe took out his revolver and fired several shots along the side of the ship and the "wild beasts" instantly backed off.

Lowe had to act quickly once again when a twist in the lowering ropes caused the stern of the boat to hit the water first while the bow was still pointed five feet upward. He clambered forward and quickly hacked through the ropes until the bow splashed down. Several women screamed but Lowe promptly told them to "shut up" as he hastened aft to put down the rudder. While Lifeboat 14 pulled away, the next starboard boat, number 12, reached the water with approximately forty on board. On the port side, Boat 9 was also making its descent, carrying another forty people, among them Ben Guggenheim's mistress, Ninette Aubart, and her maid, and Elizabeth Lines, the woman who had overheard Ismay predicting the *Titanic*'s early arrival, and her daughter, Mary.

It was now just after 1:30 a.m. Ten of the *Titanic*'s sixteen regular lifeboats had departed, carrying approximately 330 people—only a fraction of the 2,209 on board. To the passengers still on deck, the downward slope toward the bow was now very apparent. Yet many of them, the first-class men in particular, still believed that the ship would last till morning and that help would arrive before then. The lights of the nearby ship were still visible—Norris Williams was sure that he could even see the top of its mast above the glowing mast light. And a rumor had been circulating that the sister ship *Olympic* was on its way. In the Marconi Room, Jack Phillips had indeed heard from the *Olympic*, but her position was 500 miles to the east, which meant that she couldn't arrive till the following night. The German steamer *Frankfurt* had been the first to respond to the *CQD* call, but she was more than 170 miles, and many hours, away. The Cunard liner *Carpathia* was roughly 58 miles from the *Titanic* and had sent a message saying they were coming as quickly as possible and expected to be there within four hours.

Jaunty tunes continued to be played by the ship's musicians and the music was heard by those in the lifeboats as well as those on deck. Arthur Peuchen heard "Alexander's Ragtime Band" coming across the water during an awkward silence in Boat 6. The Canadian major had suggested that Quartermaster Hichens let one of the women steer so that he could join them at the oars. The quartermaster erupted at this: "I am in charge of this boat! It's your job to keep quiet and row!" A little later Captain Smith's voice was heard through a megaphone summoning

Boat 6 to return for more passengers. Hichens ignored this, saying, "It's our lives now, not theirs." Many of the women protested, but a humiliated Peuchen remained silent. "I knew I was perfectly powerless," he later recounted. "He had been swearing a good deal and was very disagreeable."

René Harris, too, heard the musicians playing "Alexander's Ragtime Band" on deck and no doubt thought of how it had been her Harry who had first introduced the tune to New York. She and her "boy" had gone toward various lifeboats as they were being loaded but when told that her husband couldn't accompany her, René had refused to board. Under her lifebelt she wore her fur coat with one arm dangling and beneath it a flannel blouse from which Harry had cut a sleeve to accommodate her broken arm. The Harrises had gone up on deck with the Futrelles at about twelve-thirty but had then become separated from them.

At one-thirty, Edith Rosenbaum found herself on the boat deck feeling a little perplexed. She had at first waited in the lounge for about forty-five minutes and had then gone up to the boat deck with some other women who were later ordered down to A deck. She had just returned to the upper deck and was wondering if she should get into a lifeboat when a man seized her arm. "What are you doing here?" he asked. "All women should be off the ship!"

As he pulled her toward a narrow stairway down to A deck, Edith recognized him as Bruce Ismay. At the bottom of the stairs, she was picked up by two crewmen who carried her to the rail of the open promenade and began to thrust her headfirst into Lifeboat 11. When both her velvet slippers fell off she insisted on being put down so she could retrieve them. One of the sailors then grabbed a toy pig she had been carrying under her arm and tossed it into the boat. Edith was very attached to the pig which played a Latin dance tune called "The Maxixe" when its tail was turned; her mother had bought it for her as a good-luck mascot after her car accident. She was eager to retrieve it but climbing into the boat in a silk dress that had a narrow skirt draped to one side was going to be awkward. Seeing her dilemma, a shipboard acquaintance named Philipp Mock stepped forward and gallantly got down on one knee. "Put one foot on my knee, and your arm around my neck," he instructed, "and from there you can jump in." Once Edith was safely on board, Mock joined her and took a seat near his married sister Emma Schabert. Edith found her toy pig lying on the floor; it had two broken legs but could still play "The Maxixe."

Edith's boat reached the water at one-forty, just as the two boats from the neighboring davits, Lifeboats 13 and 15, began to come down the side. The London schoolteacher Lawrence Beesley had been allowed into Boat 13, and the crewman in charge was Leading Stoker Fred Barrett, who had twice escaped from flooding boiler rooms that evening—once after the collision and a second time while working the pumps. As his boatload of fifty people made its descent, Barrett was once again faced with gushing water—this time from the condenser exhaust that was spouting from the hull just above the waterline. He shouted up for the lowering to stop while Washington Dodge, a doctor from San Francisco, and two crewmen hunted for the oars, which turned out to be lashed to the seats, with passengers sitting on them. Once the oars were retrieved, Dodge and a few others were able to maneuver the boat out and away from the surging exhaust stream. But the force of it pushed the lifeboat backward until the lowering lines drew taut. The crewmen struggled to free the pulleys at the bow and stern of the boat but the tightened ropes made this difficult. Suddenly, Lifeboat 15 was seen coming down directly on top of them. Cries of "Stop! Stop!" went unheard and soon the keel of Boat 15 was so close that Lawrence Beesley and a stoker in the bow of Boat 13 stood up and tried to push it away with their hands. Fred Barrett jumped toward the ropes at the stern with a knife while another crewman did the same in the bow. To shouts of "One! Two!" they hacked through the lines and freed the boat just as Lifeboat 15 splashed down beside them.

While Boat 13 rowed away, Fred Barrett looked back at the sinking liner with its shining portholes reflected on the calm, black sea and thought that the ship looked like a "great lighted theatre." Yet the water lapping at the bow railing made it very clear that this maritime drama was now entering its final act. On the boat deck all but three of the sixteen davits stood empty. The second emergency cutter, Lifeboat 2, was

An illustration of Boat 15 coming down on top of Boat 13

ready for loading on the portside bow but a crowd of stokers had already crawled over the railing into it.

"How many of the crew are in that boat?" shouted Captain Smith through a megaphone. "Get out of there, every man of you!"

Mahala Douglas then saw a solid row of men sheepishly crawl out of the boat while Chief Officer Wilde bellowed that they were all "damned cowards" who should be thrown overboard.

As the call went up for women and children to enter, Mrs. Douglas

Mahala Douglas

asked her husband, Walter, to come with her but he refused, pointing to the women who were still on the deck. When the crewmen began gesturing for Mahala to board, she turned to her husband and begged him to come with her but he replied, "No, I must be a gentleman," and turned away. Seeing Archie Butt and Clarence Moore standing nearby, she called out, "Walter, when you come, come with Major Butt and Mr. Moore because they are big strong fellows. They will surely make it." Mahala also spotted Edgar Meyer and Arthur Ryerson in the crowd, and Frank Millet was almost certainly there, too, helping usher women toward the boats as he and his friends had done for most of the last hour. As the last boats were filled, Thomas Andrews was also busy urging women to board: "Ladies, you *must* get in at once," he was overheard saying. "There is not a minute to lose. You cannot pick and choose your boat. Don't hesitate, get in, get in!"

When no more women came forward for Lifeboat 2, the "Lower Away" order was given at one-forty-five. Austrian steerage passenger Anton Kink watched as his weeping wife and four-year-old daughter cried out for him to come with them. As the boat began its descent the black-bearded Kink made a sudden dash and jumped in. Mahala Douglas felt the boat shake as Kink settled down next to his wife and child. She was sitting on the floor in front of Fourth Officer Boxhall, who was at the stern. An officer called down for Boxhall to row over to the starboard side to pick up more passengers since there was room for up to fifteen more in the boat. As they pulled around past the liner's nearly submerged bow, the fourth officer put Mahala Douglas at the tiller while he helped out with an oar. On arriving on the starboard side, Boxhall thought he sensed the lifeboat being pulled toward the ship, and, fearing the dreaded suction, ordered it to be rowed away.

On the slanting deck, crewmen then began lifting two of the Engelhardt collapsible lifeboats, numbered C and D, into the two forward-most davits, which had held Boats 1 and 2. The wooden-hulled collapsible boats had canvas sides that could be raised and clipped into place. In the Marconi Room, meanwhile, Jack Phillips had been steadily working the key on his wireless transmitter while Harold Bride wrote up the log and took messages to the captain. Other ships, including the *Baltic* and the *Virginian*, had responded to the distress call but the *Carpathia* remained the nearest ship of those that had responded. Phillips could already feel the wireless signal growing weaker when Captain Smith came in to say that the engine rooms were filling with water and that the electricity might not last much longer. At one-forty-five, Phillips sent his final message to the *Carpathia: Come as quickly as possible. Engine rooms filling up to the boilers.*

Shortly after this, the last of the *Titanic*'s rockets shot into the air and descended, emitting loud reports that sounded like cannon fire. It seemed astonishing to the *Titanic*'s senior officers that the nearby mystery ship would not both see and hear these rockets over a calm sea on such a clear night. "She cannot help but see those signals and must steam over and pick everyone up," Lightoller had said time and again to reassure anxious passengers. Now he had stopped saying it. On the steamer *Californian*, which is estimated to have been anywhere from eleven to twenty miles away, eight rockets were sighted but none were heard. A recent study has revealed that the unusually flat sea that night would have acted like a mirror that reflected and thus deadened the sound, making it inaudible beyond five to six nautical miles. Yet the rockets were definitely seen if not heard by the *Californian*, and the fact that its captain, Stanley Lord, did not wake the ship's wireless operator to find out why a ship was firing rockets in the middle of the night remains one of the most haunting "if only's" of the *Titanic* story.

At approximately one-forty, Lightoller heard that Lifeboat 4, the boat he had lowered to A deck more than an hour before, was, at last, ready for boarding. A key had been found to unlock the promenade windows but a wooden spar protruded just below the windows and had to be chopped away. While this was being done, a contingent of the *Titanic*'s most prominent passengers—Astors, Wideners, Thayers, Carters, and Ryersons—had been kept waiting, first on A deck, then in the staircase foyer, and now on the boat deck. Emily Ryerson described them as "quite a group of people we knew" and noted that "all were very quiet and self-possessed." Yet when the order came that they were to return to A deck, an exasperated Marian Thayer snapped, "Just tell us where to go and we will follow! You ordered us up here and now you're sending us back!"

The Astor party joined the Thayers and the other Main Liners as they trooped down the narrow iron steps to A deck. John Jacob Astor had taken Madeleine into the gymnasium earlier to keep her warm and they had sat together on the exercise machines. He was feeling particularly protective of her since she had been feeling ill all afternoon. When they had first gone up to A deck together after midnight, Astor had sent

Madeleine Astor

his valet back to fetch a warmer dress and a fur coat for her, and she was seen being dressed by her maid while sitting in a steamer chair. Astor had also made sure that Madeleine's pearls, engagement ring, and a few other valuable baubles were retrieved from her jewel case.

On A deck Lightoller stood on a ramp made of steamer chairs that led up to the opened windows beside Lifeboat 4. Colonel Gracie, who had been helping shepherd women into boats from the promenade, gently assisted Madeleine Astor toward Lightoller. After the second officer had placed her in the boat, Astor leaned through a nearby open window and asked Lightoller if he could accompany his wife on account of her "delicate condition." When the second officer refused, Astor asked for the number of the boat and then tossed his gloves to Madeleine. As Emily Ryerson approached the boat with her two daughters and son Jack, Lightoller said, "That boy can't go!"

"Of course, that boy goes with his mother," Arthur Ryerson insisted. "He is only thirteen!"

"Very well," Lightoller was heard to mutter, "but no more boys." On hearing this, Lucile Carter put her large hat on her eleven-year-old son's head and there was no protest as he entered Boat 4 with his mother and sister. Meanwhile, up on the boat deck, Lifeboat 10 was also being loaded. Winnipeg real-estate mogul Mark Fortune stood by it with his nineteen-year-old son, Charles, saying good-bye to his wife, Mary, and their three daughters. He was wearing his massive buffalo coat, having finally found a use for what had been a family joke during their Mediterranean holiday. Alice and Mabel Fortune pulled jewelry out of their pockets and gave it to their brother for safekeeping. "Look after Father, Charles," they called out, still smiling over the sight of Papa in his ungainly prairie coat.

Also seeing his family off in Boat 10 was Bertram Dean, a London pub owner who was emigrating to Wichita, Kansas, to open a tobacconist's shop. His wife, Eva, held their nine-week-old daughter, Millvina, in her arms, while two-year-old Bertram sat beside her. Other children were being grabbed and tossed into the boat with particular gusto by the *Titanic*'s chief baker, Charles Joughin, who was breathing whiskey-scented exhalations into the night air. Earlier, when he heard that the lifeboats were being uncovered, Joughin had mustered his thirteen assistants and filled their arms with loaves of bread to provision the boats. As the white-clad bakers processed up to the boat deck, it reminded Edith Rosenbaum of a festive parade she had once seen in Nice.

Once the bread was piled on the deck, Joughin thought that the occasion called for a drink, and so he had repaired to his cabin for a warming tipple. As the night went on, he had periodically stopped by for another nip or three. As he stood by Lifeboat 10 at one-forty-five, feeling well fortified from the cold, Joughin saw a woman in a black dress approach hesitantly, clearly nervous about having to jump across a gap of several feet, caused by the ship having developed a list to port. When at last she decided to jump, the woman screamed and fell headfirst between the ship and the boat. Instantly, Steward William Burke caught her by the ankles, saving her from a fifty-foot plunge into the sea. Several men on A deck then grabbed her shoulders and pulled the panicked woman down to the promenade as the boat began its descent. Whether she then got into another boat is unknown.

As he watched what seemed to be the last boat departing, the *Titanic*'s only Japanese passenger, Masabumi Hosono, a forty-two-year-old civil servant from Tokyo, thought of his wife and children and felt a strong urge to survive, though he did not want to do anything that would bring him disgrace. But when he saw a man jump from A deck into the lowering boat, Hosono leapt as well. Soon he and the other jumper, an Armenian named Neshan Krekorian, lay huddled together on the floor under the bow of Lifeboat 10, which now held fifty-seven people.

Boat 4 had also reached the water by this time, and Madeleine Astor could hear their Airedale, Kitty, barking from above. When she looked up as the boat pulled away, she saw the tall, stooping figure of her husband standing by the rail on the boat deck with Kitty beside him. It had taken the boat only a few minutes to reach the water since the sea was now only twenty feet below A deck. Boat 4 was then rowed aft since they had been ordered to pick up more men from an open gangway door near the stern. Emily Ryerson was shocked when she looked into the brightly lit windows and saw water washing around the legs of carved wooden bedsteads in the B-deck staterooms. From inside the ship came cracking noises that sounded like breaking china. They rowed past barrels, steamer chairs, and even doors that were being thrown down from above. There was no open gangway door to be found by the stern, but a group of stokers on the aft boat deck were watching the lifeboat's approach with interest. Two of them grabbed the lines hanging from an empty davit and slid down, the ropes burning their hands as they went. One made it into the boat; the other fell in the water and was quickly picked up.

As Boat 4 pulled away from the stern, her passengers were shocked by the sight of the liner's three massive bronze propellers slowly rising from the sea.

As the liner's deck slanted higher toward the stern,
First Officer Murdoch struggled to load Collapsible C.

THE FINAL MINUTES

G et out of this, clear out of this!" William Murdoch shouted in his stern Scottish voice as a crowd of men began swarming into Collapsible C. The first officer then raised his revolver and fired two shots into the air. Crouching on the floor of the boat, a panicked Daniel Buckley began to cry and a woman nearby threw her shawl over him and told him to lie low. Hugh Woolner saw Murdoch's gun flash as he sprinted toward the scene with Björnström-Steffansson at his heels. For the last hour, the robust Englishman and his young Swedish friend had been aggressively rounding up women and children and bustling them into lifeboats. At Collapsible C the vigorous duo began grabbing men by the ankles and hauling them out of the boat. Daniel Buckley, however, managed to escape their notice in the dark, as did four Chinese sailors who crouched under the bow.

When most of the men had been cleared out, Woolner then turned to the "Italian and other foreign women" waiting nearby (who were, in fact, mainly Lebanese) and started to hoist them into the boat, noticing how many of them went limp in his arms as he lifted them over the rail. When all the women on deck had been loaded, Woolner suggested to Steffansson that they go down to A deck in search of others. But on arriving on the promenade deck, they found it to be deserted with its ceiling lights glowing an eerie red as the power waned. No women were to be seen near Collapsible C either, according to William Carter and Bruce Ismay. Carter claimed that he and Ismay walked around calling "Are there any more women here?" for several minutes but heard no answer.

With no more female passengers to be found, the Philadelphia million-aire and the White Star managing director stepped over the rail and into Collapsible C as it was being lowered down the side.

Yet there were, in fact, nearly two hundred women and children still on board the *Titanic*. More than half of them were waiting in the third-class public rooms and corridors or on the decks near the stern. At 1:30 a.m. the gates on the stairs up from third class had been opened for women but many had chosen to remain with their men. Father Thomas Byles circulated among the third-class passengers, hearing confessions and reciting the rosary with them. At 2:00 a.m. the gates were opened for third-class men as well as women, and many more steerage passen-gers soon crowded the boat deck. As he began loading Collapsible D on the port side, Lightoller was forced to pull his revolver to clear a crowd of what he called "dagoes" out of the boat. He then formed a cordon of crewmen to prevent a rush on the boat.

As small knots of steerage women were escorted across the deck toward the last boat, there were still a few women from first class on board as well. Archibald Gracie was shocked to see Caroline Brown and Edith Evans standing by the starboard railing. He had escorted Evans and the three Lamson sisters to the staircase landing below the boat deck over an hour ago and had then gone in search of his other "unprotected" ward, Helen Candee, but discovered that she had already gone up on deck. Caroline Brown began to explain to Gracie how they had become separated from the others, but he and Jim Smith simply hustled them both toward the ring of men surrounding Collapsible D. Once they were let through, Edith Evans said to Caroline Brown, "You go first. You are married and have children." Brown was then lifted into the lifeboat, but when Evans went to follow, she was unable to clamber over the railing in her tapered skirt. "Never mind," she called out to Brown, "I will go on a later boat," and turned and hurried away down the deck. Evans had earlier told Archibald Gracie that she had been told by a fortune-teller to beware of water and that she now knew she would be drowned. Gracie had dismissed this as superstition but Edith Evans would become one of only four women from first class to perish.

René Harris had not yet boarded a lifeboat either, despite Harry's best efforts to persuade her to do so. At around 2:00 a.m. Captain Smith and Dr. O'Loughlin spotted the couple near the bridge.

"My God, woman!" the captain called out. "Why aren't you in a lifeboat?"

"I won't leave my husband," René protested.

"Isn't she a brick?" said O'Loughlin with a smile.

"She's a little fool!" the captain replied fiercely. "She's handicapping her husband's chance to save himself."

"Can he be saved, if I go?" she asked.

"Yes, there are plenty of rafts in the stern," the captain replied disingenuously, "and the men can make for them if you women give them a chance."

Before she could protest further, René felt herself being picked up and carried through the circle of crewmen.

"Catch my wife. Be careful, she has a broken arm," she heard Harry say as she was lifted over into Collapsible D. When the boat began to be lowered, her husband leaned over the rail and threw a blanket down to her.

"Harry!" she shouted.

"Good-bye, sweetheart!" he called back as the boat jerked its way down to the water—now only about fifteen feet below. René looked up and spotted Archie Butt standing beside her husband. "He was motionless," she later wrote, "without a trace of fear in his eyes." Earlier, she had noticed Archie escorting women and children toward the boats as courteously as if he were at a White House reception. René saw Frank Millet standing on the deck as well, and recalled him "wearing that same smile that he did all the way from Southampton." Frederick Hoyt, the Connecticut broker who had played cards with Millet only hours before, also noted the artist's genial expression as he helped Hoyt's wife into Collapsible D.

"Have you any message, Frank?" Jane Hoyt asked him.

"Give my love to Lily and to all my friends," Millet replied calmly.

As they stood on the portside promenade deck with the lights above them fading, Hugh Woolner and Björnström-Steffansson looked out and saw Collapsible D being lowered directly in front of them.

"Let's make a jump for it!" said Woolner. "There is plenty of room in her bows!"

The two men then climbed onto the rail at the open end of the forward promenade. Steffansson jumped down first and landed safely in the boat that was by then in the water. Woolner soon followed but hit the side of the boat with his chest and fell backward. Gripping the gunwale with his fingers, Woolner hoisted one foot out of the water and Steffansson grabbed his leg and pulled him into the boat. Woolner had barely caught his breath before a splash was heard nearby and another man swam over to the collapsible and was hauled in. Jane Hoyt threw her fur wrap over the shivering new arrival and then shrieked, "My God, it's my husband!"

"Jane!" Fred Hoyt exclaimed as he reached out to his wife. "Let me take an oar," he soon added, "it will help to warm me." Hugh Woolner later wrote that he and the three other men at the oars began to "pull like the deuce to get clear of the ship." The former Cambridge oarsman claimed he had never rowed harder. René Harris remembered that "Look out for the suction!" kept ringing in her ears as Collapsible D pulled away. It was then that she spotted two little boys sitting on the floor of the boat and passed over her blanket to be wrapped around them. The curly-headed toddlers had been put into Collapsible D by their father, who, in a strong French accent, had said that he was a "Mr. Hoffman."

May Futrelle later claimed that she was also in Boat D with René Harris. She, too, had been reluctant to leave the ship without her husband, but Jacques had finally insisted, "For God's sake go!" When May looked back up to the boat deck, she caught sight of Jacques cupping his hands as he lit a cigarette for himself and one for Colonel Astor, the match illuminating both of their faces. "I know those hands never trembled," she wrote. "This was an act of bravado. Both men must have realized that they must die."

But *did* they realize it? Most of the men left on board the sinking liner, it seems, still held hopes of escape. Jacques Futrelle himself had told his wife that he was sure he could swim to a lifeboat and be picked up. Montreal millionaire Harry Molson was seen removing his shoes as he prepared to swim for the lights of the ship he could see off the port bow. Algernon Barkworth, the justice of the peace from Yorkshire, later claimed, "I learned swimming at Eton and made up my mind if it came to the worst I would try my luck in the water." Baker Charles Joughin gathered up about fifty steamer chairs from the A-deck promenade and, with boozy purposefulness, threw them overboard one at a time for use by swimmers.

Though stories of heroic fatalism on the sinking liner are part of the *Titanic* mystique, many of them may not be entirely authentic. Ben Guggenheim is best-remembered for stating, "We have dressed in our best and are prepared to go down like gentlemen," as he and his valet stood on the sloping deck in their evening clothes. Guggenheim then gave a message to Steward Henry Etches: "If anything should happen to me, tell my wife in New York that I've done my best in doing my duty." Yet according to Etches, this encounter took place forty-five minutes after the collision, which places it at 12:25, a time when most passengers did not believe the ship was in any real danger, and no lifeboats had yet departed. Etches himself left the ship at 12:45 in Boat 5, so whether Guggenheim displayed similar sangfroid when the ship was actually going down is unknown.

In the film of *A Night to Remember,* Thomas Andrews is depicted in his final moments standing alone in the smoking room, staring blankly at the painting over the fireplace, his lifebelt cast aside. This is based on an account by Steward John Stewart, who on seeing the ship's designer asked, "Aren't you going to have a try for it, Mr. Andrews?" but the stricken man simply "stood liked one stunned." There are other reports, however, of Andrews being seen on the bridge and the boat deck after all the lifeboats had departed, so it's possible that toward the end, he thought of his wife and child and made an effort to save himself. W. T. Stead, too, is often depicted as sitting impassively in the smoking room, reading a book while the ship goes down. When Fireman George Kemish spotted Stead, "he looked as if he intended stopping where he was whatever happened." Kemish's recollection, however, was written over forty years later and it seems unlikely that at the time the stoker would have known Stead by sight. Second-class passenger Imanita Shelley recalled that while she was boarding Lifeboat 10, which left at approximately one-fifty, she saw Stead standing alone and without a lifebelt by the

Norris Williams

aft railing on the boat deck, "in silence and what seemed to me a prayerful attitude, or one of profound meditation."

Norris Williams remembered how calm it seemed after the last boats had gone. The musicians continued playing quietly, though most of the passengers had retreated upward toward .the stern. Williams thought it seemed a little peculiar to be walking around when all means of escape appeared cut off. He and his father had gone into the staircase foyer and looked down the stairwell at the greenish water climbing up the lower stairs. Out on the boat deck they saw lights from the lifeboats and Norris noted how far away many of them seemed. The calm surface of the ocean sparkled with phosphorus and reminded him of light seen through a prism. Henry Harper in Boat 3 noted that "at every stroke of the oars great glares of greenish-yellow phosphorescent light would swirl aft from the blades and drip like globules of fire from the oars. . . . I have never seen it so fine."

Others thought they had never seen so many stars in the sky. Seventeen-year-old Jack Thayer watched a davit arm grow higher against the starry sky as he stood by the starboard rail with Milton Long, the friend he had met in the Palm Room after dinner. Thayer had lost sight of his parents in the crowd going down to A deck to board Boat 4 and thought that his father had left in the lifeboat with his mother. Jack had several times been on the verge of sliding down a rope hanging from a davit but Long had told him to wait. In the silences, Jack thought of his parents and his sister and brother, of the good times in his life, and the future pleasures he might not live to enjoy.

Jack's father, meanwhile, was standing on the other side of the boat deck, having moved aft on the slanting deck with George Widener, Arthur Ryerson, and some other of his smoking room companions, Archie Butt,

Frank Millet, and Clarence Moore likely among them. Archibald Gracie and James Clinch Smith were nearby as well. When Gracie realized that all the lifeboats had left, the sensation, as he put it, "was not an agreeable one." It left him feeling breathless and he found his voice sticking in his throat. But he knew from his West Point training that if he was to survive, he could not give in to fear. "While I said to myself, 'Goodbye to all at home,' " he later wrote, "I hoped and prayed for escape."

Archie Butt and Frank Millet were no doubt experiencing similar emotions. Archie must surely have realized that the premonitions of doom that had dogged him for weeks might soon become a reality. This may have been behind the impassive gaze that Marian Thayer and René Harris had both noted. Frank Millet had written to a friend only a few months ago that he would rather sink on a warship than in a dory. And he had often said that if he could choose his manner of death, he would live his life to the fullest and end it by dying in battle. Yet an Atlantic liner sinking underneath him seemed an improbable way to die, so it is likely that Millet, like Gracie, still thought that rescue was possible.

The news that there were two more collapsible boats stowed on the roof of the officers' quarters suddenly suffused Archibald Gracie with renewed hope. He and Jim Smith hustled down to the forward starboard deck and began to lend a hand in preparing an empty davit for the collapsible boat that was lashed to the roof above. "Has any passenger a knife?" one of the men on the roof shouted down, and Gracie tossed up his penknife, thinking it an inadequate tool for such a critical task. As Gracie and Smith were leaning oars against the wall to help slide Collapsible A down from the roof, the lifeboat suddenly came crashing down, splintering the oars and sending men scurrying out of the way. Crewmen then began dragging the collapsible over to the davits to attach it to the ropes for lowering.

At the same time, Charles Lightoller was on the portside roof with about a dozen crewmen, struggling to cut the lashings and free the other Engelhardt boat, Collapsible B. Marconi operator Harold Bride had just climbed up on the roof to join them. The captain had come to the Marconi Room about ten minutes before to release Bride and Phillips from their duties. "You look out for yourselves," Smith had said. "That's the way it is at this kind of a time. Every man for himself." But Jack Phillips continued to work the wireless key even as the lights dimmed and his signal sputtered. Bride was awed by his dedication. The junior operator stepped into the sleeping quarters to retrieve his money, and when he returned, he saw a stoker trying to steal Phillips's lifebelt. In a rage, Bride grabbed the man and a scuffle ensued, which ended with Phillips slugging the stoker and knocking him down. "Let's clear out," Phillips said breathlessly, and the two men fled the wireless cabin, leaving the stoker lying on the floor. As they heard water gurgling up toward the bridge, Phillips headed aft while Bride climbed up on the roof of the officers' quarters.

Norris Williams and his father, meanwhile, were on the bridge with Captain Smith when the ship gave a sudden lurch. Norris glanced down toward the bow but could only see the foremast sticking up from the water like a tree on a floodplain. Suddenly he was engulfed in a torrent of icy seawater that washed over the ship in a wave. As he tried to swim out from the flooded bridge toward the starboard railing, Norris lost sight of his father. As the wave swept aft along the deck, it drenched those who were struggling to cut Collapsible A free from the davit ropes. On the port side, Collapsible B crashed downward and landed upside down on the boat deck.

Archibald Gracie and Jim Smith retreated up the deck from the wave but ran straight into a mass of people streaming out of the first-class entrance from the staircase. The crowd, which included some women, fled aft from the advancing water but was stopped by a railing that marked the end of the first-class promenade. Realizing they were in a tight spot, Gracie and Smith looked up to the roof over the officers' mess. Smith made a leap for the roof but fell back. Gracie tried, too, but failed, hampered by his heavy coat and lifebelt.

Just then the liner's foredeck shuddered upward and Norris Williams suddenly found himself standing high and dry on the boat deck as the water retreated. He glanced around and saw his father about twelve to fifteen feet away from him. As the word "suction" flashed into his brain, Norris yelled out "Quick! Jump!" to his father and then leapt over the rail. Others nearby did the same. At about this time, Marconi operator

Harold Bride claimed that he looked down from the roof and saw Captain Smith dive into the sea from the bridge.

A moment later the ship's bow lurched downward again, sending an even larger wave rolling aft. Harold Bride was now on the deck beside overturned Collapsible B and when the water surged toward him, he grabbed an oarlock and held on as the boat was swept from the deck. On the starboard side, a number of people had clambered into Collapsible A and two men were struggling to cut it free just as the second wave washed over it. The boat was slammed against the davit and then pushed toward the forward funnel before it drifted off half-submerged with a few occupants still inside it.

Archibald Gracie threw himself into the second wave as if riding the surf at the seashore. It lifted him up to the top of the officers' mess where he grabbed the railing, pulled himself onto the roof, and scuttled over on his stomach to the base of the second funnel. When he raised his head to look for Jim Smith, he couldn't see him or any of the others who had been on the deck only seconds before. Gracie felt a pang of guilt at being separated from his friend since they had agreed to stick together till the end. He thought that Smith might have been thrown against the wall and knocked out or washed overboard in a tangle of ropes and other debris.

Charles Lightoller scrambled toward the wheelhouse roof and dived into the sea. The icy water felt as if a thousand knives were being driven into his body. On surfacing, he saw the crow's nest on the foremast standing straight ahead of him. His first instinct was to swim toward it, but he quickly realized the folly of clinging to any part of the ship. As he started to swim away to starboard he was suddenly thrown against a ventilator shaft by a rush of water pouring down into it. He knew that the shaft went straight down to a stokehold and that the flimsy wire grating over it was all that stood between him and a hundred-foot drop. Yet each time he tried to struggle free he was pulled back against the grating. He began to feel himself drowning and sensed he had only minutes to live. Suddenly, a blast of hot air shot up the shaft and blew him free. He came to the surface gasping for air but was soon pulled down again by another inrush of water. When he finally managed to struggle away he found himself alongside overturned Collapsible B. A number of men were clinging to its back but the exhausted Lightoller could only grasp a piece of rope and float alongside it. Around him, many others floundered in the water, some swimming, others drowning, in what he called "an utter nightmare of both sight and sound."

As the *Titanic*'s bow sank lower, Lightoller could see the stern rising out of the water, "piling the people into helpless heaps around the steep decks, and by the score into the icy water." He saw the mooring cables to the first funnel strain and then snap, sending the giant funnel crashing down in a shower of sparks and soot. The cable held on slightly longer on the starboard side, which pulled the funnel in that direction, causing it to come down among scores of swimmers, missing Lightoller only by inches. Norris Williams was sure that his father had been killed by it. The funnel's fall also caused a wave that pushed overturned Collapsible B away from the ship, with Lightoller still holding on to its rope.

Jack Thayer

Only moments after he came to the surface, Jack Thayer saw the forward funnel crash down about fifteen feet away from him. There was no sign of Milton Long, who had jumped from the rail about five seconds before him. Long had slid down the side of the hull while Thayer had jumped clear, saving his life by so doing. Jack looked back at the ship and saw it surrounded by a red glare. The stern was now standing at about a thirty-degree angle with light still blazing from its portholes. To Harold Bride, who was also in the water, it looked like a duck going down for a dive. The lights then blinked once and went out. Jack Thayer could hear the rumble and roar of what he thought must be the engines and boilers being torn from their beds. For Hugh Woolner in Collapsible D, the sound was like a thousand tons of rocks tumbling down a metal chute. To others in the lifeboats it sounded like explosions and many assumed that the boilers were blowing up.

But what they heard was actually the ship being wrenched apart. Unable to bear the strain, the ship broke in two just aft of the third funnel. An unnamed passenger later told a newspaper that he felt the ship shudder beneath his feet. "It was as though someone had shouted 'The ship is sinking!' " he recalled. Then he claimed that he, Archie Butt, and Clarence Moore jumped together into the sea. When the severed bow section began its plunge, Archibald Gracie found himself swirling downward within a whirlpool. He grabbed hold of the railing at the edge of the roof and held on, even as it pulled him down farther. Then it occurred to Gracie that he might be boiled alive by scalding water pouring up from the boilers. This notion caused him to let go of the railing and to kick upward as hard as he could. As he approached the surface, broken pieces of wood were ascending around him and he grabbed hold of a small plank. When his head broke the water Gracie saw a gray vapor over the sea and a mass of tangled wreckage. The *Titanic* was nowhere to be seen. He spied a wooden crate floating in some debris and paddled toward it. Just beyond it there was a capsized boat with men on its back and he swam over and pulled himself aboard.

The boat was overturned Collapsible B, and Jack Thayer was one of those already standing on it. A wave from the sinking bow section had washed him up against it, and from its back he had had a clear view of the *Titanic*'s last moments. "The stern then seemed to rise in the air," he recalled, "and stopped at about an angle of sixty degrees. It seemed to hold there for a time and then with a hissing sound it shot right down out of sight with people jumping from the stern." Norris Williams looked up from the water and saw the three propellers and rudder outlined against the sky over his head. He then watched as the stern pivoted before it went down with seemingly no suction and very little noise. Chief Baker Joughin also claimed there was no suction. Standing right at the stern railing by the flagpole, he said, he rode it down like an elevator and then paddled away without getting his hair wet.

"She's gone," Charles Lightoller heard those around him on the overturned boat murmur like a benediction. "She's gone, lads," a crewman in Boat 3 echoed. "Row like hell or we'll get the devil of a swell." In the same boat an English businessman remembered that "we raised our hats, bowed our heads and nobody spoke for some minutes." In Boat 5, Third Officer Pitman looked at his watch and noted that it was 2:20 a.m. May Futrelle heard a Frenchwoman in her boat begin to wail but May herself didn't cry, she just felt dead. In Collapsible C, Bruce Ismay couldn't bear to watch and sat with his back turned to the sinking liner. Lucy Duff Gordon raised herself from a seasick stupor to see the black silhouette disappear in one downward rush.

Then, from across the water there came what Archibald Gracie called "the most horrible sounds ever heard by mortal man." To Hugh Woolner, it was "the most fearful and bloodcurdling wail," to René Harris it was "a sound . . . as will haunt one all one's life and into eternity." Henry Harper called it "a wild maniacal chorus" and concluded that many of the people must have gone mad as they felt the ship go down. To Edith Rosenbaum it sounded like cheering, and she recalled that a crewman in her boat encouraged them to cheer as well since it meant that all on board had gotten into lifeboats.

William Sloper was under no illusion as to the meaning of the wailing chorus. He remembered that whenever a light was lit in one of the lifeboats, it would be seen by the hundreds in the water and "immediately their massed voices would rise and fall in a tremendous wailing crescendo which reverberated off into the starlit darkness of the silent night." Lawrence Beesley thought that the cries carried with them "every possible emotion of human fear, despair, agony, fierce resentment and blind anger, mingled—I am certain of this—with notes of infinite surprise, as though each one were saying, 'How is it possible that this awful thing is happening to me? That I should be caught in this death trap?' " These "notes of infinite surprise" may have emanated most profoundly from the Gilded Age masters of the universe—Astor, Widener, Thayer, Guggenheim, Douglas, Moore, Hays, and others—who suddenly found themselves immersed in the freezing water. People used to die in shipwrecks, but this was the twentieth century. This sort of thing didn't happen any longer, particularly not to people such as them.

Vigorous activity in cold water, it is now known, only intensifies the effects of hypothermia. Those who tried to swim without lifejackets out to boats were therefore likely among the first to perish. Archie Butt may have been one of them. An unnamed stoker who made it to Collapsible B later told a newspaper reporter that after he was helped aboard the overturned boat, "a man in the uniform of an army officer crawled onto the raft, but he stiffened out at once and died. We threw him overboard to make room for a living man." If this indeed is how Archie Butt died, then for him the end came fairly quickly. It seems sadly appropriate that a man who led such a "rushing life" ended it in one final burst of frenzied exertion. His body then disappeared beneath the black surface of the water, to descend in a slow drift to the ocean floor over two miles below.

For Frank Millet, death took its time, perhaps up to half an hour or longer, as he shivered under a brilliant canopy of stars, more beautiful than any he had seen in Byzantine mosaics or Venetian frescoes, impossible to ever capture in paint. For him, there may have moments for regret, reflection, or even insight before mental confusion fogged his consciousness and cardiac and respiratory failure set in. His body was recovered ten days later, standing upright in a cork lifejacket, his white tie visible beneath the collar of his black overcoat. His face was peaceful and there were no signs of struggle on his body.

To those in the lifeboats, it seemed as if the wails of the dying would never end. As time passed it became a monotone chant, what Helen Candee called a "a heavy moan as of one being, from whom final agony forces a single sound." It reminded Jack Thayer of the high-pitched hum of insects on a summer's evening. René Harris thought of the Wailing Wall in Jerusalem. Slowly, slowly the sound grew weaker, until it finally died away into the deathly stillness of the north Atlantic night.

VOICES IN THE NIGHT

ppeal to the officer not to go back," a woman in Boat 5 implored Steward Henry Etches. "Why should we lose all of our lives in a useless attempt to save those from the ship?" Others voiced their agreement, and as the protests mounted, Third Officer Pitman gave in and ordered that Boat 5 be turned away from the cries in the water. Similar scenes were enacted in many of the other lifeboats. Seaman Thomas Jones wanted Boat 8 to return, but when those at the oars refused, he announced, "If any of us are saved, remember I wanted to go back. I would rather drown with them than leave them,"

The failure of all but two of the eighteen lifeboats to go to the aid of the dying remains another of the great "if only's" of the *Titanic* story. Many of the boats were only half-full and, had they returned quickly, could have saved dozens of lives. In the Duff Gordons' boat alone, there was room for twenty-eight more passengers. But in Boat 1, as in most of the lifeboats, the fear of being swamped by the panicked throng overruled all other instincts. "It would have been sheer madness to have returned," harrumphed Hugh Woolner in Collapsible D, only recently pulled into a boat himself.

To those who had left the *Titanic* in the early lifeboats, the cries in the water "came as a thunderbolt, unexpected, inconceivable," Lawrence Beesley later recalled. But Beesley also noted that "no-one in any of the boats . . . can have escaped the paralyzing shock of knowing that so short a distance away a tragedy, unbelievable in its magnitude, was being enacted." Yet there were some in the lifeboats who simply could not believe that any cabin-class passengers had been left behind. "I thought it was the steerage on rafts and that they were all hysterical," claimed one first-class passenger. Mary Eloise Smith, an eighteen-year-old U.S. congressman's daughter, thought that the cries were from "seamen or possibly steerage who had overslept, it not occurring to me that my husband and my friends were not saved." Yet twenty-four-year-old Lucian Smith, whom Mary Eloise had married only two months earlier, was indeed one of those not saved.

In Boat 4, most of the women realized that their husbands and sons could be among those struggling in the icy water, since they had waved good-bye to them only half an hour before. With Quartermaster Perkis at the tiller, Marian Thayer, Madeleine Astor, and Emily Ryerson and her younger daughter began rowing back determinedly, despite a few protests in their boat. Seven men were pulled into Boat 4, all of them crew or stewards. One passenger, the wife of a New York stockbroker, recognized her bedroom steward as he was hauled aboard. Two of the rescued men soon died, and several others lay moaning and delirious for most of the night.

In Boat 14, Fifth Officer Lowe was quite certain that it would be "suicide" to row into the tumult and decided that he would wait until the crowd "thinned out" before returning. Lowe had taken charge of four other lifeboats and had ordered them tied together with Boat 14, about 150 yards away from the sinking liner. Daisy Minahan, the sister of the Wisconsin doctor who was one of those howling in the water, was less than impressed with the conduct of the young fifth officer. She claimed that Lowe had been making flippant remarks and swearing so much that he must have been drinking. When she and a few others begged him to transfer passengers and go back to rescue swimmers, he replied, "You ought to be damn glad you are here and have got your own life." When Lowe at last began moving passengers into the other boats, he yelled at Daisy, "Jump, God damn you, jump!" earning her permanent enmity.

But Lowe's language was genteel compared to that of Quartermaster Hichens in Boat 6. When the horrifying cries came across the water, several passengers pleaded with Hichens to return, but the quartermaster refused, saying there would only be a lot of "stiffs" there. This upset a number of the women, but Arthur Peuchen could only say resignedly, "It is no use arguing with that man. It is best not to discuss matters with him." While the major sat glumly at his oar in a lifeboat less than half-full, most of his shipboard coterie—Harry Molson; Hudson and Bess Allison and their two-year-old daughter, Loraine; Mark Fortune and his nineteen-year-old son;

Fifth Officer Lowe

the bachelor trio known as "the Three Musketeers"; Charles Hays, his son-in-law, and his twenty-two-year old assistant—all either drowned or slowly froze to death.

Almost an hour had passed by the time Fifth Officer Lowe finally maneuvered Boat 14 into the wreckage. By then most of the wailing had subsided and only three or four men were rescued. One very large man, a first-class passenger named W. F. Hoyt, was pulled from the water bleeding from the nose and mouth and died shortly afterward. As they prepared to leave the scene, a floating door was suddenly spotted with what appeared to be a small Japanese man lashed to it. He looked frozen stiff and Lowe said, "What's the use? He's dead, likely, and if he isn't there's others better worth saving than a Jap." Eventually Lowe relented and the man was pulled into the boat, where several women began rubbing his chest, hands, and feet. Within seconds he opened his eyes, said a few words that no one understood, and then stood up and stretched. He soon took an oar and began rowing so diligently that Lowe had to admit that he was ashamed of what he'd said about "the little blighter." The rescued man was actually Chinese, one of eight Donaldson Line crewmen traveling in third class, four of whom had secreted themselves in the bow of Collapsible C.

In the dark, Lowe did not catch sight of the twenty or more people who had taken refuge on the partly submerged Collapsible A, Norris Williams among them. As he clung to the collapsible's gunwale, Norris felt his fur coat weighing him down and quickly shrugged it off. He then made his way into the boat and found that he was able to stand in it even though the water was waist high. Someone near the bow organized a head count which soon faltered when it came to those who didn't understand English. It was then proposed that they put up the collapsible's canvas sides and try to bail out the boat. A passenger next to Norris became enthusiastic about this idea and asked the man ahead of him if he could borrow his bowler hat for bailing. The man refused, insisting, to Norris's bemusement, that without his hat he would catch cold in the night air. But any hopes of bailing were abandoned when after much pulling it was discovered that the supports for the sides were broken and the canvas shredded. After this, it seemed as if only God could help them and when someone suggested a prayer, they stood together in the water with bowed heads. One of the most devout of the shivering supplicants was Rhoda Abbott, a seamstress and Salvation Army soldier who had jumped from the deck with her two teenaged sons but had lost them in the chaos near the plunging bow.

They prayed on the back of overturned Collapsible B as well. When the cries in the water died away, a crewman near the stern took a quick poll of the faiths of those around him and then led the group in the Lord's Prayer. This heartened Archibald Gracie, who had been intimidated by the rough-looking men around him and had feared that he might receive "short shrift" if they decided the boat needed to be lightened. Gracie had averted his eyes as swimmers were fended off with language that, in his words, "grated on my sensibilities." As Fireman Harry Senior approached the collapsible he was hit over the head with an oar but went around to the other side and climbed on. Baker Charles Joughin was pushed off as he tried to board, but he, too, swam around the boat until he was recognized by one of the cooks, who reached out and clasped his arm. As Algernon Barkworth breaststroked toward the collapsible in Eton-trained style, someone shouted "Look out, you will swamp us!" but Barkworth crawled aboard anyway, dripping like a wet sheepdog in his fur coat. The Yorkshire justice of the peace became the

Approximately twenty-eight men found refuge on the back of overturned
Collapsible B. It was later photographed by the crew of a ship from Halifax.

third first-class passenger, along with Gracie and Jack Thayer, among the
roughly twenty-eight men on the overturned collapsible. Wireless operator Harold Bride was crowded in near the stern, next to Jack Thayer,
with someone sitting on his feet. The Irish bagpiper Eugene Daly was
one of approximately six third-class passengers who had also crawled
aboard. Baker Joughin claimed that he simply hung on to the boat from
the water, insulated by the alcohol he had drunk. The other men kneeled
or crouched on the slippery ribs of the collapsible's hull, and a few used
boards and an oar to paddle away from the wreckage.

Second Officer Lightoller soon took charge of the boat, much to
Gracie's relief. When the second officer learned that one of the Marconi men was on board, he asked Harold Bride what ships had replied
to the distress calls. The junior wireless operator said that the *Carpathia*
was the nearest one and that it should arrive within three hours. This
raised everyone's spirits and a crewman organized shouts of "Boat Ahoy!
Boat Ahoy!" which reached peak volume when green flares were seen in

the distance. These, however, were being lit by Fourth Officer Boxhall, who had taken a box of them into Boat 2. When the flares disappeared, Lightoller soon put a stop to the shouting.

In Boat 1, Cosmo Duff Gordon likewise told Henry Stengel to quit his incessant shouts of "Boat Ahoy." Cosmo was worried about his wife, who was stretched out in the boat, seasick and shivering from the cold. Mabel Francatelli soon lay down next to "Madame," as she called her employer, and from time to time, Lucy roused herself to reassure Cosmo that she was all right. She also tried occasionally to make light conversation and at one point teased Franks about the odd assortment of clothes she was wearing. "Just fancy," she said, "you actually left your beautiful nightdress behind you." For Fireman Robert Pusey this proved to be too much. "Never mind about your nightdress, madam," he retorted, "as long as you have got your life." Another fireman joined in. "You people need not bother about losing your things for you can afford to buy new ones." Seeing "Madame" stretched out in her fur coat and pink velvet designer mules made this all too apparent. "What about us?" the fireman continued. "We have lost all our kit and our pay stops from the moment the ship went down." "Yes, that's hard luck if you like," replied Sir Cosmo. "But don't worry, you will get another ship. At any rate I will give you a fiver towards getting a new kit." He could not then have imagined how this small gesture of noblesse oblige would come to haunt him.

In Boat 6, Margaret Brown had doffed her sables to free her up for rowing. She had encouraged the other women to row as well, defying the quartermaster who railed at her from the stern. But Robert Hichens had chosen the wrong group of women to bully. In addition to the forceful Mrs. Brown, the plucky Mrs. Candee, and the voluble Berthe Mayné, there were two English suffragettes on board, Elsie Bowerman and her mother, Edith Chibnall. Both were active members of Sylvia Pankhurst's Women's Social and Political Union, the most militant of Britain's votes-for-women organizations. Edith was one of ten women who had accompanied Mrs. Pankhurst on a 1910 deputation to Parliament that had resulted in arrests after a scuffle with police. She had also donated a banner for a Hyde Park demonstration that read "Rebellion to tyrants is obedience to God."

A full-scale rebellion against one male tyrant was soon under way in Boat 6. The women tried to taunt the quartermaster into joining them at the oars, but Hichens refused, preferring to stand at the tiller shouting out rowing instructions and doom-filled warnings that they could be lost for days with no food or water. Eventually Boat 16 came near and the two lifeboats tied up together. Margaret Brown spotted a chilled, thinly clad stoker in the adjoining boat and after he jumped over into Boat 6 to help with the rowing, she wrapped him in her sables, tying the tails around his ankles. She then handed him an oar and instructed Boat 16 to cut them loose so they could row to keep warm. Howling curses in protest, Hichens moved to block this but an enraged Mrs. Brown rose up and threatened to throw him overboard. The fur-enveloped stoker reproached Hichens for his foul language in the broadest of Cockney accents: "Soy, don't you know you are talking to a loidy!"

"I know who I'm talking to and I am commanding this boat!" the quartermaster spluttered as Boat 6 rowed away under Margaret Brown's direction.

Ella White was appalled by the hapless rowing in Boat 8 and tried to set the pace by counting out strokes while waving her illuminated cane. This only succeeded in annoying the men at the oars, but Marie Young loyally noted that Mrs. White's electric cane was "treasured above all" since they had no other source of light in the boat. The piteous cries from a twenty-two-year-old Spanish newlywed, Maria Josefa "Pepita" Peñasco, calling out for her husband Victor, became so vexing for those in Boat 8 that the English aristocrat, the Countess of Rothes, left the tiller to take her in her arms and comfort her. Pepita and Victor Peñasco were a wealthy young honeymooning couple from Madrid who, when in Paris, had decided to take the maiden voyage of the *Titanic* as a lark without telling their families. Another passenger remembered that Pepita and Victor "were just like little canaries ... they were so loving ... but she was saved and he perished."

At thirty-three, Noëlle, the Countess of Rothes, had been the

Noëlle, Countess of Rothes, in 1905 with her young son, Lord Leslie

chatelaine of Leslie House, a ten-thousand-acre estate near Fife, since marrying the heir to this ancient Scottish seat in 1900, and her take-charge manner had caused Seaman Jones to put her at the tiller of Boat 8. While she went to comfort Pepita, Noëlle asked her husband's cousin, Gladys Cherry, to take over the helm. When the dreadful moans of the dying came across the water, the countess put her hands over the Spanish bride's ears. Noëlle and Gladys both backed Seaman Jones when he proposed returning to rescue swimmers, but Gladys recalled that the others "would have killed us rather than go back." She also remembered the beauty of the stars that night but stated, "That icy air and stars I never want to feel or see again."

Edith Rosenbaum also recalled how keenly the cold was felt by those in her lifeboat. To distract the children in Boat 11, Edith would occasionally twist the tail of her toy pig and play "The Maxixe." William Sloper, however, actually found himself too warm as he pulled on an oar in Boat 7. The Shetland pullover and woolen suit he was wearing beneath his winter overcoat and lifebelt were causing him to drip with perspiration. Seeing Dorothy Gibson shivering nearby in the polo coat she had put on over her silk evening dress, Sloper removed his overcoat and put it around her shoulders. In Boat 5 Karl Behr took a break from rowing to rub Helen Newsom's stockinged feet, which were wet from the water in the bottom of the boat. The man next to Behr nudged him and revealed a small nickel-plated revolver in the palm of his hand. "Should the worse come to the worst," he said calmly, "you can use this after my wife and I have finished with it." Behr thanked him politely and only later thought about how strange the offer was.

On half-submerged Collapsible A, circumstances truly were life and death, with the latter taking a heavy toll. A man behind Norris Williams asked if he could rest his arm on his shoulder and Norris agreed. Over time his grip loosened, and when Norris looked at his face, the man gave him a weak smile and fell dead in the water. As a faint glow appeared in the eastern horizon, hopes of rescue began to rise but they were not enough to save a mother and daughter who drifted away lifeless in each other's arms.

On overturned Collapsible B two men had died from the cold during the night and one of them had fallen overboard. Algernon Barkworth thought to himself how quickly any horror of the dead disappears at such times. And even one less man lightened the burden on their precarious raft which was slowly sinking beneath them. Shortly before dawn there was a shout from the stern, "There is a steamer coming behind us!"

"All you men stand steady!" commanded Lightoller, "I will be the one to look astern!" He then looked but did not confirm the good news. Shooting stars and lights from the other lifeboats had raised many false alarms during the night. Soon, however, Archibald Gracie saw in the distance what was unmistakably the mast lights of a steamer. Behind the lights were large white shapes that one man suggested were fishing boats from the Grand Banks of Newfoundland. As the sun rose, Gracie saw that they were icebergs.

With the dawn came a breeze that sent waves washing over the boat and Lightoller began to doubt whether the collapsible would last until the *Carpathia* reached them. He had lined up the men two abreast along the keel and now called out "Lean left!" or "Lean right!" to counteract the swells. As the sky grew brighter, they suddenly spotted four of the *Titanic*'s lifeboats tied up together about eight hundred yards away. The men shouted and Lightoller fished an officer's whistle out of his pocket and blew a shrill blast. Boats 4 and 12 untied from Boat 14 and Collapsible D and began to inch toward them. To Seaman Samuel Hemming in Boat 4 it looked as if the men were standing on a slab of ice.

"Come over and take us off!" shouted Lightoller when the boats came within hailing distance. The overturned collapsible was by then so low in the water that the wash as Boat 12 drew near almost caused it to capsize. Lightoller began unloading the men one at a time; four or five went into Boat 4, the rest into Boat 12. The boat shook dangerously as each man made his leap. Baker Joughin paddled over to the boat, claiming to have been in the water the whole time. The second officer was the last to leave, and before doing so he hoisted the body of the dead man into Boat 12. Archibald Gracie massaged the lifeless body's head and wrists but rigor mortis had already set in. Lightoller soon made his way to the stern of Boat 12 and took the tiller as the now heavily loaded boat lumbered toward the rescue ship.

For the half-frozen survivors on Collapsible A, the sight of the *Carpathia*'s mast lights in the early dawn light kindled new hope. They cheered and on a count of three began shouts of "Boat Ahoy."

"We can see a ship now," said Olaus Abelseth, a Norwegian-born farmer from North Dakota, to a man he was holding up by one shoulder. Abelseth had recognized him as a man from New Jersey who had been in his compartment on the Boat Train to Southampton.

"Who are you?" the man from New Jersey responded blankly. "Let me be. Who are you?"

Abelseth continued to hold him up but within half an hour he was dead. As the sun rose, Norris Williams couldn't help noticing what a beautiful, sparkling morning it was. He could see the scattered lifeboats in the distance and reflected on how little was left from the greatest ocean liner ever built.

In Boat 14, Fifth Officer Lowe had hoisted a sail and was making good time toward the *Carpathia*, even while towing Collapsible D behind them. Hugh Woolner soon saw Lowe heading the boat toward a group of people who seemed to him to be standing up in the water. "They were a party of fourteen or so," he recalled, "among them a black-haired woman and two corpses." Rhoda Abbott, the only female to have survived in Collapsible A, was the first to be taken off. René Harris watched as this small woman dressed all in brown "sank into the bottom of the boat like a drowned bird." When Norris Williams clambered into Boat 14, his legs felt as if thousands of needles were piercing them. Finally, only three corpses were left in the half-submerged collapsible. Two of them appeared to be crewmen; the other was a man in evening clothes. Lowe checked to make certain they were dead and then set the boat adrift. As the collapsible floated off, a white lifebelt covered the face of the lifeless man in evening clothes. A month later, the *Oceanic* would recover the abandoned collapsible almost two hundred miles away from where the *Titanic* sank. Still wearing the white tie and tails he had worn to dinner on the *Titanic*'s last night, Thomson Beattie, the last of "the Three Mus-keteers," was given a burial at sea.

When one of the *Carpathia*'s rockets was first spotted from Boat 6, the ever-contrary Quartermaster Hichens dismissed it, saying, "That is a falling star." After it became clear that it was indeed a ship, Hichens stated, "No, she is not going to pick us up. She is to pick up bodies," and ordered that the rowers let the boat drift. But the women at the oars were having none of it. "Where those lights are lies our salvation," said Helen Candee, voicing what they were all thinking, and with renewed spirit they began pulling hard toward the *Carpathia*.

When the sun came up fully, the ice field began to glow in mauves and corals, a breathtaking sight. There was one iceberg with a double peak about two hundred feet high. To Lucy Duff Gordon the illumi-nated bergs looked like giant opals, and May Futrelle noted how they glistened like rock quartz, though one of them, she thought, was doubt-less the murderer. The scene reminded Hugh Woolner of photographs of an Antarctic expedition. Seven-year-old Douglas Spedden raised a few smiles in Boat 3 by exclaiming to his nurse, "Oh Muddie, look at the beautiful North Pole with no Santa Claus on it!" Daisy Spedden recorded in her diary that as their boat was rowed toward rescue, "the tragedy of the situation sank deep into our hearts as we saw the *Carpathia* stand-ing amidst the few bits of wreckage with the pitifully small number of lifeboats coming up to her from different directions."

After racing through the night to the *Titanic*'s distress position, the

222 | HUGH BREWSTER

Carpathia had spotted Fourth Officer Boxhall's green flares and had headed for them. "Shut down your engines and take us aboard," Boxhall shouted up as the *Carpathia* drew alongside Boat 2 at 4:10 a.m.

"I have only one sailor," he added, as the boat tossed on the choppy swells.

"All right," came back the voice of the *Carpathia*'s captain, Arthur Rostron.

"The *Titanic* has gone down with everyone on board!" Mahala Douglas shrieked from beside the tiller and Boxhall promptly told her to "shut up," a reproach that she later thought was justified. Yet after helping his passengers onto the rope ladder that was lowered from the *Carpathia*, Boxhall, too, would become emotional. After being escorted to the bridge, the twenty-eight-year-old fourth officer with the boyish face confirmed with Captain Rostron that the *Titanic* had indeed gone down. As he began giving details, Rostron interrupted to ask how many people were left on board when she sank.

"Hundreds and hundreds! Perhaps a thousand! Perhaps more!" Boxhall burst out, his voice breaking. "My God, sir, they've gone down with her. They couldn't live in this icy water."

"Thank you, mister," the captain replied with characteristic calm. "Go below and get some coffee and try to get warm."

In the *Carpathia*'s dining saloons, coffee, hot brandy, and sandwiches were being served to Mahala Douglas and the other numbed survivors from Boat 2. Stewards had taken their names and given them blankets, and a doctor with medical supplies was stationed in each of the three dining saloons. These arrangements had been requested by the captain, and they represented only a few of the entries on a long list of orders that he had issued to his department heads shortly after receiving the *Titanic*'s distress call. And it was only by chance that the *CQD* call was received at all. The *Carpathia*'s wireless operator, Harold Cottam, had quit for the night but had left his earphones on as he was unlacing his boots. Once alerted about the *CQD* call, the forty-two-year-old captain immediately ordered that the *Carpathia* head for the *Titanic*'s distress position and told Cottam to inform the *Titanic* they would be there in four hours. By putting on top speed, they made it in only three and a half, maneuvering their way around icebergs spotted by the extra lookouts posted in the crow's nest, bow, and wing bridge.

Rostron had also ordered that bosun's chairs and canvas ash bags be positioned by the rope ladders to hoist up the women and children. Lucy Duff Gordon and Mabel Francatelli were both swung up in bosun's chairs, after Boat 1, the second boat to arrive, came alongside at 4:40 a.m. Once on deck, Lucy recalled, she and Franks "clung to each other like children, too exhausted to speak, only realizing the blessed fact that we were saved." Lucy drank some hot brandy but felt too ill to eat. After taking a sedative, she fell asleep in a first-class cabin offered by *Carpathia* passengers and did not wake till the next morning.

As Lucy drifted off to sleep, the sixteen remaining boats continued to make their way toward the *Carpathia*. Henry Harper in Boat 3 was struck by how tiny the Cunarder looked compared to the *Titanic* but thought that he had never seen a finer sight. Daisy Spedden, meanwhile, was growing increasingly annoyed with a "fat" woman in Boat 3, who, as she later wrote, "had been dreadful all along for she never stopped talking and telling the sailors what to do, and she imbibed from her brandy flask frequently, never offering a drop to anyone else." As they approached the *Carpathia*, the fat woman stood up to be the first off, and it gave Daisy great satisfaction to pull her down by the lifebelt and see her land on the floor of the boat with her heels in the air. She was held there, seething, until they were alongside the *Carpathia*, when, in Daisy's words, "we were all charmed to let her go up in the sling first." Henry Harper recorded that when a "woman of substantial size" stepped toward the bosun's chair, another woman, dressed only in a nightgown and kimono, suddenly sat up and pointed at her. "Look at that horrible woman!" she cried out. "She stepped on my stomach! Horrible creature!" According to Harper, the woman in the kimono had been lying unseen on the bottom of the boat the whole night. Her identity is unknown, but many researchers believe that the "fat" woman could only have been the Main Line millionairess Charlotte Cardeza.

Collapsible C, with Bruce Ismay aboard, approached the *Carpathia* at approximately 5:45 a.m. Once on board, Ismay stood apart from the other passengers, speaking to no one. Dr. Frank McGee, the *Carpathia*'s surgeon, approached him and suggested he go into the dining saloon and get something warm to drink but Ismay replied that he didn't want anything. Noting his distraught expression, the doctor urged him again to go into the dining saloon and Ismay snapped, "No. If you will leave me alone I will be much happier here." He then added, "If you will get me in some room where I can be quiet, I wish you would." A steward took Ismay to one of the doctor's examining rooms where he remained until the ship arrived in New York. William Carter, meanwhile, remained on deck, waiting anxiously for his wife and children.

Edith Rosenbaum recalled that when Boat 11 arrived it almost collided with another lifeboat as they were tossed about in the waves. The babies and children in Boat 11 went up first in the canvas ash bags and Edith was then quickly hoisted in a bosun's chair, which bumped and scraped along the side of the ship. When Boat 14 drew alongside at around 7:15 a.m., Norris Williams was able to climb up the rope ladder even though his feet were numb. A steward handed him a tumbler of brandy which he quickly emptied and as the alcohol's warmth radiated through him, he suddenly felt very hungry. He managed to hobble to one of the ship's galleys where the cooks made him what he thought was the best meal he had ever tasted. On finishing it, Norris spied an invitingly warm space behind one of the stoves, crawled in with his blanket, and fell fast asleep.

Boat 14 arrived with Collapsible D still in tow. During the night, Fifth Officer Lowe had called out encouraging words to the women in the collapsible behind him, completely winning over René Harris. As the sun rose, she looked to where the voice came from and saw "a young man of six feet two, very slender and sinewy. . . . His face was clear cut and of the fine British race. . . . His cap was tilted boyishly to one side. He looked like a college boy out on an early morning lark." This slightly romantic fixation on Harold Lowe helped distract René from the gnawing fear that her own beloved "boy" was now lost to her forever. Once on the *Carpathia*, she followed a group of steerage women to the crowded third-class dining saloon. She sat there silently for some time before a

Lifeboat 14 approaches the *Carpathia* with Collapsible D in tow.

steward found her and apologized for putting her with the third-class passengers. "What difference does it make?" René thought.

René's friend May Futrelle was surprised to see some male passengers among the women in the *Carpathia*'s first-class dining saloon, and this caused her to make a rapid search of all the public rooms in the hope that her "Jack" might be in one of them. She then went out on deck to see the remaining lifeboats arrive, and as each boat came alongside, she kept hoping that every big man she spied might be her husband. On discovering that Jacques Futrelle was not on board, she would return to the dining saloon to await the next boat.

William Carter had spotted his wife and daughter as Boat 4 came alongside but could not see his son. When he shouted down for him, eleven-year-old Billy Carter lifted up the brim of his mother's large hat and called up to his anxious father. It had been a long, cold, and arduous night for the most socially prominent of the *Titanic*'s ladies in Boat 4. But the news that awaited them on the rescue ship was far worse. Madeleine Astor, Marian Thayer, and Emily Ryerson would soon learn that they were widows, and Eleanor Widener would discover she had lost both her husband and her son. Of the nine guests who had attended the Widener dinner party the evening before, only four were left alive. A very fragile Madeleine Astor was soon escorted to the dining saloon and attended to by Dr. McGee. Marian Thayer waited on deck as the last boats came in, anxiously looking for her husband and son.

Boat 8 was the next to arrive, at around 7:30 a.m., followed by Boat 6, which had to make several attempts to come alongside on account of the rising waves. After Helen Candee was swung up the side, she was assisted to the hospital where her broken ankle was treated. Margaret Brown was given a cup of hot coffee as she stepped onto the deck, and she was soon impressed by how many of the *Carpathia*'s passengers came forward to offer clothing, toiletries, and the use of a stateroom. On entering the dining saloon, she spied "our brave and heroic quartermaster" gesticulating to a small group as he described how difficult it had been to discipline the occupants of his boat. On seeing Mrs. Brown, however, Hichens, in her words, "did not tarry long but made a hasty retreat."

After 8:00 a.m., only Boat 12 remained on the open sea, precariously overloaded with about seventy-five passengers, including those rescued from Collapsible B. Lightoller ordered a few people to move toward the stern which helped raise the bow, but still the gunwales remained only inches above the water. Archibald Gracie was squeezed in at the bow between Algernon Barkworth and the body of the dead man that Lightoller had put on board. A woman passed him a steamer rug which he threw over his head and he and Barkworth and a crewman huddled under it for warmth. As the sea became rougher, one wave and then another splashed over the bow. Just as the boat looked as if it might founder, Lightoller managed to coax it onto one long swell that took it right into calmer waters in the lee of the *Carpathia*. Archibald Gracie had no trouble clambering up the rope ladder and said that he felt like kissing the deck in gratitude. Harold Bride, too, managed to climb up to the deck but promptly collapsed and was carried to the hospital to be treated for frostbitten feet. Jack Thayer spied his mother waiting on the deck and embraced her. She was overjoyed to see him but shocked that he had no news of his father.

Charles Lightoller, punctilious to the end, saw that all his passengers were boarded before climbing up himself, becoming the last *Titanic* survivor to board the *Carpathia.* On deck a knot of women stood around Captain Rostron asking if he was sure that there were no more boats.

"Could not another ship have picked them up?" one distraught woman demanded.

"Was it not possible that he might have climbed onto an iceberg?" queried another.

Lightoller thought to himself that there was no kindness in holding out hope where he knew there was none.

May Futrelle heard an officer on deck say, "This is the last of the *Titanic*'s boats." But even then she did not give up. Only when the *Carpathia* blew its whistle and began to move away did she fully realize that her husband was gone.

Captain Rostron of the *Carpathia* was nicknamed "The Electric Spark"
on account of his energetic decisiveness.

THE SHIP OF SORROW

MONDAY, APRIL 15, 1912, 8:40 A.M.

Please don't!" René Harris called out as the *Carpathia*'s musicians gathered by the piano in the dining saloon. To May Futrelle, sitting beside her, it looked as if they were about to play a hymn. The musicians dispersed, but something that May found even more harrowing followed. An Episcopalian clergyman came into the dining saloon and read the service for the burial of the dead from the Book of Common Prayer. This was at the request of Captain Rostron, a prayerful man himself, who thought it would give comfort to the bereaved. But for May, "the shock and finality of it were awful." The minister, Reverend Father Roger Anderson of Baltimore, finished with a prayer of thanksgiving for the living, many of whom were by then quietly weeping. Margaret Brown looked around the room at the survivors, "speechless, half-clad, their eyes protruding, hair streaming down, those who only twelve hours before, were immaculately groomed and richly gowned."

During the service, the *Carpathia* circled over the area where the *Titanic* had gone down. Arthur Peuchen went out on deck and stood by the bow railing looking for any sign of his friends. He saw some deck chairs and lifebelts and streams of granular, reddish-brown cork, but no bodies. Peuchen assumed they had drifted off with the wind that had come up that morning. He also saw a striped barber's pole bobbing in the waves which puzzled him since the barbershop had been on C deck. He concluded that it must have been blown out of the ship by the explosions he had heard during the sinking.

From the bridge, Captain Rostron also noted floating masses of insulating cork but was surprised by how little wreckage there was. He did see one body, a man floating on his side in a life preserver, his head half-submerged. But with the sea rising, Rostron was eager to be on his way to New York and signaled to the *Californian*, which had arrived an hour before, to continue the search. The Leyland steamer had heard the news by wireless early that morning and had slowly made its way through the ice to the scene. The *Californian* searched the area for an hour or more but saw only stray bits of wreckage and some of the *Titanic*'s lifeboats that Rostron had set adrift after taking thirteen of them on board.

That morning Captain Rostron had considered several places he might land his more than seven hundred unexpected passengers. He'd first considered the Azores so that he could continue to the Mediterranean as scheduled; then Halifax, which was the nearest port. But on seeing the survivors come aboard, many of them in a distressed state and some in need of medical attention, it soon became clear that he should take them directly to New York. Rostron decided to visit Bruce Ismay to discuss the decision with him but the shattered White Star chairman quickly gave his agreement to whatever the captain thought was best. It was Rostron who had earlier prompted a dazed Ismay to send a wireless message notifying the White Star Line's New York office about the accident. To Philip Franklin, the U.S. vice president of White Star's parent company, the International Mercantile Marine, Ismay had written:

Deeply regret advise you *Titanic* sank this morning after collision iceberg, resulting serious loss life. Full particulars later. Bruce Ismay.

"Captain, do you think that is all that I can tell him?" Ismay asked as he gave the note to Rostron.

"Yes," said Rostron in reply.

By then Philip Franklin already knew that the *Titanic* was in trouble. He had been awakened just before 2 a.m. by a telephone call from a newspaper reporter informing him that the *Titanic* had struck an iceberg and had radioed for assistance. Franklin rang off and telephoned the

White Star dock and was told that reporters had been calling there as well. On telephoning the Associated Press, Franklin was informed that a report on the *Titanic*'s distress calls had already gone out—in time for the morning papers. At 3 a.m. he cabled Captain Haddock of the *Olympic,* urging him to make every effort to contact the *Titanic* and advise him of her position. By 8 a.m. crowds had already started to gather outside the White Star offices on lower Broadway.

As the *Carpathia* turned its bow toward New York, the captain found that the ice field continued for many miles, stretching toward the horizon. While he proceeded slowly around its perimeter, the giant bergs caught the morning sun, a sight that stirred Rostron to wax poetic when he wrote of it later: "Minarets like cathedral towers turned to gold in the distances . . . and some seemed to shape themselves like argosies under full sail." Helen Candee, too, admired the stunning white vista as she reclined with her ankle bandaged, pondering what she called "nature's implacable strength." Archibald Gracie, meanwhile, lay wrapped in blankets on a sofa in the lounge, feeling rather awkward without his clothes. Daisy and Frederic Spedden had looked after Gracie when he first arrived—"half-frozen and completely unnerved," in Daisy's description—and had taken his clothes to be dried in a bake oven. But after a few hot brandies the colonel had rallied, and whenever Daisy drew near, he would ask plaintively for his trousers, saying he couldn't possibly move without them. Gracie had suffered a blow to the head and there were cuts and bruises on his legs that would be sore to the touch for several days. Eventually his dry but salt-stained clothes were returned to him and he went off to nap in a borrowed cabin.

The Speddens spent the rest of the day tending to those in need and Daisy recalled heartrending scenes as women frantically sought their missing children. Margaret Brown tried to help a woman who kept screaming out for her child and she eventually asked the doctor to give the distraught woman a sedative since she was pulling out strands of her hair in panic. Soon the only children left unclaimed were the two French toddlers who had been put aboard Collapsible D by a "Mr. Hoffman." Margaret Hays, the young New Yorker who had carried her little dog into Boat 7, was fluent in French and had taken charge of the two boys. The curly-haired waifs, aged three and two, were soon seen playing on deck with Margaret's Pomeranian, one of three dogs to have survived.

After napping for almost an hour behind a stove in the galley, Norris Williams had awakened and gone out on deck just as the *Carpathia* was departing. But with his legs still feeling very numb and painful, he made his way to the ship's hospital. A surgeon who was helping Dr. McGee examined Norris and expressed grave concern about the state of his legs. He thought that amputation might be necessary and cheerfully ventured that this could even be done on board before the ship reached New York. But there was a chance, he thought, that the young tennis player might be able to save his legs if he were to exercise them continually. Norris seized on this option and resolved to walk the decks day and night. First, however, he found a change of clothes and steeped himself in a hot bath.

Jack Thayer had been lent a pair of pajamas and a bunk and as he climbed into bed he was still aglow from the hot brandy given to him on arrival—his first-ever alcoholic drink. His mother was resting in Captain Rostron's cabin, which she shared with Eleanor Widener and Madeleine Astor. René Harris was given the use of a stateroom along with two other women, one of them Ninette Aubart, whom she soon befriended. The distraught young Frenchwoman was grieving the loss of Ben Guggenheim and feeling afraid about landing in a strange country where she did not speak the language.

Captain Rostron paid another visit to Ismay's room that morning. He had received a wireless message from the *Olympic* proposing that the *Titanic*'s passengers be transferred to her. Rostron thought that putting the survivors into boats for a second sea transfer was a very bad idea. Even the sight of a ship that so closely resembled the *Titanic* might stir up panic among the survivors. Ismay agreed emphatically—the *Olympic* should stay out of sight.

On board the sister liner, however, Frank Millet's friend Daniel Burnham had been told that they were steaming to the rescue of the *Titanic*'s passengers, and he was preparing to give up his suite to Frank and Archie Butt. He could use the time on board with Frank to prepare him for the next meeting of the Lincoln Memorial Commission. In a letter waiting for Frank in New York, Burnham had written, "The rats swim back and begin to gnaw at the same old spot the moment the dog's back is turned," the "rats" being several congressmen who were still pushing for John Russell Pope's design over that of Henry Bacon. The letter had concluded, "I leave the thing confidently in your hand."

When a list of the *Titanic*'s survivors was posted on the *Olympic*'s notice board the next morning, however, Burnham saw that Millet's name was not on it. In his diary entry for April 16, the ailing architect recorded the news of the *Titanic*'s loss and noted that "Frank D. Millet, whom I loved, was aboard of her . . . and probably [has] gone down." Burnham himself would die two weeks later, but the classical white temple he had championed for the Lincoln Memorial would prevail—a tribute to the architect's persistence and that of the friend he loved.

The *Olympic*'s Marconi operators were relaying all the messages from the *Carpathia* to stations onshore, due to the Cunard liner's limited wireless range. Marconi forms had been distributed to the survivors that morning but many of their messages would not be sent for another day or two—if at all. Captain Rostron had instructed that the first priority was to transmit a list of the survivors. The *Carpathia*'s chief purser and his assistant were busy compiling the names of passengers while Lightoller worked on the list of the surviving crew and engine room staff and a senior steward gathered the names of the cooks and stewards. The grim tally would come to 712 people rescued from a ship that had held 2,209. Over two-thirds of those on board the *Titanic* had perished.

But this news had not yet reached New York. The morning edition of the *New York Herald* announced: THE NEW TITANIC STRIKES ICEBERG AND CALLS FOR AID, VESSELS RUSH TO HER SIDE. The *New York Times* went further and said that the liner was actually sinking. This sent anxious relatives down to White Star's offices at No. 9 Broadway—among them Ben Guggenheim's wife, Florette; John Jacob Astor's son, Vincent; and J. P. Morgan's son, John Pierpont Jr. ("Have just heard fearful rumor about *Titanic* with iceberg," the financier had wired his son from the spa in Aix. "Hope for God sake not true.") Philip Franklin knew little more than was in the newspapers but he and his staff provided reassurances that the *Titanic* would not sink and her passengers were safe. Ismay's "Deeply regret advise you" cable had not been received by him

Philip Franklin (inset) reassured those making inquiries at the White Star offices in New York that the *Titanic*'s passengers were safe.

and, unaccountably, would not arrive till Wednesday morning. At 9:30 a.m. Franklin announced to the press that the *Titanic* was still afloat. At mid-morning there was a rumor out of Montreal that the damaged liner was slowly being towed to Halifax, and by noon White Star had arranged to send a train there to pick up passengers. That afternoon many newspapers ran stories headed ALL SAVED FROM TITANIC AFTER COLLISION. Philip Franklin meanwhile continued to send wireless messages to Captain Haddock of the *Olympic*, asking him to contact the *Titanic* and advise him regarding the landing of the passengers.

By early afternoon the *Carpathia* had passed the last of the ice and could begin to pick up speed, but at 4:00 p.m its engines were stopped. Father Anderson then appeared on deck in his clerical garb, followed by

Carpathia crewmen carrying four corpses sewn into canvas bags. These were the bodies of two male passengers, one fireman, and one seaman, that had been brought aboard from the lifeboats. Each of the canvas bags in turn was laid on a wide plank and covered with a flag. As the words "Unto Almighty God we commend the soul of our brother departed, and we commit his body to the deep" were read aloud, the bodies were tipped into the sea one at a time. A large crowd stood nearby with heads bared. The canvas bags had been weighted so that the bodies would fall feet first but one of them struck the water flat. A *Carpathia* passenger wrote that he would never forget the sound of that splash.

One of those buried at sea was first-class passenger William F. Hoyt, the heavy man who had been pulled into Boat 14 and died shortly thereafter. When May Futrelle learned that a large man had been lifted into one of the lifeboats, she questioned the crew of Boat 14 but soon realized that the man they described could not have been her husband. She also heard that Archibald Gracie had been pulled under with the ship and worked up her courage to ask him if he had suffered as he was being dragged down. Gracie reassured her that if he had never come up, he would have had no more suffering, giving May some comfort that perhaps Jacques had not endured an agonizing death.

That afternoon Charles Lightoller had a serious talk with the three other surviving officers, Pitman, Boxhall, and Lowe, about what lay ahead. It was agreed that their best hope for escaping what Lightoller called "the inquisition" that awaited in New York was to immediately board the *Cedric*, scheduled to sail for Liverpool on Thursday. Their case was taken to Bruce Ismay who sent a message to Philip Franklin suggesting that the *Cedric* be held for the *Titanic*'s crew and himself. Ismay also asked that clothes and shoes be put on board for him. The cable was signed "Yamsi," his coded signature for personal messages.

Ismay took only soup for dinner that evening in his room—a room, he later insisted, that was merely a storeroom where Dr. McGee kept his medicines, not a private cabin. For many of the other rescued passengers, a search began after dinner for places to sleep. Women with children were given first priority for staterooms and Daisy Spedden noted in her diary that a nice man gave up his cabin to her and her son Douglas, her maid, and Miss Burns, while an elderly gentleman took in her husband, Frederic. Edith Rosenbaum made a bed for herself on one of the tables in the dining saloon while other women slept in the lounges, using sofa cushions as pillows. The men found refuge wherever they could, mainly in the smoking rooms, where they curled up on the floor, the tables, or on the upholstered benches. Norris Williams found that the smoking room benches were not long enough for him to sleep on for any length of time, but this suited him since he was getting up every two hours to exercise his legs anyway.

In the wireless room, the work of transmitting survivors' names continued, but the young operator, twenty-one-year-old Harold Cottam, was feeling the strain. He had been at his key for the last twenty-four hours and at one point had snapped, "I can't do everything at once. Patience please." Someone told Harold Bride, who was resting in the hospital with a sprained ankle and frostbitten feet, that Cottam was getting a bit "queer." Bride offered to help and managed to hobble up to the wireless room where he sat on the bed with his foot propped up on a pillow, organizing the traffic while Cottam continued transmitting. That night they passed on 321 names of first- and second-class passengers, promising that the list of third-class passengers and crew would follow the next day. At one point, Cottam said to the *Olympic*'s operator, "Please excuse sending but am half asleep." One of the names wrongly keyed in due to his fatigue was a "Mr. Mile," which would cause Frank Millet to be reported as among the survivors the next day. But at Russell House in Broadway, Lily Millet already had a deep sense of foreboding that her husband was gone.

It was not until 6:20 p.m. on the evening of April 15 that a message to the White Star offices in New York from the *Olympic* delivered the shattering news that the *Titanic* had sunk. Philip Franklin was so shocked that it took him several minutes to pull himself together. After telephoning two IMM directors, one of whom was J. P. Morgan Jr., he went to speak to the waiting reporters. Franklin began reading the *Olympic*'s wireless message aloud but got no further than the second line and the words "*Titanic* foundered at 2:20 a.m." when the room suddenly emptied out as the newsman charged off to call in the biggest story of the new century.

At 8:00 p.m. President and Mrs. Taft were sitting at Chase's Theater in Washington, waiting for the curtain to go up on a comedy called *Nobody's Widow*. A White House messenger arrived with an envelope for the president that was carried into their private box. Within minutes, the first couple had left the theater and were being driven back to the White House. The president went directly to the telegraph office in the executive offices next door and began reading the latest press bulletins. Taft's round and normally genial face looked ashen, his jowls hung in folds. He telegraphed Philip Franklin to inquire as to whether Major Butt was among the rescued. A similar message was sent to the Marconi station at Cape Race, Newfoundland. Before returning to the White House, Taft asked the telegraph operator to keep him informed of all developments during the night.

THE NEXT MORNING Lucy Duff Gordon awoke to light streaming in through the portholes and was surprised to find herself in an unfamiliar cabin. A stewardess came in with tea, and on seeing her instead of her Irish stewardess from the *Titanic*, Lucy suddenly remembered where she was. As memories of the disaster flooded back, she buried her face in the pillows and wept. A woman from the next cabin later helped her to dress, and the two of them went out on deck, where they encountered small groups of survivors, all of them discussing the tragedy. "All that day and for the remainder of the voyage until we arrived in New York," Lucy wrote, "the *Carpathia* was a ship of sorrow as nearly all were grieving over the loss of somebody."

At breakfast in the first-class dining saloon, Margaret Brown suggested to those at her table that a fund should be started for "the poor foreigners who, with everything lost, would be friendless in a strange country." This met with a positive response though Margaret soon found that not many of the men were willing to actually pledge money to her idea. But there was general agreement among the survivors that a fund should be started to express the gratitude of the rescued to Captain Rostron and his crew. At a meeting held at three that afternoon in the dining saloon, almost all of the cabin-class survivors turned up and $4,000 was pledged on the spot. It was agreed, however, that the needs of the destitute should be met first, and Margaret Brown, her friend Emma Bucknell, and two others were appointed to a committee for that purpose. A resolution of thanks to God and to the captain and his crew was drafted and signed by the newly formed Committee of Survivors, which included, among others, Karl Behr, Mauritz Björnström-Steffansson, Algernon Barkworth, Isaac Frauenthal, Frederic Spedden, and Frederic Seward, with Margaret Brown as its sole woman. The resolution also promised to thank the *Carpathia*'s officers and crew in a more tangible way and by Thursday approximately $10,000 had been raised. Money was distributed to the captain and crew before landing, and a silver cup for the captain and medals for the officers and crew would be presented when the *Carpathia* returned from the Mediterranean in late May.

In this spirit of giving, Cosmo Duff Gordon remembered that he had promised "a fiver" to the men in Lifeboat 1. Since he was without his checkbook he asked Franks to find some notepaper and write out bank drafts for him. The Duff Gordons then arranged for a presentation on deck and asked the crewmen to wear their lifebelts—causing alarm among several women when they appeared carrying them. Lucy brought along her lifebelt so that everyone could sign it as a souvenir. Group photographs of the twelve survivors from Boat 1 were then taken by a *Carpathia* passenger, Dr. Frank Blackmarr. A number of those on deck at the time thought the whole occasion was inappropriate—a few even claimed that someone called out "Smile!" as the photo was being snapped, which is likely untrue. But it did fuel rumors that "the lord and lady" had escaped in their own private boat, a story that would be repeated once they were ashore.

Edith Rosenbaum, however, was completely won over when she finally met the famous Lucile in person. "Are you the one giving such interesting reviews in *Women's Wear*?" Lucy asked Edith and then told her how much she had admired her stylish clothes on the *Titanic*. Edith recorded that they swapped fashion information and that Lucy regretted that "all her models [designs], as well as my own, had gone to the bottom of the sea, but we acknowledged that pannier skirts and Robespierre collars are at a discount in mid-ocean."

The small contingent from Lifeboat 1 poses for a souvenir photograph.
Lucy stands at center, in front of Cosmo, and beside Mabel Francatelli.

Dorothy Gibson also found that new apparel was difficult to come
by in mid-ocean and so continued to wear the white silk evening dress
she had donned for dinner on Sunday night. The prettiest girl sported
a large diamond ring on her engagement finger, given to her by Jules
Brulatour, the head of Eastman Kodak and an investor in Éclair Films,
who was planning to marry Dorothy as soon as he could divorce his wife.
There is a twinge of disappointment in William Sloper's account as he
acknowledges this. Sloper had seen Alice Fortune (whom he had once
called his "Canadian girlfriend") come aboard from the lifeboat with
her sisters and their mother, Mary, who was in a state of near collapse. A
sympathetic Dr. McGee had arranged for the Fortunes to use his cabin
and an adjoining consulting room. Not wanting to intrude on their grief,
Sloper left Alice alone until Thursday when he knocked on her cabin
door to offer assistance in finding accommodation in New York. With a
tear-stained face, Alice assured him that they were being met by friends
from Winnipeg. Just before closing the door, she reminded him of the
prediction made by the fortune-teller in Cairo.

Norris Williams finally became acquainted with Karl Behr on the
rescue ship and recalled that Behr and Helen Newsom and the Beckwiths were very kind to him. By taking walks every two hours, Norris

felt his legs improve each day, and a few months later he was back on the tennis circuit. In 1914 he and Behr would compete together on the U.S Davis Cup team, and Williams would also become a U.S. singles champion, a Wimbledon doubles champion, and an Olympic gold medalist. Norris met another survivor on board who told him that he had been bringing home a prized dog on the *Titanic* and had gone to the kennels and released all the dogs a half hour before the ship went under. Norris described to him how when he was swimming away from the sinking liner he

Norris Williams made a full recovery from his ordeal and became a tennis champion.

had spied the black face of a French bulldog in the water. This was no doubt Gamin de Pycombe, the French bulldog that Edith Rosenbaum had tucked into bed in Robert Daniel's stateroom after the collision. Daniel himself was rescued from the water, though his bulldog was not. The fact that three dogs had been saved from the *Titanic* when people were lost was a touchy subject among the survivors. On seeing a man (likely Henry Harper) cuddling his dog on deck, May Futrelle described him as the kind of man who would rather save a dog than a child. In addition to Harper's Pekingese and Margaret Hays's "little doggie," the third surviving canine was Elizabeth Rothschild's Pomeranian, carried by her into Boat 6.

ON TUESDAY NIGHT a violent thunderstorm broke over the *Carpathia*. Karl Behr was jolted awake by a deafening crash and thought the ship had struck an iceberg. His immediate thought was to find Helen Newsom, and so he raced out onto the deck. There he saw flashes of lightning and with great relief returned to his bed on a smoking room table. Others who awoke to the lightning thought that distress rockets were once again being fired. The storm was followed by rain and fog that lasted for the next two days. This dismal weather kept most people indoors, and the mournful blasts of the foghorn on Wednesday seemed to echo the doleful mood on the "ship of sorrow." Crowded into the public rooms, there was little for the survivors to do but talk—and talk they did. Accounts of the disaster were repeated and embellished with each telling. But one of the most disturbing stories would prove to be true. Emily Ryerson described to Mahala Douglas and some others how Bruce Ismay had showed her an ice warning message on Sunday and told her they were going to put on more speed. The news that ice warnings had been received and the ship had not slowed down spread quickly, and a group that included Lawrence Beesley sought out one of the surviving officers, who confirmed that this was indeed the case. Learning that the collision could have been avoided filled Beesley with a sense of hopelessness. And resentment toward Bruce Ismay, who remained secluded in his cabin, continued to grow.

With a historian's eye, Archibald Gracie attempted to separate truth from fantasy as he listened to the survivors' stories, a potential book beginning to form in his mind. Second Officer Lightoller and Third Officer Pitman regularly stopped by the small cabin Gracie shared with Hugh Woolner to discuss various aspects of the disaster. All agreed that the explosions heard during the sinking could not have been the ship's boilers blowing up. From the discovery of the severed wreck in 1985 we now know that the "explosions" were actually the sound of the ship being wrenched apart. But Gracie and Lightoller firmly believed that the ship had sunk intact—a view that would become the prevailing opinion for the next seventy-three years. Gracie thought that Norris Williams and Jack Thayer, "the two young men cited as authority . . . of the break-in-two theory," had confused the falling funnel for the ship breaking apart. But both Williams and Thayer knew exactly what they had seen, as did some other eyewitnesses. On the *Carpathia*, Jack Thayer described the stages of the ship's sinking and breaking apart to Lewis Skidmore, a Brooklyn art teacher, who drew sketches that were later featured in many newspapers. The inaccuracies in

Skidmore's drawings, however, only bolstered the belief that the ship had, in fact, sunk intact.

And what of the most famous *Titanic* legend of all—that the band played "Nearer My God to Thee" as the ship neared its end? It's often claimed that this was a myth that took hold among survivors on the *Carpathia* and captivated the public in the aftermath of the disaster. None of the musicians survived to confirm or deny the story, but Harold Bride noted that the last tune he heard being played as he left the wireless cabin was "Autumn." For a time this was believed to be a hymn tune by that name, but Walter Lord proposed in *The Night Lives On* that Bride must have been referring to *"Songe d'Automne,"* a popular waltz by Archibald Joyce that is listed in White Star music booklets of the period. Historian George Behe, however, has carefully studied the survivor accounts regarding the music that was heard during the sinking and has found credible evidence that "Nearer My God to Thee" and perhaps other hymns were played toward the end. Behe also recounts that the orchestra's leader, Wallace Hartley, was once asked by a friend what he would do if he ever found himself on a sinking ship. Hartley replied, "I don't think I could do better than play 'O God, Our Help in Ages Past' or 'Nearer My God to Thee.' " The legendary hymn may not have been the very last tune played on the *Titanic* but it seems possible that it was heard on the sloping deck that night.

Margaret Brown had little time for swapping *Titanic* stories since she was devoting most of each day to helping steerage passengers in need. Gladys Cherry wrote that she and Noëlle Rothes also "helped in seeing after these poor distressed souls, and it has helped us so much." Daisy Spedden, too, worked tirelessly with "the people," as she called them, cutting up blankets to make clothes for children who had escaped only in nightclothes. In a letter, Daisy wrote, "The number of widows is pitiful to say nothing of the motherless and fatherless children." More pointedly she noted, "We spend our time sitting on people who are cruel enough to say that no steerage should have been saved, as if they weren't human beings!" Margaret Brown, too, found that not everyone supported her altruism. Two of the women on her committee were approached by Dr. McGee as they made their way down to the third-class decks one morning. "Madam, we have the situation under perfect control," he said to one of them regarding the steerage passengers, adding that "cutting up blankets would not soothe their tortured minds." Since the doctor had just emerged from the room of Bruce Ismay, the committee-women suspected that he was taking orders from the "secluded pluto-crat," as Margaret Brown had dubbed him, and this simply increased their resolve to do more. A sign was posted in the third-class dining saloon stating that the members of the committee would be available to give aid at regular hours each day. Many survivors came forward and, in Margaret Brown's words, "unburdened their sorrows that lay like a weight upon their breasts."

To Mrs. Brown, the attitude of the men who had been rescued was "pathetic," and she recalled that they all tried to explain how they were saved "as if it were a blot on their manhood." René Harris remembered that when Dr. Frauenthal came to examine her bandaged arm he began explaining how he had been rescued, and she assured him that he need not apologize for saving his life. René was less understanding when she learned that the *Titanic*'s three professional gamblers had survived. The cardsharp who had been pointed out to her on Sunday approached her not long after she came on board and said, "Do not grieve. It is God's

A group of women on the *Carpathia* sew blankets into clothes for children. Hard at work among them is Noëlle, Countess of Rothes (see arrow).

will." René gave him such a scalding reply that whenever the gambler caught sight of her on the ship, "he would run away from me as if from a fury."

The resentment of the widowed women toward the male survivors caused Arthur Peuchen to ask Lightoller for a note confirming that he had been ordered into a lifeboat. The second officer obliged and wrote that Major Peuchen had "proved himself a brave man." Unbeknownst to the major, the question of how he had survived was already preoccupying his home city of Toronto. By Tuesday morning the sinking of the *Titanic* was headline news everywhere, and in the Toronto papers Major Peuchen was conspicuous as the only male in the "Saved" column. Based solely on the information that the survivors were mainly women and children, the disaster was already being hailed as a triumph for chivalry and Anglo-Saxon male fortitude. But this placed any man who had survived under immediate suspicion of cowardice. An editorial in the *Toronto Star* observed that Peuchen's escape was "a subject of universal discussion in Toronto" and that "the dispute is hotly waged and participated in by everybody young and old."

In Washington, friends of Archie Butt, Frank Millet, and Clarence Moore were proclaiming that without a doubt they would have been the last men to leave the ship. " 'Poor Butt' was the universal comment," reported the *Washington Times*. "And perhaps the greatest compliment those who had known the military aide were able to bestow," the newspaper continued, "found expression in the inevitable afterthought, 'I'll bet he died like a man.' " Another newspaper reported that "the employees of the White House were in a nervous condition which unfitted them for work during the days of uncertainty concerning Archie's fate." President Taft, too, was preoccupied by the fate of his aide and frustrated by his inability to receive word of whether Archie might be on board the rescue ship. On Tuesday, Taft instructed the secretary of the navy to send out two scout cruisers, the *Salem* and the *Chester*, to establish radio contact with the *Carpathia*.

In New York, the city was in the grip of *Titanic* fever. Flags flew at half-staff, the Henry Harris theaters were dark, and even Macy's department store had closed out of respect for Isidor and Ida Straus. Police had been called in to control the crowds in front of the White Star office at 9 Broadway. Alex Macomb, a sailor in the U.S. Navy on leave in the city, sent his mother a description:

> The scene in front of the steamship office was a tragedy in itself. As the list of those known to have been saved was printed on a large bulletin board, you could hear cries of joy and relief from various parts of the throng massed in front of the office. When they started the list of those who had not been heard of, cries of "Oh! Oh God!" could be heard everywhere, and the hysterical women seemed to fill the whole city with their screams. I have never seen anything so heart rending in my life.

In London similar scenes played out as names were posted at Oceanic House, White Star's London office, near Trafalgar Square. Southampton was the hardest-hit city of all since that was where most of the crew and victualing staff lived—of whom only 212 out of 885 had survived. "In the humbler homes of Southampton," the *Daily Mail* reported, "there is scarcely a family that has not lost a relative or friend. Children returning from school appreciated something of the tragedy, and woeful little faces were turned to the darkened, fatherless homes."

In their fog-shrouded limbo on board the *Carpathia*, the *Titanic*'s survivors had little idea of the impact the news of the disaster was having ashore. On Thursday morning, Daisy Spedden noted that "the people," who had been fairly calm over the last two days, were becoming excited and nervous, and she had to admit that the prospect of landing made even her weak in the knees. By late afternoon crowds had begun gathering in Battery Park and at the liner piers in lower Manhattan.

Sailor Alex Macomb had noted in his letter to his mother that the *Carpathia* was due to arrive on Thursday night, "and you can imagine the scene when the vessel gets in. I wouldn't miss it for anything."

Crowds waited at Pier 54 after the *Carpathia* entered New York harbor.

TWO CONTINENTS STIRRED

Mary Adelaide Snider was in a jam. She had spent most of the day trying to get a press pass to Pier 54, where the *Carpathia* was due to dock that evening—but there were none to be had. The city authorities had decided that access to the pier would be restricted to six news services, ten New York newspapers, and two London dailies. Special pleading that she had come all the way from Canada to cover the story for the *Toronto Evening Telegram* hadn't helped her in the slightest. There were hundreds of newsmen—and they *were* all men, she noticed—trying to get onto the pier as well. The lucky ones had already tucked their pier passes into their hatbands. Others had hired tugboats and were out in the harbor waiting to meet the *Carpathia*.

But Mary was not about to let this most plum of all assignments defeat her. She hadn't become the *Telegram*'s first female reporter and worked her way out of the women's pages for nothing. That afternoon she had hired the boyfriend of her hotel chambermaid, an out-of-work bartender named George, to help her navigate the waterfront. George had managed to get her through the police lines across West Street, but after two blocks their way was blocked by a dense crowd; by evening there would be more than thirty thousand people clogging the streets around Pier 54. Through the drizzling rain, Mary noticed an ambulance turning into the pier gates ahead and told George to flag down the next ambulance he saw. A minute later he spotted one slowing down to show its credentials to the police, and Mary raced into the street toward it.

"Please take me on the pier, Doctor," she said breathlessly through the window, to a young intern who pointed her to the doctor in charge. "I've been at the Customs House all day. I cannot get a pass," Mary explained, turning toward the doctor. She added hurriedly that she had come down from Canada, and if she failed to make the assignment, her paper would think it was on account of her sex.

"Jump in," replied the doctor, "but mind, you're a nurse."

Mary climbed aboard, and, as she later described it, "the ambulance entered the portals which were closed to multi-millionaires. The walls of Jericho had fallen before the small voice of pleading. The reporter was on the pier."

Over the past three days the press fever over "the story of the century" had been further stoked by the silence from the *Carpathia*. The rescue ship's wireless operators had refused to accept outside inquiries, including one from President Taft, while they relayed survivor names and messages. Some papers resorted to speculation and outright invention to provide details on the tragedy that had taken fifteen hundred lives. A few even accused the *Carpathia* of deliberately withholding information.

The reporters in tugs began coming alongside the *Carpathia* not long after it passed the Ambrose Lightship at around five that afternoon. Daisy Spedden was on deck and heard them "shouting all sorts of cold-blooded, heartless questions about the disaster." Some of the newsmen had megaphones while others held up placards with questions like "Is Mrs. Astor there?" Several reporters waved fifty-dollar bills, trying to entice some of the *Titanic*'s crewmen to jump overboard and be picked up from the water. When the boat carrying the harbor pilot drew near, Captain Rostron spied journalists on it and instructed two of his crewmen to pull up the rope ladder behind the pilot as he climbed aboard. One newshound made a jump for it anyway, but missed and fell in the water. When the ship stopped briefly at the quarantine station, however, another reporter made a successful leap onto the deck but Rostron had him brought to the bridge where he was kept until the ship docked.

Standing at the very end of the pier, Mary Snider saw the *Carpathia* emerge out of the darkness and rain, illuminated by flashes from photographers' magnesium flares. But the rescue ship went right past her, heading north toward the White Star Line terminal. The passengers standing on her decks thought the *Carpathia* might be going to dock there but soon they saw the *Titanic*'s lifeboats being lowered over the side. Four of them were loaded onto the deck of a tugboat and nine others were put in the water to be towed behind it. That these few boats were all that remained of the great liner seemed highly poignant and as one reporter noted, "A deep sigh arose from the multitude."

As the *Carpathia* slowly returned to Pier 54, an expectant hush fell over the crowd. Among them were Frank Millet's two sons, Laurence, twenty-seven, and Jack, twenty-three. Laurence, who lived in New York and worked on Wall Street, carried a flask of whiskey and a box of cigars, two things he thought his father would welcome after his ordeal. His younger brother, Jack, had come down from Harvard on Monday and stayed with him all week. The news that their father was on the list of those rescued had buoyed their spirits, though they knew that nothing was certain until he walked down the gangway. Also waiting in the crowd was Major Blanton Winship, who had been a housemate of their father's at Archie Butt's home in Washington. Winship was one of several people sent to New York by President Taft with instructions to wire the White House with any news regarding Archie Butt as soon as the *Carpathia* docked. The president was still preoccupied with the fate of his aide, even though he was resigned to the fact that he had likely not survived. In a note sent on Wednesday to the British ambassador, Taft had written, "Archie was like my younger brother. His character was transparently sweet and loyal. We mourn his going deeply but when I heard of the number lost and the number saved, I knew he was one of those who went down."

At the White House that morning, Taft had met with Senator William Alden Smith of Michigan, who was also heading to New York for the *Carpathia*'s arrival. Smith was carrying subpoenas requiring J. Bruce Ismay and the *Titanic*'s officers and crew to give testimony at a U.S. Senate inquiry into the disaster. The senator had read Ismay's intercepted "Yamsi" wireless messages that revealed his intention to spirit himself and the *Titanic*'s crew out of American jurisdiction as quickly as possible. Smith intended to head this off and hand Ismay the subpoena in person, and Taft had offered the senator his full support for the investigation.

At approximately 9:30 p.m. Mary Snider saw what she later described as "the black-hulled ship warped in. Flashlight flares from the tugs alongside showed the passengers crowded on deck . . . Three or four of the wounded were first carried out on blanket-covered stretchers." Helen Candee was one of those carried off the ship, and she was taken directly to hospital by ambulance to receive treatment for her broken ankle. The next day she visited her son Harold in another New York hospital and found that he was recovering well from the plane crash that had caused her to hurriedly book passage home on the *Titanic*.

Ripples of anticipation ran through the subdued crowd as survivors began walking down the covered gangway. Among the first to appear was a young woman with disheveled hair and heavy-lidded eyes who seemed ready to drop from exhaustion. As she answered the customs inspectors' questions, a man in the crowd suddenly cried out "Dorothy! Dorothy!" and rushed forward and swept her into his arms. As Dorothy Gibson laid her head weakly on his shoulder, Jules Brulatour carried the prettiest girl all the way along the pier and down into a waiting taxicab. Only a few minutes later, Madeleine Astor appeared with her stepson Vincent Astor, who had gone on board to greet her. She was wearing a white sweater and appeared very pale under the white lights. Colonel Astor's secretary William Dobbyn wrote, "I never saw a sadder face or one more beautiful, or anything braver or finer than the wonderful control she had of herself." There was no need for the ambulance and nurse they had brought for Madeleine, and to avoid the press she was taken down a freight elevator to a waiting limousine.

Philip Franklin was one of the first to slip up the gangway to the *Carpathia* after she docked. Having hardly slept since he was awakened early on Monday morning, the IMM executive now had the task of telling Bruce Ismay that more trouble awaited. He had been in Ismay's room only a few minutes when William Alden Smith and another senator arrived to serve Ismay with a summons to appear before a U.S. Senate investigation. Lightoller and the other officers were also served with warrants for the pending inquiry which Lightoller considered "a colossal piece of impertinence."

Outside on the pier, René Harris's brother waited nervously in the crowd. He dreaded having to tell his sister that Harry had not been saved. But when René came down the gangway, she simply announced to him and the others waiting for her, "I have come alone," and everyone understood that she already knew that her "boy" was gone. The arrival was harder for May Futrelle. When she walked alone into a New York hotel room where family members were waiting, there was shock and dismay, particularly from her teenaged daughter, who was expecting to see her father. Laurence and Jack Millet, too, began to worry when so few men were seen leaving the ship. Jack joined a line of people seeking information and heard a man ahead of him ask if there was any news of Frank Millet. When he overheard that his father was not among the survivors, Jack cried out "My God!" and burst into tears.

Mary Snider was beginning to worry about finding a Canadian to interview when suddenly she spied the man all of Toronto had been talking about. "Carelessness, gross carelessness!" Arthur Peuchen was proclaiming to a clutch of reporters. "The captain knew we were going into an ice field, and why should he remain dining in the saloon when such danger was about?" After days of confinement, the major was a man ready to talk. Mary elbowed her way in beside Peuchen, whom she described as "stalwart, sunburnt and manly-looking," and managed to secure the promise of an interview for that evening. All through his reunion with his family and till after midnight in a suite at the Waldorf-Astoria, Peuchen told his story again and again as Mary Snider and other reporters scribbled furiously. "I have a clear conscience" and "It was my training as a yachtsman that saved me" and "If there is room for one more let it be a woman, I am no coward" are just some of the quotes attributed to the major in the next day's editions. Mary Adelaide Snider filed three stories under her byline about the *Carpathia*'s arrival, a highlight to a career that earned her the encomium that she was "quite equal to a man and possibly far more brilliant."

In another suite at the Waldorf that evening, William Sloper's brother had to forcibly push a scrum of reporters out the door. While on the rescue ship, William had written an account of his experiences, which he wanted to save for his hometown paper, the *New Britain Herald,* and for Connecticut's largest paper, the *Hartford Times.* The next morning, several New York tabloids ran nasty references to Sloper, and one paper later claimed, "William T. Sloper, son of a prominent Connecticut banker, was rescued from the *Titanic* disguised in a woman's nightgown." Sloper, like some other male survivors, would spend years living down this accusation.

But it would be Lucy Duff Gordon who would make the most disastrous press blunder of the night. The Duff Gordons had been greeted at the pier by a party that included interior designer Elsie de Wolfe and her companion Bessie Marbury, and whisked off to a suite at the Ritz that Elsie had filled with flowers and where new clothes for them were laid out on the beds. Champagne, bouquets, and congratulatory messages kept arriving at the suite, and over dinner Lucy delivered a colorful account of their escape from the *Titanic*. Among those at the table was Abraham Merritt, the editor of Hearst's *New York American* for which Lady Duff Gordon wrote a fashion column. Later that evening, Merritt telephoned Lucy and said that Mr. Hearst was insisting on having her story for the next morning's paper and asked her if he could tell it as he heard it. Still heady from champagne and relief, Lucy gave her assent. Merritt then telephoned his recollection of Lucy's narrative to a reporter, who wrote it up under Lady Duff Gordon's name, burnished with such choice quotations as Lucy saying to Cosmo while the lifeboats were being loaded, "Well, we might as well take the boat; it will be only a pleasure cruise until morning."

This set other reporters to questioning why there had been so few passengers in Lifeboat 1. A *Titanic* crewman, who had not been in the lifeboat but had heard stories about it, told one newspaper that a wealthy man in "the millionaire's boat" had offered the crew a reward if they would row away quickly from the sinking liner and that the crewmen were later given £5 bank drafts on the rescue ship. Denials were issued by those who had actually been in Boat 1 but rumors that an English lord had bribed crewmen to row away from the cries of the drowning only gained momentum. When picked up by the press in Britain, where class antagonisms were running high, the story would cause a sensation.

While the Duff Gordons drank champagne at the Ritz that Thursday night, Margaret Brown was still on the *Carpathia*, helping out with the steerage passengers. Immigration and health officials had come on board to spare the *Titanic*'s third-class survivors the customary hiatus at Ellis Island, but it was after eleven o'clock before the first of them began to leave the ship. Still wearing the black velvet suit she had donned after the collision, "Queen Margaret," as some in first class had dubbed her, worked to organize the disembarkation of the steerage women and help with their travel arrangements. The Countess of Rothes was doing likewise, and one passenger of particular concern for her was Rhoda Abbott, who was unable to walk due to her ordeal in Collapsible A. Although Rhoda assured the countess and Margaret Brown that she would be looked after by the Salvation Army, she was transferred by ambulance to New York Hospital at Noëlle's expense and later to a hotel room that Mrs. Brown arranged for her. The small, slim countess eventually walked down the gangway and into the arms of her husband Norman, the Earl of Rothes, and before long, she, too, was in a suite at the Ritz-Carlton. But Margaret Brown remained on the ship, where she improvised beds in the lounge for the remaining steerage women and spent the night with them. The next day her brother, who had come from Denver to greet her, came on board and told Margaret that her ailing grandson—the reason she had come home on the *Titanic*—was recovering well. This encouraged her to stay in New York, where she set up headquarters for the *Titanic* Survivors' Committee in her suite at the Ritz-Carlton.

At breakfast on Friday morning a crowd of curious hotel guests gathered around Arthur Peuchen in the Waldorf-Astoria's dining room and made him recount his story once again. In the hotel's largest ballroom, meanwhile, seven U.S. senators were preparing to question J. Bruce Ismay, the first witness to appear before the U.S. Senate investigation. As he began his testimony that morning, Ismay still seemed shaken by the disaster, and his voice was almost a whisper as he expressed his "sincere grief at this deplorable catastrophe" and offered his full cooperation to the inquiry. Yet his answers were guarded and often prefaced with "I presume" or "I believe" and concluded by "More than that I cannot say"—giving his testimony an air of evasiveness. His claims that he was simply a passenger like any other and that the *Titanic* was not pushed to its maximum speed were greeted with skepticism by the senators and

J. Bruce Ismay (at center) was the first witness called to testify at the Senate Inquiry in the East Room of the Waldorf-Astoria.

with open hostility by the press. The Hearst newspapers famously dubbed him J. "Brute" Ismay and ran his photograph framed by those of *Titanic* widows. Edith Rosenbaum was among the few survivors who thought that the White Star chairman was being made a scapegoat and made a point of telling reporters that it was Ismay who had put her into a lifeboat.

The tabloid villain of the story was followed by its newly minted hero. Captain Arthur Rostron made only a brief appearance in the Waldorf's ballroom since the *Carpathia* was due to resume its voyage to the Mediterranean that evening. The energetic, blue-eyed Rostron won over the senators with his description of how he had raced to the *Titanic*'s distress position even though, as he acknowledged, it was at some risk to his own ship and its passengers. Senator Smith responded by telling the captain "Your conduct deserves the highest praise." Rostron would later receive a Congressional Gold Medal and a "Thanks of Congress" resolution.

Senator William Alden Smith

In the afternoon, it was Second Officer Lightoller's turn to answer questions, the first of nearly two thousand he would be asked by this committee and the British inquiry that followed. Throughout his testimony, Lightoller acquitted himself well and skillfully steered criticism away from Captain Smith and the White Star Line even while he considered the American inquiry to be "nothing but a complete farce." The second officer came to have particular contempt for Senator Smith, whose ignorance of nautical matters led to him being ridiculed by the English press as "Watertight Smith" for asking whether the watertight compartments were meant to shelter passengers. The *London Globe* called Smith "a gentleman from the wilds of Michigan" who felt it necessary "to be as insolent as possible to Englishmen." British resentment toward America's waxing power was captured by the poet Wilfrid Scawen Blunt, who wrote in his diary that if anyone had to drown it was best that it be American millionaires. To the English elites, the U.S. inquiry seemed to be yet another example of American muscle flexing. But a Labor parliamentarian, George Barnes, noted more dispassionately that "it may be humiliating to some to have an [American] inquiry into the loss of a British ship but . . . the average person realizes that Americans get to work very quickly, and the average person, I think, is rather glad it is so."

As the Senate inquiry wrapped up its first day of hearings at the Waldorf-Astoria on Friday, April 19, Arthur Peuchen and his family left the hotel to board an overnight express train for the journey home. At Toronto's Union Station the next day a large crowd waited to catch a glimpse of the man who had survived the tragedy that, according to the *Toronto Globe*, "has stirred two continents as they have not been stirred in a century." Also greeting the Peuchens was a large headline in Saturday's *Toronto World:* MAJOR PEUCHEN BLAMES CAPTAIN WHO WENT DOWN WITH HIS SHIP. In the article that followed, the major accused Captain Smith of "criminal carelessness." At the Peuchen home on Jarvis Street, a telegram awaited requesting that the major give testimony before the Senate inquiry in Washington the following Tuesday. After two days at the Waldorf-Astoria, the hearings were to reconvene on Monday in the U.S. capital. Although utterly fatigued, Peuchen made arrangements to leave the following day. Before his departure, however, he found time to talk to one more reporter, to correct what certain newspapers had attributed to him. "I have never," he asserted, "spoken an unkind word about Captain Smith."

On the following morning, as the major and his wife prepared to leave for Washington, the *Titanic* furnished a ready theme for Sunday's sermons. At Peuchen's own church, St. Paul's on Bloor Street, his friend and neighbor Archdeacon H. J. Cody pronounced, "The men of our race have not forgotten how to die . . . sacrifice for a chivalrous ideal is one of the finest features of our history." This theme was echoed in countless pulpits on both sides of the Atlantic. The Reverend Dr. Leighton Parks, of St. Bartholomew's on Park Avenue in New York, could not resist a poke at the women's suffrage movement by noting that while the men of the *Titanic* sacrificed themselves for women and children, "those women who go about shrieking for their 'rights' want something very different."

Major Peuchen took the stand before the Senate subcommittee on the afternoon of Tuesday, April 23. His testimony reads as if he were self-assured and even a little self-satisfied, but according to the *New York Times,* he seemed nervous and there were occasional pauses for him to recover his composure. At the end he asked to make a statement in which he repeated his denials of ever having said "any personal or unkind thing about Captain Smith." He went on to state,

> I am here, sir, more on account of the poor women that came off our boat. They asked me if I would not come and tell this court of inquiry what I had seen, and when you wired me, sir, I came at once, simply to carry out my promise to the poor women on our boat.

At least one of the "poor women" in Boat 6 would have greeted Peuchen's statement with a derisive snort. Margaret Brown was already miffed that she had not been asked to testify before the Senate inquiry given her prominence on the Survivors' Committee and the acclaim she was enjoying as a heroine of the *Titanic.* And as a supporter of women's suffrage, Margaret was not shy about using her newfound fame to wade into the debate over gender equality swirling around the disaster. (One newspaper poet noted how the cry of "Votes for women" had become "Boats for women/ When the brave/ Were come to die.") Margaret Brown stated in an interview that while " 'Women first' is a principle as deep-rooted in man's being as the sea . . . to me it is all wrong. Women demand equal rights on land—why not on sea?"

In fact, the "women and children first" protocol for abandoning ship was not a particularly ancient one. It began with the HMS *Birkenhead,* a British troopship that was wrecked off Cape Town, South Africa, on February 26, 1852. The soldiers famously stood in formation on deck while the women and children boarded the boats, and only 193 of the 643 people on board survived. Hymned as the "Birkenhead drill" in a poem by Rudyard Kipling, it became a familiar touchstone of Britain's imperial greatness and AS BRAVE AS THE BIRKENHEAD was a much-used heading in UK *Titanic* press coverage. A story that Captain Smith had exhorted his men to "Be British!" further burnished the oft-cited claim that Anglo-Saxon men had not forgotten how to die.

It would be up to the blunt-spoken Ella White, one of only two women called to testify at the Senate inquiry (though five others gave affidavits) to throw some cold water on the selfless chivalry of the *Titanic*'s men:

> They speak of the bravery of the men. I do not think there was any particular bravery, because none of the men thought it was going down. If they had thought the ship was going down, they would not have frivoled as they did about it. Some of them said, "When you come back you will need a pass," and, "You can not get on tomorrow morning without a pass." They never would have said these things if anybody had had any idea that the ship was going to sink.

Chivalrous or not, there was no denying that of the 1,667 men on board, only 338, or 20.27 percent, had survived as compared with a 74.35 percent survival rate for the 425 women. On April 21 the bodies of the *Titanic*'s victims began to be pulled out of the north Atlantic by the *Mackay-Bennett*, a cable ship that had been sent out from Halifax with a hundred tons of ice and 125 coffins on board. The *Mackay-Bennett*'s captain described the scene as resembling "a flock of sea gulls resting on the water. . . . All we could see at first would be the top of the life preservers. They were all floating face upwards, apparently standing in the water." John Jacob Astor's body was found floating with arms outstretched, his gold pocket watch dangling from its platinum chain. To the ship's undertaker it looked as if Astor had just glanced at his watch before he took the plunge. It is often written that Astor's body was found mangled and soot-covered and that he must therefore have been crushed when the forward funnel came down. Yet according to three eyewitnesses, Astor's body was in good condition and soot-free, and like most of the other floating victims, he appeared to have died of hypothermia.

On April 25 the body of the Buffalo architect Edward Kent was recovered. In the pocket of his gray overcoat was the silver flask and ivory miniature given to him by Helen Candee on the grand staircase, and these were later returned to her by Kent's sister. Frank Millet's body was found on the same day and identified by the initials F. D. M. on his gold watch. The next evening the *Mackay-Bennett* left for Halifax with 190 bodies on board, another 116 having been buried at sea. A second ship, the *Minia*, had arrived on the scene, but after a week's search it retrieved only seventeen bodies, and two other ships would find only an additional five. The *Mackay-Bennett* landed in Halifax on April 30 to the tolling of church bells and flags flying at half-staff. Horse-drawn hearses took the bodies from the dock to a temporary morgue set up in a curling rink.

Frank Millet's eldest son, Laurence, had been waiting in Halifax for the *Mackay-Bennett* to arrive and at midnight was allowed to view his father's body. Early the next morning he accompanied the casket to Boston on a train which also carried the bodies of Isidor Straus and a twenty-one-year-old passenger named Richard White. Heads were bowed at Boston's North Station as the coffins were wheeled along the platform. Millet's body was then taken to the chapel at Mount Auburn Cemetery in Cambridge, where a funeral service was held that afternoon. On viewing the body after the service, Jack Millet wrote to his mother in Broadway that his father's face was undamaged and had a calm expression. He also noted, "We are so used to long absences that I can not quite get used to thinking that we shall never see him again." Meanwhile, Major Blanton Winship remained in Halifax, sent there by President Taft to examine every corpse in search of Major Butt, though Archie's body was never recovered.

At Frank Millet's funeral "Nearer My God to Thee" was not played, though the hymn was ubiquitous at most other *Titanic* memorials. It was sung by a congregation of twenty-five hundred at London's Westminster Chapel on April 25, during a commemorative service for W. T. Stead that was attended by such notables as future prime ministers David Lloyd George and Ramsay MacDonald. The dowager Queen Alexandra sent a representaive and a message of condolence, and the service ended with the "Hallelujah Chorus." Psychic messages had already been received from Stead in the afterlife reporting that it was he who had requested that the *Titanic*'s musicians play "Nearer My God to Thee." The hymn also concluded a packed memorial service for Major Butt held in his hometown of Augusta, Georgia, on May 2. President Taft delivered an emotional tribute to his aide, giving an outline of Archie's life and praising his loyalty and cheerfulness and noting that "never did I know how much he was to me until he was gone." He also spoke of Archie's devotion to his mother and said, "It always seemed to me that he never married because he loved her so." At another large memorial service held in Washington three days later by Archie's Masonic Lodge, Taft broke down during his eulogy and could not continue. The entire assemblage then stood and sang with great emotion "Nearer My God to Thee," the hymn that Archie had chosen for his funeral because it appealed to his sentimental side.

It would be another hymn that would cause tears at the service for James Clinch Smith, held in the same small white church in St. James, Long Island, that had seen Stanford White's funeral six years before. After "O God, Our Help in Ages Past" was sung, Archibald Gracie mentioned to one of Smith's sisters that it was the last hymn played at the Sunday service on the *Titanic*. She was very affected by this and told Gracie it was Jim's favorite hymn and the first tune he had learned to play on the piano as a child. Gracie included this anecdote in *The Truth About the Titanic*, a book that he did not live to see published. On December 4, 1912, Archibald Gracie died from health conditions degraded by the hypothermia and shock he had experienced when the *Titanic* sank. From "our coterie" only Helen Candee, Hugh Woolner, and Mauritz Björnström-Steffansson remained alive by the end of 1912. Helen Candee wrote romantically of "the Two" in her article for the May issue of *Collier's* magazine, but the affair with Woolner did not continue on land, and in August of 1912 he married the young widow of an American.

Edith Rosenbaum also wrote about her *Titanic* experiences and described for readers of *Women's Wear Daily* how her new friend Lady Duff Gordon "made her escape in a charming lavender bath robe, very beautifully embroidered, together with a pretty blue veil." The questionable taste of this description was barely noticed amid the furor surrounding Cosmo Duff Gordon's supposed bribery of the crewmen in Boat 1. In England the story had blown up into a huge scandal and Lucy described the scene that greeted them when they stepped off the *Lusitania* in mid-May:

All over the [train] station were newspaper placards—"Duff Gordon Scandal" . . ."Baronet and Wife Row Away from the Drowning" . . ."Sir Cosmo Duff Gordon Safe and Sound While Women Go Down on *Titanic*." Newsboys ran by us shouting, "Read about the *Titanic* coward!"

Making matters worse was the testimony given the week before at the British Wreck Commissioner's Inquiry by Charles Hendrickson, one of the firemen in Boat 1. He claimed that he had suggested they row back to pick up survivors, but Lady Duff Gordon had protested, saying they would be swamped, and Sir Cosmo had backed her up. The British Inquiry had begun on May 2 and was being presided over by John Bigham, First Viscount Mersey. In a bid to clear their names, the Duff Gordons offered to appear before the inquiry—the only passengers to do so. Cosmo was scheduled to testify first on Friday May 17, and Lucy noted the day before in a letter to Margot Asquith that he "shuts himself in the library for hours on end, dear man, worrying and looking a fright when he emerges, he is so downcast." Margot Asquith and many other society friends packed the gallery at the Scottish Hall on Monday, May 20, for "Lucy's day in court." The women were dressed in their new spring frocks and hats—to the *New York Times* correspondent, the scene resembled "a fashionable matinee in aid of a popular charity." Lucile wore a black ensemble with a white lace collar, and a hint of mourning was suggested by her large black hat and veil. When called, she spoke clearly, emphatically denying Hendrickson's testimony and what the "clever reporter" had put into the *New York American* story. She denied hearing any cries of the drowning after the *Titanic* sank, though years later in her autobiography she would recall that "the air was rent with awful shrieks."

Lucy's time before the inquiry was brief since she followed Cosmo who had already been grilled for several hours that morning and on the preceding Friday. Cosmo's aristocratic reticence did not make him a particularly forceful witness in his own defense. When asked if it occurred to him that more people could have been saved in Boat 1, he replied, "There were many things to think about, but of course it quite well occurred to one that people in the water could be saved by a boat, yes." His harshest questioner was W. D. Harbinson, the counsel for the seafarers' union, who took direct aim at class privilege. At one point he had to be cautioned by Lord Mersey "not to try to make out a case for this class or that class or another class, but to assist me in arriving at the truth." When Harbinson asked Cosmo if a fair summation of his position was "that you considered when you were safe yourselves that all the others might perish," Lord Mersey interrupted again to object to the unfairness of the question and to point out, "The witness's position is bad enough."

The Duff Gordons' friends were supportive, as was some of the press coverage. One journalist wrote that "Torquemada never placed his victims more unfairly on the rack of the Inquisition than have Sir Cosmo and Lady Duff Gordon been placed on the rack of cross-examination." In his report, Lord Mersey found that "the very gross charge" against Sir Cosmo was unfounded, but this was not enough to vindicate the Duff Gordons in the court of public opinion. As Lucy later noted, "A great deal of the mud that was flung stuck to us both. For myself, I did not mind . . . but I minded very much for Cosmo's sake. To the end of his life, he grieved at the slur which had been cast on his honor." The whole affair, in her words, "well-nigh broke his heart and ruined his life." With her customary insouciance, Lucy claimed that the notoriety actually helped her business. ("Now all the women of London seem to want a nightdress like the one that could compel Lady Duff Gordon's admiration in such an hour of peril," *Women's Wear Daily* noted on June 4, 1912.) Certainly, the next few years were good ones for Lucile Ltd., and when the Great War diminished the European appetite for fashion she focused her activities on New York, and in 1915 opened a Chicago salon as well. Cosmo stayed with Lucy for a time in America but when a Russian gigolo she dubbed "Bobbie" became a permanent part of the household, he stormed off to England in the spring of 1915 and lived apart from her until his death in 1931.

Lord Mersey's report found that J. Bruce Ismay had also been unjustly vilified and noted that if the White Star chairman had not jumped into Collapsible C, "he would merely have added one more life, namely, his own, to the number of those lost." But Ismay, too, suffered keenly from the social ostracism directed toward him and after resigning as president of the International Mercantile Marine and chairman of the White Star Line in June of 1913, spent most of the remainder of his life out of the public eye. In private, his wife, like Lucy, would remark that the *Titanic* had ruined her husband's life.

The only real blame assigned by Lord Mersey's report was toward Captain Lord and the officers of the *Californian*, concluding that their ship was only between five and ten miles away from the *Titanic* and that if they had come to the rescue on first seeing the distress rockets "[they] might have saved many if not all of the lives that were lost." Stanley Lord lost his job with the Leyland Line, and until his death in 1962 tried to clear his name. In recent decades his case has been championed by a legion of defenders known as "Lordites," who argue that the *Californian* was either not "the mystery ship" seen by the *Titanic* or was too far away to have reached the *Titanic* in time. But it is undeniable that if the *Californian*'s wireless set had been turned on, the *Titanic*'s distress call would have been heard and the ship could have taken action. The report of the U.S. Senate inquiry recommended that wireless on ships should be in operation twenty-four hours a day. It also proposed that ships carry enough lifeboats for everyone on board, that regular lifeboat drills be conducted, and that crewmembers should be skilled in the lowering and operation of lifeboats.

Lord Mersey's report, by contrast, had to step gingerly around the issue of lifeboats since the inquiry was conducted by the British Board of Trade, whose outdated regulations had allowed a ship the size of the *Titanic* to carry only sixteen regular lifeboats. But Mersey did recommend that lifeboat capacity be based on the maximum number of people a ship could carry rather than its gross tonnage. His report also found no evidence that third-class passengers had been treated unfairly, despite that fact that 532 of the 710 aboard were lost. Lord Mersey is often accused of wielding the whitewash brush for finding neither Captain Smith nor the White Star Line responsible for the disaster. Lightoller's insistence that Smith was simply following standard nautical procedure in maintaining full speed and trusting the lookouts to spot the ice in time clearly swayed the inquiry, though Mersey noted that this practice would "without doubt be negligence in any similar case in the future."

His exoneration of the White Star Line may have been influenced by a fear that assigning blame would lead to lawsuits that would cripple the line and damage the reputation of British shipping to the benefit of the French and German liners. Dozens of lawsuits were filed nevertheless, particularly in the United States, and the total sum demanded for all claims came to almost $17 million. The claims encompassed everything from $8 for a pair of Dorothy Gibson's satin slippers and $50 for Eugene Daly's bagpipes, to $5,000 for William Carter's new Renault and $14,000 for Charlotte Cardeza's Burmese ruby ring. Suits were also filed for loss of life: For being deprived of their husbands, René Harris sued for a million dollars, May Futrelle for $300,000, and Lily Millet for $100,000, though much less was actually received since the final amount distributed to all claimants came to only $664,000.

René Harris received a $50,000 settlement for the loss of Henry B. Harris, a far cry from a million but even this sum was welcome since the Harris theatrical enterprise was on the verge of bankruptcy. René was advised to liquidate and live on her assets but she insisted that Harry wouldn't have wanted it that way. Despite being told that "there was no such thing as a woman in the theater business" René convinced her creditors to give her a chance to make the company solvent—and she succeeded far beyond anyone's expectations. For twenty years she filled the Harris theaters with hit plays and helped launch the careers of such stars as Helen Hayes, Barbara Stanwyck, Dame Judith Anderson, and the playwright Moss Hart. Similarly, René's friend May Futrelle found herself having to repay publishers' advances for books that Jacques would now never write. She, too, managed to pay off her husband's debts and generate income through licenses of his existing works and by her own writing.

One modest expense that the White Star Line was happy to cover was a transatlantic ticket for Marcelle Navratil, the mother of the two curly-haired "*Titanic* orphans" who were being looked after in New York by Margaret Hays. After seeing a photograph of her sons in a French newspaper, Mme. Navratil contacted the White Star Line, who arranged passage to New York from her home in Nice. Over the Easter holiday in April, Marcelle's estranged husband, Michel Navratil, had disappeared

The *Titanic* "orphans," Michel Navratil, age three,
and his two-year-old brother, Edmond

with the boys and was taking them to America on the *Titanic* under the
alias "Louis Hoffman." On May 16 Marcelle was reunited with her sons
and two days later they returned home together on the *Oceanic*.

On the same day that Marcelle Navratil arrived in New York, a
brand-new movie entitled *Saved from the Titanic* was announced on
the marquees of the city's nickelodeons. The ten-minute silent film had
been made in three weeks at Éclair's studios in New Jersey and starred
a real-life survivor of the shipwreck, Miss Dorothy Gibson, wearing the
same white silk dress and black pumps in which she had escaped from
the sinking liner. Dorothy had at first been unwilling to relive her ordeal
so soon after the disaster and according to one newspaper there were
times during the filming when she had "practically lost her reason by
virtue of the terrible strain she had been under." The one-reeler, which
was produced by Jules Brulatour, would be Dorothy's last film since she
then embarked on a career in opera. This would prove to be short-lived,
as would her marriage to Brulatour in 1917. Following a generous divorce
settlement in 1919, the prettiest girl retreated from public attention and
was never seen on stage or screen again.

Margaret Brown, however, was only warming up to the spotlight. A
photograph of her presenting a silver loving cup to Captain Rostron on

This image of Dorothy Gibson appeared on the poster for *Saved from the Titanic.*

May 29 was carried in newspapers around the world. The ceremony took place on the *Carpathia* after its return from the Mediterranean, and gold, silver, and bronze medals were given to Rostron and his officers and crew on behalf of the *Titanic* survivors. Margaret also made a personal gift to the captain of the small turquoise Egyptian tomb figure she had tucked into her pocket before leaving her *Titanic* stateroom. A trip home to Denver in April had turned into a victory lap for the heroine of the *Titanic,* with a luncheon being given in her honor at the home of a once-frosty grande dame of Mile High society. To the *Denver Times* Margaret modestly noted that "I simply did my duty as I saw it. . . . That I did help some, I am thankful and my only regret is that I could not have assisted more." Margaret continued to chair the *Titanic* Survivors' Committee for the rest of her life, and in 1920 she laid floral wreaths on all the *Titanic* graves in Halifax when a shipboard fire during a crossing caused her to land there unexpectedly. She also raised funds for the Women's *Titanic* Memorial in Washington, D.C., just one of the dozens of statues, plaques, fountains, and even buildings erected in memory of the sinking on both sides of the Atlantic.

The largest *Titanic* memorial of all is the Widener Library at Harvard University, erected by Eleanor Widener in memory of her son Harry, in which his rare book collection is carefully preserved. Among the many memorials in Southampton, England, is a bronze plaque to the ship's postal workers cast from the *Titanic*'s spare propeller. A proposal for a monument in memory of Archie Butt and Frank Millet was issued from the White House within days of the *Titanic*'s sinking. It was President Taft's idea, and he agreed to chair the committee and make the first donation toward it. Several hundred of Frank and Archie's friends followed suit—the list of donors reads like a Gilded Age Who's Who, with such names as sculptor Daniel Chester French, architects Henry Bacon and Cass Gilbert, industrialists Henry Clay Frick and Charles L. Freer, urban parks creator Frederick Law Olmsted, and decorative artist Louis Comfort Tiffany.

It was first thought that the memorial might take the form of a bronze tablet on the White House grounds but sculptor Daniel Chester French wrote to Lily Millet in early July that he and architect Thomas Hastings were at work on something that would likely take the form of a fountain. At the end of January 1913, President Taft approved the design for the Butt-Millet Memorial Fountain to be located in a leafy glade on the Ellipse just beyond the South Lawn of the White House. Daniel Chester French, who would later sculpt the large seated figure of Abraham Lincoln for the Lincoln Memorial, created two bas reliefs for the fountain's central shaft that rises from a basin of Tennessee marble. On its north side, facing the White House, a knight in armor representing Chivalry

The Butt-Millet Memorial Fountain near
the White House

was carved in honor of Archie Butt; on the south side, looking toward the Lincoln Memorial, a classical maiden with a palette and brush symbolizing Art, commemorates Frank Millet. Around the rim of the basin an inscription reads:

> In memory of Francis Davis Millet—1846–1912—and Archibald Willingham Butt—1865–1912, This monument has been erected by their friends with the sanction of Congress.

The Butt-Millet Memorial Fountain was completed by October of 1913, but there is no record of any dedication ceremony for it. By then Woodrow Wilson had replaced William Taft as president. During the fall election—the one that Archie Butt had been dreading—Theodore Roosevelt made a third-party bid for the presidency, splitting the Republican vote and allowing the Democrats to capture the White House. In his inauguration address President Wilson lauded America's prosperity, but proclaimed that "evil has come with the good and much fine gold has been corroded. With riches has come inexcusable waste." America and the world were changing. Deference for wealth and privilege was on the wane, and Gilded Age excess was out of fashion—for the time being at least. Labor unrest, suffragette marches, waves of New World immigrants—all were harbingers of a modern world struggling to be born.

"It takes a terrible warning," William Alden Smith had declared at the U.S. Senate Inquiry, "to bring us back to our moorings and senses." The *Titanic* disaster did no such thing, of course. The "story of the century" would soon be overshadowed by far greater horrors in the fields of Flanders. But in the twenty-first century, quite remarkably, this Edwardian shipwreck has become our most-invoked metaphor for calamity, a byword for human arrogance and folly. In an age when Greek myths and biblical stories are no longer part of common understanding, the *Titanic* has become one of our most potent modern parables. Expressions like "rearranging the deck chairs" and "hitting the iceberg" are used daily and need no explanation. For politicians it has become a rite of passage to be perched on the liner's plunging stern by newspaper cartoonists. The story of the giant ship that sank on its maiden voyage is so rife with symbolism that if it hadn't actually happened, we might have had to invent it.

Yet it did happen, on that cold, clear April night in 1912. And it happened to real people—stokers, millionaires, society ladies, parsons, parlormaids—people who displayed a full range of all-too-human reactions as the events of the night unfolded. The recollections of those who survived, conflicting and embroidered though they often are, allow us to place ourselves on that sloping deck and ask, "What would *we* do?"

The unsinkable story sails on.

Postscript

TITANIC AFTERLIVES

J ust how long *did* their hearts go on? Of the 712 people who avoided death in the early morning of April 15, 1912, five lived to be one hundred or more and at least a dozen lived into their nineties. Despite exceptional longevity for a few, tragedy stalked the lives of so many *Titanic* survivors that it has often encouraged superstitious speculation of the "hand of fate" variety.

There are at least seven known deaths by suicide among the survivors, and *Titanic* researcher Philip Gowan has found evidence for as many as seven or eight more, though none of them, so far as is known, were directly *Titanic*-related. **Dr. Washington Dodge,** the San Francisco physician and civic politician who helped push Boat 13 away from the condenser exhaust, shot himself in the forehead in 1919 after a breakdown caused by business and investment problems. In March of 1927, **Dr. Henry Frauenthal** leapt to his death from the balcony of his New York apartment following months of depression fueled by his wife's mental illness. Lookout **Frederick Fleet** hung himself from a clothesline in 1965 in despair over the death of his wife. Quartermaster **Robert Hichens,** the man at the ship's wheel when Fleet spotted the berg and who later became the tyrant of Boat 6, plotted a murder-suicide in November of 1933 in Torquay, Devon. But he was so drunk on the chosen night that he only succeeded in wounding the man he believed had wronged him and failed to kill himself, though he did attempt to cut his wrists while under arrest. Hichens was released from prison in 1937 and died in 1940. On September 22, 1945, **Jack Thayer,** aged fifty, was found in his car with his wrists and throat slashed. The reason most often given for his suicide is that he was depressed over the loss of his son in the Pacific War. His mother, **Marian Thayer,** died of natural causes on April 14, 1944, the thirty-second anniversary of the *Titanic*'s collision with the iceberg.

It seems a particularly cruel twist of fate that **Douglas Spedden,** the much-beloved only child of **Daisy and Frederic Spedden,** should have been struck by a car and killed in August of 1915, three years after the family were all saved from the *Titanic*. The couple had no other children and lived on in Tuxedo Park until their deaths—Daisy died in 1950 and Frederic in 1947. (Daisy had, for a time, employed **Ellen Bird,** the English maid to **Ida Straus.**) As a Christmas gift for Douglas in 1913, Daisy wrote a story about their European travels and voyage on the *Titanic*, with Douglas's toy polar bear as the narrator. The manuscript was discovered by a relative, Leighton Coleman III, and published in 1994 as the children's picture book *Polar the Titanic Bear*.

Eleven-month-old **Trevor Allison,** the only surviving member of his family, also did not live to see adulthood. The Allison baby was carried off the *Carpathia* by his English nursemaid, **Alice Cleaver,** who had taken him into Boat 11. The Allison family blamed Alice Cleaver for the deaths of **Bess Allison** and two-year-old **Loraine Allison,** believing that Bess must not have known that the baby had left with the nurse and thus likely searched for him until it was too late. Alice claimed that she had told Mrs. Allison she was taking the baby with her. Major Peuchen said that he saw Bess Allison get out of a lifeboat with Loraine and go in search of her husband. **Trevor Allison** was raised by Hudson's brother, George Allison, and his wife Lillian but died of ptomaine poisoning at the age of eighteen in August of 1929. In 1940 a woman named Loraine Kramer appeared on a national radio program claiming to be **Loraine Allison.** Her story of how she had survived the *Titanic* proved to be far-fetched, however, and she was dismissed as an impostor by the Allison family.

Perhaps the most heartrending of all survivor stories is that of **Helen Walton Bishop,** the nineteen-year-old newlywed from Dowagiac,

Michigan, who left her lapdog Frou Frou behind before boarding Boat 7 with her husband. Helen was likely pregnant on the *Titanic*, since on December 8, 1912, she gave birth to a baby boy, who died two days later. The following November, Helen suffered a severely fractured skull in an automobile accident and was not expected to live. She recovered with a metal plate placed in her skull but her mental condition was seriously altered and this led to a divorce in January of 1916. Three months later Helen was injured from a fall while visiting friends in Danville, Illinois, and on March 15, 1916, she died and was buried in her hometown of Sturgis, Michigan. Her death at the age of twenty-three made the front page of the *Dowagiac Daily News*. Ironically a story about the remarriage of her former husband, **Dickinson Bishop,** appeared on the same page.

RHODA ABBOTT (1873–1946)

Rhoda Abbott (sometimes called "Rosa"), who was rescued from half-submerged Collapsible A, is the only woman to have survived the night in the icy water. She spent two weeks in New York Hospital after being carried off the *Carpathia* and lived with respiratory problems for the rest of her life. Rhoda also grieved deeply the loss of her two sons, sixteen-year-old **Rossmore** and fourteen-year-old **Eugene**. She had taken the two boys back to England in 1911 to live with her mother after separating from Stanton Abbott, a middleweight U.S. boxing champion. But the two boys became homesick for America and she was returning with them to Providence, Rhode Island, on the *Titanic*. In December of 1912 she married an old friend from England, George Williams, and lived with him in Jacksonville, Florida, until 1928, when the couple returned to England. There George suffered a stroke and Rhoda cared for him until his death ten years later. She died of heart failure on February 18, 1946.

MADELEINE ASTOR (1893–1940)

Nineteen-year-old **Madeleine Astor** gave birth to **John Jacob Astor VI** on August 14, 1912. She had inherited the income from a $5 million trust fund and the use of the Astor mansion on Fifth Avenue and "Beechwood" in Newport so long as she did not marry again. But on June 22, 1916, Madeleine relinquished any claim to the Astor fortune when she married her childhood friend, the independently wealthy William Karl Dick (1888–1953). They had two sons but divorced in 1933 after Madeleine began an affair with a twenty-six-year-old Italian prizefighter named Enzo Fiermonte, whom she had hired to teach boxing to her boys. To the horror of her family and Palm Beach society, she married Fiermonte in November of 1933 and endured five stormy years before divorcing him for "extreme cruelty" in 1938. Two years later, the always frail Madeleine died of heart disease at the age of forty-seven and was buried in New York's Trinity Cemetery, not far from the first husband she had last seen standing on the deck of the *Titanic*. Madeleine's eldest son, **John Jacob Astor VI,** spent many years battling his half brother, Vincent Astor, for a larger share of the family wealth and died in 1992.

LÉONTINE PAULINE "NINETTE" AUBART (1887–1964)

Several Guggenheim family members awaited the arrival of the *Carpathia*, and it is believed that they arranged accommodation for **Ninette Aubart** and her maid in New York and kept the news of her existence hidden from **Ben Guggenheim**'s widow, Florette. Ninette and her maid took the *Adriatic* to Liverpool on May 3 and proceeded from there to Paris. She filed a claim of $12,220 for her belongings and $25,000 for injuries against White Star, though like most claimants, she received far less. Ninette Aubart married three times and had at least one child, a son, before her death in October of 1964, in Paris. One of her husbands was believed to have been a member of the French Cabinet, and René Harris recalled in her 1932 *Liberty* article that on a visit to Paris she was invited to tea by her *Carpathia* roommate, who was by then married to "one of the outstanding figures in the French capital."

LAWRENCE BEESLEY (1877–1967)

Lawrence Beesley wrote a successful book, *The Loss of the SS Titanic*, that was published in late 1912. A devout Christian Scientist, he also wrote in a church journal about how his faith had sustained him during the disaster, as did another Christian Scientist on board, Second Officer

Charles Lightoller. Beesley corresponded with Walter Lord while he was researching *A Night to Remember* and visited the set during the filming of the 1958 movie based on the book. He died on February 14, 1967, at the age of eighty-nine.

KARL BEHR (1885–1949)

Karl Behr and **Helen Newsom** were married in March of 1913 and had three sons and one daughter. Karl continued to play tennis through 1915, competing with **R. Norris Williams** and being ranked in the top ten of U.S. players. He later went into banking and became vice president of Dillon, Read & Co. of New York and was also on the board of several companies, among them Goodyear Tire and Rubber and the National Cash Register Company. After his death, on October 15, 1949, Helen married Dean Mathey, a tennis player and friend of Karl's; she died in 1965.

JOSEPH BOXHALL (1884–1967)

After testifying at both the U.S. and British inquiries, **Joseph Boxhall** became the fourth officer on the *Adriatic*. During World War I he served on cruisers and a torpedo boat and was promoted to the rank of lieutenant commander. After the war, he married Marjory Beddells, the daughter of a Yorkshire industrialist and the marriage was a happy one, though they had no children. Boxhall returned to the merchant service in 1919, became a chief officer, though never a captain, and retired in 1940. He served as a technical advisor on the film *A Night to Remember*, to the surprise of those who knew him since, until then, he had been reluctant to talk about the *Titanic*. He died at the age of eighty-three, on April 25, 1967, the last of the *Titanic*'s surviving officers, and his ashes were scattered over the ocean near where the *Titanic* had gone down.

GEORGE BRERETON (1874–1942)

Professional gambler **George Brereton** (also known as Brayton, Bradley, etc.) befriended passenger **Henry Stengel** on board the *Carpathia* and later tried to involve him in a horse-racing scam in New York. Brereton died of a gunshot wound to the head in 1942 and is believed to be another of the *Titanic*'s suicides. His cardsharp companion **Charles Romaine** died after being hit by a New York taxi in 1922. What became of **Harry Homer** is unknown.

HAROLD BRIDE (1890–1956)

Harold Bride was still in the *Carpathia*'s wireless room with **Harold Cottam** when Guglielmo Marconi came on board at Pier 54 to personally congratulate the two operators. Bride sold his story to the newspapers, and a photograph of him being carried off the *Carpathia* with bandaged feet was widely printed. After returning to England, he resumed work as a wireless operator and during World War I served on the small steamer *Mona's Isle* as a telegraphist. He married in 1919 and had three children, and later moved to Scotland, where he worked as a salesman and died at the age of sixty-six, on April 29, 1956.

MARGARET BROWN (1867–1932)

Margaret Brown continued to travel and work on behalf of the issues she supported, such as women's suffrage, literacy for children, historic preservation, and the *Titanic* Survivors' Committee. During World War I, she worked with the American Committee for Devastated France to rebuild damaged towns on the Western Front and also helped provide care for wounded soldiers, which resulted in her being awarded the French Legion of Honor. Her husband, J. J. Brown (who had said of his wife after the disaster, "She's too mean to sink") died in 1922, and legal wrangles over his will consumed much of her time and money over several years. Always fascinated by the theater, Margaret began studying acting in the Sarah Bernhardt tradition in her late fifties and even toured in a play made famous by "the divine Sarah." On October 26, 1932, while staying at the Barbizon Hotel in New York, she died of a cerebral hemorrhage at the age of sixty-five. An autopsy revealed that she had a significant brain tumor. After her death, a *Denver Post* reporter named Gene Fowler wrote a highly fanciful account of her life and dubbed her "Molly" Brown, which later led to the Broadway musical *The Unsinkable Molly Brown*, which became a movie starring Debbie Reynolds.

FRANCIS M. BROWNE (1880–1960)

Francis M. Browne became Father Browne SJ after his ordination in 1915, at which time he was immediately assigned as chaplain to the Irish Guards who were serving on the Western Front. There he was wounded several times and his lungs were damaged by mustard gas. After the war he was sent to Australia so his health could recover, a trip he documented carefully with his camera. On his death in 1960, an archive of more than forty-two thousand photographs was left to the Irish Jesuits, and this extraordinary legacy has since been featured in books and exhibitions.

DANIEL BUCKLEY (1890–1918)

After his testimony before the U.S. Senate Inquiry, **Daniel Buckley** was assailed as a coward for hiding under a woman's shawl in a *Titanic* lifeboat. Yet during World War I he served his adopted country as an infantryman and was killed in 1918. He is buried in his hometown of Ballydesmond in County Cork.

EMMA BUCKNELL (1852–1927)

At the age of eighteen, **Emma Ward**, the daughter of a clergyman, had become the third wife of William Bucknell, a wealthy Philadelphian who was forty-one years her senior. The marriage produced a son and three daughters, but in his seventies Bucknell became irascible and stingy toward his wife and family, despite his considerable wealth, which had provided the principal endowment for Bucknell University in Lewisburg, Pennsylvania. Fortuitously, Bucknell died in 1890, leaving Emma a wealthy widow and allowing her the time and means to travel. After the *Titanic* disaster, Emma was outspoken about the ill-prepared crew and poor lifeboat provisions, and she was reportedly affected by the trauma of the disaster for the rest of her life. She divided her time between a home in Clearwater, Florida, and her Adirondack retreat on Saranac Lake, where she died of heart failure on June 27, 1927.

HELEN CANDEE (1859–1949)

Helen Candee recovered from the broken ankle she received while climbing into Boat 6, although she had to walk with a cane for a year.

After publishing "Sealed Orders," her account of the disaster, in *Collier's* magazine in May 1912, she tried to put the *Titanic* behind her, though she requested $10,000 for personal injury and $4,646 for lost possessions in a class-action lawsuit against the White Star Line. In October of 1912 her large and lavish book on tapestries, simply called *The Tapestry Book*, was published and became her best-known work. In 1917, at the age of fifty-eight, she became a volunteer nurse with the Italian Red Cross and tended wounded soldiers in field hospitals just behind the battle lines. In Milan she helped care for a wounded young American ambulance driver named Ernest Hemingway, whose love affair with one of Helen's coworkers helped inspire his novel *A Farewell to Arms*. In the 1920s Helen was drawn to travels in the Far East and wrote two acclaimed books, *Angkor the Magnificent* and *New Journeys in Old Asia*. In 1930 she returned to her love of textiles for her eighth and final book, *Weaves and Draperies: Classic and Modern*. During her seventies she continued to travel and often wrote articles for *National Geographic*. By age eighty, as she became physically weaker, she lived with her daughter Edith and in the summers visited her cottage in York Harbor, Maine. It was there, on August 23, 1949, at the age of ninety, that her productive, event-filled life drew to a close.

CHARLOTTE CARDEZA (1854–1939)
The largest claim for lost possessions was made by **Charlotte Cardeza,** who submitted a detailed inventory of the vast wardrobe she had brought on board, which she valued at £36,567 2s ($177,352.75). Charlotte continued to travel the world until the 1930s, when declining health caused her to settle in at Montebello, her Main Line mansion. When she died at the age of eighty-five, on August 1, 1939, the bulk of her estate was left to her son, **Thomas Cardeza** (1875–1952), who in his mother's name endowed a foundation to study blood diseases at Thomas Jefferson University.

PAUL CHEVRÉ (1866–1914)
The official opening of the Château Laurier Hotel in Ottawa was postponed due to the death of **Charles Hays,** and a rather subdued ceremony

was held on June 12, 1912. Sculptor **Paul Chevré**'s bust of Prime Minister Wilfrid Laurier was installed in the lobby though Chevré himself would die less than two years later. His obituary claimed that he survived the sinking of the *Titanic* but never recovered from the shock of it.

EUGENE DALY (1883–1965)

Irish bagpiper **Eugene Daly** retained his love of music throughout his life, later taking up the flute when his wife objected to the sound of the pipes. He arrived penniless off the *Carpathia* and worked at various jobs in New York before going to war in 1917. His Irish girlfriend accepted his proposal and married him before he left for France. The couple returned to Ireland in 1921 when Eugene's mother was dying and stayed on in Galway, where their only daughter, Marion (Mary), was born. Mary and her husband emigrated to America in 1952, and after his wife's death in 1961, Eugene came over to join them and died in New York on October 30, 1965.

ELIZA GLADYS "MILLVINA" DEAN (1912–2009)

Two-month-old **Millvina Dean,** her mother **Eva Georgetta "Ettie" Light Dean** (1879–1975), and two-year-old brother **Bertram Dean** (1910–1992), returned to England aboard the *Adriatic,* where Millvina became the "pet of the liner," with passengers vying to be photographed holding her. The family moved in with Ettie's parents near Southampton, where Millvina and Bertram were educated with the support of a small stipend from a survivors' fund. Millvina did not discover that she had been on the *Titanic* until she was eight and her mother was planning to remarry. Millvina herself never married; she was a cartographer's assistant during World War II and later worked in the purchasing department of a Southampton engineering firm. In her seventies she became a *Titanic* celebrity and was in great demand to appear at conventions, exhibitions, and on radio and TV programs. During the final years of her life she became the last *Titanic* survivor and continued to graciously sign autographs and tell her story. She died on May 31, 2009, after a short illness, and her ashes were scattered in Southampton harbor, the scene of the *Titanic*'s departure ninety-seven years before.

MAHALA DOUGLAS (1864–1945)

Mahala Douglas continued to live in Walden, the large house she and her husband **Walter Douglas** had built on Lake Minnetonka, and at her winter home in Pasadena, until her death at the age of eighty-one, on April 21, 1945. Her husband's body was recovered by the *Mackay-Bennett*, and she is buried next to him in the Douglas family mausoleum at the Oak Hill Cemetery in Cedar Rapids, Iowa.

LADY DUFF GORDON (1863–1935)

The 1920s didn't roar for **Lucy Duff Gordon** since Jazz Age flappers found her romantic gowns passé. As Cecil Beaton wrote, "The era of elaborate ornamentation was over. . . . It was a far cry from Lucile's pastel chiffons to the jerseys and short skirts with which Chanel replaced them." Lucy didn't understand how the postwar world had changed and fired designer Edward Molyneux from her Hanover Square salon for producing sleeker, more modern designs. By 1923 Lucile Ltd. was bankrupt. It was left to the ever-kind **Sir Cosmo Duff Gordon** to explain how her capital had disappeared—as usual, Lucy blamed her business partners. Lucy continued to write her fashion columns and sometimes created designs for private clients from her small flat, in the way that she had started her career so many years before. "She had to learn . . . to get on buses, perhaps in the rain, and go to cocktail parties," recalled her granddaughter. It didn't help that her sister, **Elinor Glyn** (1864–1943), was enjoying great success in Hollywood as a screenwriter and even as a director. (When Clara Bow starred in the screen adaptation of Elinor's novel *It*, she was dubbed "the 'It' Girl," "It" being a coded term for sex appeal.) In 1932 Lucy published her autobiography, *Discretions and Indiscretions,* which became a bestseller. In it she describes her experiences on the *Titanic* and the scandal that followed. Lucy died of breast cancer in a Putney, London, nursing home on April 20, 1935, at the age of seventy-one, four years to the day after Cosmo's death. They are buried together in Brookwood Cemetery near London. In recent years, exhibitions of Lucile fashions at the Victoria and Albert Museum in London and New York's Fashion Institute of Technology have provided some recognition of Lucy's place in the history of fashion.

ALICE FORTUNE (1887–1961)

Alice Fortune's shipboard flirtation with **William Sloper** was likely intended to be little more than that, since on June 8, 1912, she married lawyer Charles Holden Allen, to whom she was already engaged. The couple had one daughter and lived in Fredericton, New Brunswick, and in Montreal. They retired to their summer home in Chester, Nova Scotia, and Alice died there on April 7, 1961. Her mother, **Mary Fortune** (1851–1929), did not remarry and died in Toronto in March 1929, aged seventy-seven. Older sister **Ethel Fortune** (1883–1961) was haunted by dreams of her brother **Charles Fortune** flailing about in the icy water. She married Toronto banker Crawford Gordon in 1913, and their son, Crawford Gordon II, was responsible for producing the prototype of the Avro Arrow aircraft in the 1950s. Ethel died in Toronto on March 21, 1961. The youngest sister, **Mabel Helen Fortune** (1888–1968), married a jazz musician from Minnesota and had one son, but the marriage was short-lived. Mabel soon met a woman from Ottawa and lived with her in Victoria, British Columbia, for the rest of her life.

LILY MAY FUTRELLE (1876–1967)

May Futrelle returned to "Stepping Stones," the house on the harbor in Scituate, Massachusetts, and it is said that on every April 15 she would throw flowers into the Atlantic in memory of her husband, **Jacques Futrelle.** In the 1930s she taught creative writing in Boston and New York and was a national chair of the American League of Pen Women. She also hosted a radio show called *Do You Want to Be a Writer?* May died in Scituate at the age of ninety-one and is buried there.

DOROTHY GIBSON (1889–1946)

William Sloper wrote that he was invited to the wedding reception for **Dorothy Gibson** and **Jules Brulatour** in 1917 but was unable to attend. The prettiest girl's affair with Brulatour had been made public in May of 1913 after Dorothy had struck and killed a pedestrian while driving Brulatour's car. After Dorothy and Brulatour separated in 1919, she lived for a time in Manhattan and moved to France with her mother in 1928. She later became involved in Fascist politics but changed her affiliations during World War II and was arrested by the Germans in Italy as a suspected resistance supporter and imprisoned in Milan. Dorothy escaped in 1944 and died of heart failure at the Ritz in Paris on February 17, 1946, at the age of fifty-six. No print of *Saved from the Titanic* has survived; the only existing film from Dorothy's movie career is a one-reel comedy, *The Lucky Holdup*, which premiered just before she sailed on the *Titanic*.

HENRY SLEEPER HARPER (1864–1944)

"Louis, how *do* you keep yourself looking so young?" is how **Henry Harper** reportedly greeted *Carpathia* passenger Louis Ogden shortly after he arrived on the rescue ship. It's possible that a similar insouciance regarding disaster contributed to the Harper & Brothers publishing firm's slide into receivership in 1899 while Henry was a director. Henry kept a desk there for a time after the company was sold but increasingly had less to do with the firm. He and his wife, **Myra Harper,** had no children and liked to spend about six months of every year traveling abroad. Henry also loved the outdoors and became involved in protecting the Adirondack forests from logging. After surviving the *Titanic*, the Harpers continued to travel and while in America divided their time between New York City and a summer home in Winter Harbor, Maine. When Myra died in 1923, Henry married again and in his sixties fathered a son, also named Henry. Henry Sleeper Harper died on March 1, 1944, in New York City, after a two-year illness. His bowler hat was photographed still sitting on a bed in his stateroom during the filming of the *Titanic* wreck for James Cameron's 3D documentary *Ghosts of the Abyss*. Harper's Egyptian manservant, **Hammad Hassab,** returned to Egypt and continued to work as a dragoman through Thomas Cook and Sons. His calling card read, "Hammad Hassab, Dragoman, Having the distinction of being a survivor from the wreck of the *Titanic*."

IRENE (RENÉ) HARRIS (1876–1969)

"Mrs. Harris was rich, racy and of infinite good humor," remembered playwright Moss Hart of the woman who produced his first play in 1925. The twenties roared for René (who by then had become Renée), with song-and-dance man George M. Cohan regularly filling the Hudson Theater along with other hit shows. This allowed her an apartment on Park Avenue, a home in Palm Beach, and a yacht with a crew of four. Her social circle included Irving Berlin and Douglas Fairbanks and Mary Pickford, and she had a string of male admirers, three of whom became husbands, though never for long. "I have had four marriages—but really only one husband," she claimed, referring to her first, whom she always called "Henry B." Renée would keep her "infinite good humor" but lose everything else when the Depression hit the theater business particularly hard. In 1932 she was forced to sell the Hudson Theater, for which she had once been offered a million, for only $100,000, and even that did not cover her debts. Down to only the clothes on her back, Renée moved in with her sister and survived the Depression directing children's plays for the WPA's Federal Theater Project and selling the occasional magazine story. By the early 1950s she was living in a one-room apartment in a hotel in Manhattan and spending summers at a retirement home for theater people on Long Island. She became a good friend of Walter Lord's when he was working on *A Night to Remember* but was unable to sit through a screening of the 1958 movie version as she found it too realistic. On the fiftieth anniversary of the sinking in 1962, she gave an interview to NBC radio and attended a memorial service at New York's Seamen's Church with her old friend **May Futrelle** and some other survivors. Walter Lord encouraged her to finish writing the story of her remarkable life, and she was hard at work on it in late August of 1969, when she collapsed and was rushed to hospital. Renée died on September 2, 1969, at the age of ninety-three. All who knew her had to agree with the final notice she received in *Variety*, which said "The lady was something special."

MASABUMI HOSONO (1870–1939)
The *Titanic*'s sole Japanese survivor was assailed for having brought shame on his country in the eyes of the West. In 1913 he lost his government job, though he was eventually rehired. **Hosono** wrote a description of his *Titanic* experience in which he (incorrectly) claimed that he was the last person to get into the last boat. He died on March 14, 1939.

VIOLET JESSOP (1887–1971)

Stewardess **Violet Jessop** had the distinction of surviving the *Olympic*'s collision with the British cruiser *Hawke* on September 20, 1911, and the sinking of both the *Titanic* and the third sister ship, *Britannic*, when it was sunk in the Aegean while serving as a hospital ship in 1916. Her memoir, *Titanic Survivor*, was edited by liner historian John Maxtone-Graham and published in 1997. Violet died in May of 1971 in Great Ashfield, Suffolk.

CHARLES LIGHTOLLER (1874–1952)

Despite his staunch defense of Captain Smith and the White Star Line, the *Titanic*'s senior surviving officer was never made a captain of any White Star ship. **Charles Lightoller** did become a full commander in the Royal Navy during World War I and on returning to White Star after the war was made chief officer of the *Celtic*. Realizing he was never going to achieve a better posting, Lightoller retired after twenty years of service, and he and his wife for a time ran a guesthouse. He purchased and refitted a steam motor launch, which was dubbed the *Sundowner*, and on June 1, 1940, the sixty-six-year-old Lightoller took the *Sundowner* across the Channel to rescue men from the beaches of Dunkirk. During World War II he would lose two of his three sons in combat. Charles Lightoller died on December 8, 1952, at the age of seventy-eight.

HAROLD LOWE (1882–1944)

Harold Lowe confessed to **Margaret Brown** on the *Carpathia* that he regretted the swearing in the lifeboat that had so upset **Daisy Minahan.** He also had to retract from his testimony at the U.S. Inquiry that he had fired his pistol to prevent "Italian immigrants" from jumping into Boat 14, after a complaint was filed by the Italian embassy. (He explained that he meant "immigrants of the Latin race.") In September of 1913, Lowe was married, and the couple had two children, a boy and a girl. During World War I he became a commander in the Royal Naval Reserve, but like the other surviving officers from the *Titanic* never achieved a command in the merchant service. Lowe retired to his native Wales and died on May 12, 1944. He is buried at Llandrillo Yn Rhos, Colwyn Bay, North Wales.

BERTHE MAYNÉ (1887–1962)

Hélène Baxter and her daughter **'Zette** seemingly bonded in their grief with **Quigg Baxter**'s lover, **Berthe Mayné**, since she stayed in Montreal with the Baxter family for a brief time before returning to Europe and resuming her career as a singer. She never married and eventually retired to a comfortable house in a suburb of Brussels, bought for her by a wealthy admirer. As an elderly woman, she would sometimes mention that she had been on the *Titanic* with a young Canadian millionaire, but was never really believed. Only after her death did a nephew discover a shoebox filled with letters, photographs, and clippings revealing that "Tante Berthe's" story was actually true. **Hélène Baxter** (1862–1923) died in 1923 in Montreal, and her daughter, **Mary Hélène ('Zette)** (1885–1954), left her husband Dr. Fred Douglas in 1923, remarried, and died in Redlands, California, in 1954.

DAISY MINAHAN (1879–1919)

By April 24, 1912, **Daisy Minahan** and her sister-in-law **Lillian** were back in Green Bay, Wisconsin, and on May 2 **Dr. William Minahan**'s body, recovered by the *Mackay-Bennett*, was shipped home for burial. Not long after the funeral, Daisy was admitted to a sanatorium for pneumonia. In 1918 she moved to Los Angeles, and died there on April 30, 1919, at the age of forty. Her sister-in-law, **Lillian Minahan** (1875–1962), also moved to California, where she married twice more. She died in Laguna Beach, California, in 1962, at the age of eighty-six.

JOHN PIERPONT MORGAN (1837–1913)

On Wednesday April 17, 1912, **J. P. Morgan** received a flood of messages at the spa in Aix in honor of his seventy-fifth birthday. He wired his thanks in return but added "Greatly upset by loss *Titanic*... my heart ... very heavy." The International Mercantile Marine had not been a financial success for years, and now it was associated with this shocking tragedy. Morgan died in his sleep on March 31, 1913, at the Grand Hotel in Rome, where a year before he had met with Frank Millet to discuss the American Academy. Flags on Wall Street flew at half-staff and the stock market closed for two hours in his honor.

In November 1926, the IMM sold the Oceanic Steam Navigation Co., Ltd., of which the White Star Line was a major part, to the Royal Mail Group for £7 million. In 1932 the White Star Line once again became an independent company, but it merged with the Cunard Line in 1934 to become Cunard–White Star.

MARIA JOSEFA ("PEPITA") PEÑASCO (1889–1972)

Maria Josefa Perez de Soto y Vallejo Peñasco y Castellana, to use her full, aristocratic name, was met at Pier 54 by the ambassador of Uruguay at the request of her family, and she and her maid, **Fermina Oliva y Ocaña** (1872–1969), were taken to the Waldorf-Astoria. Pepita's father soon arrived in New York and took Fermina to Halifax with him in search of his son-in-law's body, but no corpse identified as being that of **Victor Peñasco** was recovered. Pepita married a Spanish baron six years later and had two sons and a daughter and lived a comfortable life similar to the one she would have had with Victor. Fermina continued to work for her for some years and then retired to live with her sister and work as a dressmaker, dying in 1969, at the age of ninety-six.

ARTHUR PEUCHEN (1859–1929)

Major Peuchen's promotion to lieutenant colonel and commanding officer of the Queen's Own Rifles went ahead as planned in May of 1912 despite rumors to the contrary. He retired from Standard Chemical in 1914 and for the first year of World War I was commander of the Home Battalion of the Queen's Own. From 1915 to 1918 he lived in London, where his son was a lieutenant in the Royal Field Artillery and his daughter married an officer from the same regiment. He returned to Canada after the war. In a family memoir, a nephew recalls that "the backlash of the *Titanic* disaster played havoc with my uncle's enterprises." He further claimed that Peuchen eventually lost most of his money and that even "Woodlands" on Lake Simcoe had to be sold. "Years after, when I would mention my uncle," he recalled, "people would say, 'Oh yes, he's the man who dressed in women's clothes to get off the *Titanic.*'" Peuchen certainly sustained losses in 1924 after the collapse of the Home Bank, and it is believed that for a time he lived in a lumbermen's dormitory in

Hinton, Alberta, where he owned tracts of forest. But he died at his home in a fashionable Toronto neighborhood on December 7, 1929. In 1987 his wallet was retrieved from the ocean floor and inside it were a few business cards and some streetcar tickets.

HERBERT PITMAN (1877–1961)

In July of 1912 **"Bert" Pitman** became the third officer on the *Oceanic*, and later served on the *Olympic* but in the purser's office, due to his deteriorating eyesight. During World War II he worked aboard the troopship SS *Mataroa* as a purser, and in March of 1946 was given an MBE (Member of the British Empire) award for his wartime service. He retired shortly after this to Pitcombe, Somerset, and died there on December 7, 1961, aged eighty-four.

EDITH ROSENBAUM (RUSSELL) (1879–1975)

"I'm accident prone," **Edith Rosenbaum** once noted. "I've had every disaster but bubonic plague and a husband." It took Edith several years to recoup her *Titanic* losses—she submitted a large claim for her missing merchandise but was compensated for only a fraction of its worth. In 1916–17 she became a war correspondent for the *New York Herald*, and after the war changed her name to Russell since the French fashion industry was boycotting those with German-sounding names. During the 1920s Edith continued her fashion importing and writing for magazines. She traveled extensively, weathering other catastrophes, such as car accidents and tornadoes, and once danced with Benito Mussolini and raised dogs for Maurice Chevalier. In the mid 1940s she made London her home base, living at Claridge's and then at the Embassy House Hotel. She made a lifelong friend in the young actor Peter Lawford and became godmother to the children he had with presidential sister Patricia Kennedy Lawford. Edith, too, befriended Walter Lord, bequeathing him her "good luck" musical toy pig. In 1958 she served as an advisor to William MacQuitty, the producer of the film *A Night to Remember*, and tried to persuade him to allow her to design the costumes. In old age Edith became increasingly eccentric and litigious and died in a London hospital on April 4, 1975, at the age of ninety-five.

LUCY NOËLLE MARTHA, COUNTESS OF ROTHES (1878–1956)

Noëlle Rothes (pronounced Roth-*ez*) was hailed as "the plucky little countess" in the aftermath of the disaster, following tributes to her in the newspapers by Seaman Jones and other survivors from Lifeboat 8. Noëlle and her husband, Norman, escaped from the press attention by traveling across the country to Pasadena, California, where the earl had planned to acquire a citrus farm. It was this prospect that had brought Noëlle and her husband's cousin, **Gladys Cherry** (1881–1965), to make the crossing on the *Titanic*. In the end, the Earl of Rothes decided not to settle in California and the couple returned to Scotland, where Noëlle had been proclaimed a national heroine by the newspapers. She was sympathetic to the grilling that Seaman Thomas Jones and Steward Alfred Crawford had received at the British Inquiry and sent each of them an engraved silver pocket watch. Seaman Jones eventually gave the countess the brass number 8 from the lifeboat, mounted on a plaque. The Earl of Rothes was wounded twice in World War I, and after the war both his health and finances deteriorated, requiring the sale of Leslie House in 1919. Norman died in March of 1927, and on December 22 of that year, Noëlle married an old family friend, Colonel Claude Macfie, and went to live with him in the village of Fairford, Gloucestershire. In the early 1950s, while corresponding with Walter Lord regarding *A Night to Remember*, she recalled that when dining at a London restaurant in the spring of 1913, she had been suddenly overcome with emotion. Soon she realized that the orchestra was playing the "Barcarolle" from *The Tales of Hoffmann*, a tune she had last heard played in the Palm Room on the night of the sinking. Noëlle died of heart failure on September 12, 1956, at the age of seventy-seven. Her cousin-in-law and traveling companion, Gladys Cherry, married a man named George Pringle and died in Godalming, Surrey, on May 4, 1965.

EMILY RYERSON (1863–1939)

On April 22, 1912, **Emily Ryerson,** her three daughters, and son John attended a funeral service in Philadelphia for the two **Arthur Ryersons,** father and son. Emily soon devoted herself to charity work, and during World War I worked on a fund for French orphans and wounded soldiers which won her the Croix de Guerre. She also traveled with President Herbert Hoover on a goodwill tour of South America. On a visit to China in 1927, the sixty-four-year-old Emily met and later married forty-five-year old Forsythe Sherfesee, a financial advisor to the Chinese government, and the couple made their home in Cap Ferrat. While traveling in Montevideo, Uruguay, in 1939, Emily suffered a fatal heart attack and her body was brought back to Cooperstown for burial in the Ryerson family plot overlooking Lake Otsego.

WILLIAM SLOPER (1883–1955)

William Sloper went home to New Britain, Connecticut, and became a managing partner in a private investment firm. He married a widow, Helen Lindenberg, in 1915 and helped raise her three daughters. In 1949 he published a biography of his father, *The Life and Times of Andrew Jackson Sloper*, which is today most noteworthy for its chapter on his own *Titanic* experiences. William died on May 1, 1955, and is buried in Fairview Lawn Cemetery, New Britain.

ELEANOR WIDENER (1861–1937)

After returning to Philadelphia by private train, **Eleanor Widener,** like **Emily Ryerson,** had to prepare funerals for both her husband and her son. At the dedication ceremony for the Harry Elkins Widener Memorial Library at Harvard in June of 1915, she met Dr. Alexander Rice, a physician and keen explorer. They married that same year and on their honeymoon embarked on a five-thousand-mile expedition in a steam launch deep into South America. The couple mapped and explored much of the Amazon wilderness and they returned to South America several more times in search of the source of the Orinoco River. They also traveled in India and Europe, and Eleanor died in Paris of a heart attack on July 13, 1937.

RICHARD NORRIS WILLIAMS (1891–1968)

R. Norris Williams recuperated well from being half-frozen in a submerged lifeboat. He went to Harvard that fall and soon won several national singles and doubles tennis championships, a doubles trophy at

Wimbledon, and a gold medal at the 1924 Olympics. When Collapsible A was recovered by the *Oceanic* in mid-May 1912, Williams's fur coat with a whiskey flask in its pocket was recovered and returned to him. He served with distinction during World War I and was awarded the Chevalier de la Legion d'Honneur and the Croix de Guerre. He later became an investment banker in Philadelphia and died on June 2, 1968, aged seventy-seven.

HUGH WOOLNER (1866–1925)

Only four months after the *Titanic* disaster, **Hugh Woolner** married Mary Alaia Dowson, the widow of an American. The couple had a son the next year and went on to have five daughters. Woolner's reputation for unsavory financial dealings was reinforced by a 1916–17 court case in which he was accused of exerting undue influence in the drawing up of the will of an elderly woman with a large estate. Woolner and his wife later divided their time between Hungary and England after they inherited a home in Budapest belonging to one of Hugh's relatives. He died there on February 13, 1925, of respiratory failure, at the age of only fifty-eight. Woolner's *Titanic* sidekick, **Mauritz Håkan Björnström-Steffansson** (1883–1962), stayed in America and in 1917 married Mary Pinchot Eno, a young woman introduced to him by **Helen Candee.** The couple had no children and lived in a large Manhattan town house. On his death, on May 21, 1962, Björnström-Steffansson left behind a sizeable fortune from his father's pulp empire and his own investments.

NOTES

ABBREVIATIONS

ET: Encyclopedia Titanica website

FDM to CWS: Francis Davis Millet letters to Charles Warren Stoddard, Charles Warren Stoddard Collection, Special Collections Research Center, Syracuse University Library

TDH: *The Titanic Disaster Hearings: The Official Transcripts of the 1912 Senate Investigation*, edited by Tom Kuntz

OBT: *On Board RMS Titanic: Memories of the Maiden Voyage*, edited by George M. Behe

ST: *The Story of the Titanic as Told by Its Survivors*, edited by Jack Winocour

TIP: Titanic Inquiry Project website

PROLOGUE: A RARE GATHERING

1 *"a noble apartment"* The Shipbuilder, 1912, in Foster, *Titanic Reader*, p. 32.

2 *"the unsinkable subject"* Lord, *Night Lives On*, p. 1.

2 *"a rare gathering"* Futrelle, in OBT, p. 288.

2 *"a small world bent on pleasure"* Duff Gordon, *Discretions*, p. 162.

3 *"an exquisite microcosm"* Lord, *Night Lives On*, p. 6.

3 *"as if some great"* Strange [Oelrichs], in King, *A Season of Splendor*, p. 439.

3 *"The thought occurs that the* Titanic *is"* Lord, in Ballard, *Discovery of the Titanic*, p. 7.

CHAPTER 1: AT THE CHERBOURG QUAY

5 *"the porters scurrying around"* Williams, *"CQD."*

6 *"made a god of punctuality"* Lehr, *"King Lehr,"* p. 164.

6 *"Obnoxious, ostentatious"* Sharpey-Schafer, *Soldier of Fortune*, pp. 130–31. See full text pages 307–308.

7 *"Millet," he once wrote* Twain, in Sharpey-Schafer, *Soldier of Fortune*, p. 16.

7 *"Millet was an artist"* Charles Francis Adams, in Sharpey-Schafer, *Soldier of Fortune*, p. 16.

7 *"Inertia is not one of Millet's faults"* Torrey, "Frank D. Millet, N.A.," *Art Interchange* 32, no. 6 (June 1894): 167, cited by Simpson, *Reconstructing the Golden Age*, pp. 414–15.

8 *"this perfection of a village"* Henry James, "Our Artists in Europe."

10 *"I want a gem"* Morgan Library website.

10 *"Pierpont Morgan...is carrying loads"* The Letters of Henry Adams, vol. V, p. 377, in Strouse, *Morgan*, p. 457.

12 *"pre-eminent example"* and quotes to follow, *Belfast Telegraph*, June 1, 1911, in Foster, *The Titanic Reader*, pp. 254–55.

13 *"I hope that here will eventually be"* New York Times, April 7, 1912.

13 *"Pierpont will buy"* in Auchincloss, *Vanderbilt Era*, p. 199.

14 *"If this sort of thing goes on"* Millet in Sharpey-Schafer, *Soldier of Fortune*, pp. 130–31.

14 *"had the entrée to every house"* New York Times, March 31, 1912.

CHAPTER 2: A *NOMADIC* HIATUS

17 *departure at 5:30* This time was noted in the diary of Daisy Spedden.

17 *"Riding the waves"* Williams, *"CQD."* It's most likely that the tender did not actually go into the outer harbor until after the *Titanic* was sighted, but remained behind the breakwater, as recalled by Margaret Brown and Edith Rosenbaum.

19 *"pawing every girl in sight"* Kaveler, *The Astors*, p. 148. The author was told this by women from Astor's set.

19 *"It is very questionable"* Town Topics, in Kaplan, *When the Astors Owned*, p. 56. It should be noted that the Astors often received harsh coverage in *Town Topics*, since they did not pay off the publisher, Colonel Mann, to be kept out of its pages.

19 *"pneumatic road improver"* Kaplan, *When the Astors Owned*, p. 62.

20 "a walking chandelier," Ibid., p. 31.

20 *"the poor old lady"* "After Holbein," in New York Stories of Edith Wharton, Robinson, ed., p. 360.

21 *"Mother Force has let no grass"* Town Topics, in Kaplan, *When the Astors Owned*, p. 157.

21 *"continued rumors"* New York Times, August 2, 1911.

22 *"best gol-durn"* and *"built me a home"* in Iversen, *Molly Brown*, p. 55.

24 *"cold, gray atmosphere"* and *"evil forebodings"* Brown, *Newport Herald*, May 28–29, in OBT, p. 217.

25 *"just a sideline"* and *"I never"* Russell [Rosenbaum], "By the Grace of God."

26 *Shortly before 7 p.m.* Passenger Marian Wright wrote in a letter that the ship arrived at Cherbourg at 7:00, and this conforms with several other passenger recollections.

26 *"the master palace of the sea"* and *"actively ill"* Brown, in OBT, p. 217.

26 *"the tender [began] pounding"* and *"as it shook"* Rosenbaum memoir, 1934, Charles Pellegrino website.

CHAPTER 3: THE PALM ROOM

29 *"a very distinct start"* Williams, *"CQD."*

29 *"All right"* and following dialogue Rosenbaum memoir, 1934, Charles Pellegrino website.

30 *"At the entrance"* Ramon Artagaveytia letter, in OBT, p. 91.

31 *"snapped like thread"* O'Donnell, *Last Days of the Titanic*, p. 94.

31 *"A voice beside me said"* Ibid., p. 94.

31 *"Instead of the radiant"* and *My heart sank* Jessop, *Titanic Survivor*, p. 119.

33 *"Of course there is"* Williams, April 10, 1912, letter. in OBT, p. 87.

34 *"It is a monster"* Rosenbaum, letter to Shaw, April 11, 1912.

34 *"As we sat down to dinner"* Browne, in O'Donnell, *Last Days of the Titanic,* p. 95.

36 *"had not learned its intonation"* Ibid., p. 94

37 MAJOR BUTT'S SUIT A WONDER *New York Times,* March 3, 1912.

38 *"I never reread or correct"* Abbott, *Taft and Roosevelt,* vol. 2, p. 656.

38 *"in case of accident of any kind"* Ibid., p. 848.

39 *"two old Southern"* Abbott, *Letters of Archie Butt,* p. 109.

39 *"endless tennis and swimming"* Ibid., p. 69.

39 *"everyone joined in the water fight"* Ibid., p. 72.

40 *"Phillips had worn his spurs in the water"* Ibid., p. 73. William Phillips (1878–1968) would become undersecretary of state from 1922 to 1924 and again during the Franklin Roosevelt administration, 1933–1936.

40 *"GEORGIA recognizes New England's right"* Ibid., p. 132.

41 *"each day I seem to miss Mother the more"* Ibid., p. 151.

42 *"My hat is in the ring"* Abbott, *Taft and Roosevelt,* vol. 2, p. 345.

42 *"3,213,600 ear-splitting citizens"* and *"Do you wonder that our nerves"* Ibid., p. 765; *"saucy little brats"* Ibid., p. 760.

42 *"I hate to leave the Big White Chief"* Ibid., p. 847.

42 *"My devotion to the Colonel"* Ibid., p. 812.

42 *"Don't forget that all my papers"* and *"as I always write you in this way"* Ibid., p. 848.

44 *"in a depressed"* and *"If I do not see it"* Behe, *"Archie,"* vol. 3, p. 602.

44 *"It was hard to realize"* Dodge, *Loss of the Titanic.*

CHAPTER 4: "QUEER LOT OF PEOPLE"

47 *"I have the best room"* Millet in Sharpey-Schafer, *Soldier of Fortune,* pp. 130–31.

48 *"the two men had a sympathy"* Leigh Palmer, *Washington Times,* April 19, 1912.

48 *"We looked at each other"* Katz, *Love Stories,* p. 203.

49 *"spoons"* to *"between us two"* Ibid.

49 *wanting to hug the marble* Engstrom, *Francis Davis Millet,* p. 65.

50 *"a great double bed"* Katz, *Love Stories,* p. 206.

50 *"Byronic mold,"* *"reading chatting, writing,"* and *"the realization of"* Ibid., p. 207. The artist A. A. Anderson (1847–1940) studied art in Paris and became a successful portraitist. After marrying the wealthy heiress Elizabeth Milbank in 1887, he and his wife became major philanthropists. Anderson also bought a ranch in Wyoming and became a pioneering Western conservationist and aviator.

50 *"Miss you? Bet your life"* FDM to CWS.

50 UBI BOHEMIA FUIT? Engstrom, *Francis Davis Millet,* p. 67.

51 *"Come Charlie, come!"* FDM to CWS.

51 *"spooning frightfully"* FDM to CWS.

51 *"our hero"* Engstrom, *Francis Davis Millet,* p. 111.

51 *"smoking rooms"* Sharpey-Schafer, *Soldier of Fortune,* pp. 130–31.

53 *"a Nancy boy"* Hustak, *Titanic: The Canadian Story,* p. 58.

53 *"an old dragoman"* Harper, *The Outlook,* in OBT, p. 316.

54 *"We are changing ships"* Hustak, *Titanic: The Canadian Story,* p. 26.

54 *"almost inseparable"* Ibid., p. 24.

55 *"black velvet with* passementerie*"* Abbott, *Letters of Archie Butt,* vol. 1., p. 161.

55 *"pulchritude of the male"* Abbott, *Taft and Roosevelt,* vol. II, p. 589.

55 *"as handsome as a young Greek athlete,"* Ibid., p. 653.

55 *"has been camping," "cat of a mother,"* and *"never really cared"* Behe, *"Archie,"* vol. 3, p. 12.

55 *"a terrific blow to me"* Behe, *"Archie,"* vol. 2, p. 248.

55 *"it was the same old story"* Ibid., p. 151.

56 *"I shall not mention her again"* Ibid., p. 248. The marriage of Mathilde Scott Townsend (1885–1949) to Peter Goelet Gerry (1879–1957) (whom Archie termed "an anemic millionaire") did not last. In 1925, she married the patrician, but homosexual, Benjamin Sumner Welles (1892–1961), who succeeded William Phillips as FDR's undersecretary of state in 1937. Welles resigned in 1943 to avoid revelations about his homosexuality being made public. Mathilde died of peritonitis in Switzerland six years later. The Townsend mansion in Washington is today the Cosmos Club.

56 *"such fun doing the shops"* Abbott, *Taft and Roosevelt,* vol. II, p. 799.

56 *a strenuous one-day, ninety-eight-mile gallop* This was dreamed up by the president to demonstrate that an order requiring army officers to ride ninety miles in three days was not unduly harsh.

56 *dubbed "Oscar Wilde"* Bradley, *Imperial Cruise,* p. 50.

56 *"he is such a good housekeeper"* Behe, *"Archie,"* vol. 3 , p. 229.

57 *"on the older man"* Washington Times*,* April 19, 1912.

57 *"between the years 1884 and 1888"* Eckley, *Maiden Tribute,* p. 104.

58 *"love of a cabin"* and *"a splendid, monstrous, floating Babylon"* Estelle Stead, *My Father,* p. 341–42.

59 [WE] DEMAND THAT INIQUITY Eckley, *Maiden Tribute,* p. 63.

59 *"had pleasure in giving my assent"* Ibid.

59 *"There's a man in the room!"* Ibid., p. 56.

59 *"because in the streets"* Ibid., p. 86.

60 *"a posing somdomite* [sic]*"* Ellmann, *Oscar Wilde,* p. 412.

60 *"if all persons guilty"* Stead, *Review of Reviews* 11 (June 1895), pp. 491–92.

60 *"I am glad to remember"* Eckley, *Maiden Tribute,* p. 226.

61 *"I still don't like this ship"* Hyslop, Forsyth, and Jemima, *Titanic Voices,* p. 118.

CHAPTER 5: QUEENSTOWN

64 *"sunny and big hearted"* and *"a wonderful, ringing laugh"* Bullock, *Titanic Hero,* p. 30.

64 *"There go my pals"* Ibid., p. 44.

64 *"Our esteem for him"* Jessop, *Titanic Survivor,* p. 117.

64 *"nothing but work all day long"* to *"without any"* Hyslop, Forsyth, and Jemima, *Titanic Voices,* p. 115.

65 *"I wish that God"* and *"Aren't you going to"* Eckley, *Maiden Tribute,* p. 7.

66 *"She is a magnificent ship"* Spedden diary, *Titanic Commutator,* p. 47.

67 *"So you see it would be impossible"* Eaton and Haas, *Titanic: Triumph and Tragedy,* p. 100.

68 *"the ruling lights"* and *"give his ears"* Lightoller, in ST, p. 275.

69 *"What fort is that?"* to *"call them a 'Gang,' Sir?"* O'Donnell, *Last Days of the Titanic,* p. 95.

70 *"It's a good place"* Minahan letter, in OBT, p. 55.

70 *"live-wake"* Connaught Telegraph, May 25, 1912, ET.

70 *"A Nation once again!"* in Molony, "A Tender Named America," ET.

70 *"nothing could have given"* Beesley in ST, p. 18.

72 *"Goodbye, I will give you copies"* O'Donnell, *Last Days of the Titanic,* p. 95.

72 *"Nothing is left to chance"* Ibid., p. 98.

72 *"we gathered ... to pray"* Ibid., p. 95.

73 *"I'm going down"* Hyslop, Forsyth, and Jemima, *Titanic Voices,* p. 111.

73 *"at least this lot"* Eaton and Haas, *Titanic: Triumph and Tragedy,* p. 101.

CHAPTER 6: FELLOW TRAVELERS

75 *"all take their exercise"* Brown, in OBT, p. 217.

75 *"silver lake"* René Harris, "Her Husband Went Down with the Titanic," *Liberty,* April 23, 1932.

75 *the Titanic's kennels* The location of the kennels is thought to have been aft on the boat deck because the *Olympic* had one in this area after 1912. But they may have been located belowdecks, near the third-class galley, a convenient place for feeding the dogs kitchen scraps. Beveridge, *Titanic: Ship Magnificent,* p. 222.

75 *She [Kitty] wandered away* From the notes of Katherine Force and Dr. Reuel Kimball, April 22, 1912, Charles Pellegrino website.

76 *"the first time a member"* Behe, *"Archie,"* vol. 2, p. 159.

76 *"she thought [he] looked"* Ibid.

76 *"If I could live"* Kaplan, *When the Astors Owned,* p. 11.

78 *"swinging black Amazons"* Chicago Tribune, August 17, 1893, in Larson, *Devil in the White City,* p. 314.

79 *"the strangest gathering"* Ibid.

80 *"that God-damned swamp"* Engstrom, *Francis Davis Millet,* p. 346.

81 *"full dress was always en règle"* Gracie, in ST, p. 121

81 *"was a subject"* Ibid., p. 122.

82 *"Quite as important"* Dress, May 1912.

82 *"almost spell-bound"* Marcus, *Maiden Voyage,* p. 72.

83 *"My dear fellow"* Ibid.

84 *"It was to gain a much needed rest"* Gracie, in ST, p. 121.

86 *"invariably circulated"* Gracie, in ST, p. 122.

86 *"wincing at [Gracie's] approach"* Lord, *Night Lives On,* p. 44.

86 *"the men of my coterie"* Gracie, in ST, p. 122.

88 *"If I am shipwrecked"* OBT, p. 543.

88 *"certain persons"* Lord, *Night Lives On,* p. 39.

88 *"If saved"* Jay Yates (J. H. Rogers) bio, ET.

CHAPTER 7: PRIVATE LIVES

91 *"quiet modesty"* New York Times, April 24, 1912.

92 *"Jim sails today"* Ibid.

94 *"Where's your wife"* to *"buxom brunette"* From Smith testimony at Thaw trial, in Mooney, *Evelyn Nesbit and Stanford White,* p. 223.

95 *"I did it because"* and *"He had it coming"* and *"Oh, Harry"* Uruburu, *American Eve*, p. 282.

95 STANFORD WHITE, VOLUPTUARY AND PERVERT Baker, *Stanny*, p. 377.

96 *"the most exquisitely lovely"* Irvin S. Cobb, in Ibid., p. 386.

97 *"the revolting details"* Ibid., p. 388.

97 *"Stanny White was killed"* Ibid., p. 397.

97 *"There was surely"* Auchincloss, *Vanderbilt Era*, p. 183.

98 *"would seduce Saint Anthony"* and *"semi-respectable spree"* Engstrom, *Francis Davis Millet*, p. 147.

98 *"his compulsions"* Lessard, *Architect of Desire*, p. 212.

99 *"practically the only"* Williams, *"CQD."*

99 *An auction was held:* Two additional numbers were added to the auction pool called the high and low fields, for which everyone had to pay full price. The high field number won when the ship's run exceeded the highest number in the pool and the low field was a winner when fewer miles were covered than the lowest number in the pool. Informal pools called decimal pools, where ten numbers were drawn from a hat, also took place.

100 *"The ship is as firm"* Edith Harper, *Stead the Man*, p. 244, in Marcus, *Maiden Voyage* p. 72.

100 *"powerful five-feet-five"* Candee, "Sealed Orders."

101 *"The Parisian café"* Henry Julian, in OBT, pp. 81–82.

101 *"of all the brothers"* Unger and Unger, *The Guggenheims*, p. 64.

102 *"Papa, you must have"* Ibid., p. 228.

102 *"one of the handsomest"* New York Times, October 25, 1894.

102 *"the Googs"* Davis, *The Guggenheims*, p. 218.

104 *"well-known in Brussels"* Belgian newspaper *Nieuws*, cited in Hustak, *Titanic: The Canadian Story*, p. 39.

105 *"crossed [a] thick ice-field"* and *"another ice-field"* "Marconigrams Sent and Received by Captain Smith," ET.

105 *"They are out of our way"* Boxhall testimony, U.S. inquiry, TIP.

CHAPTER 8: SHIPBOARD COTERIES

107 *"I took a Turkish bath this morning"* Spedden diary, *Titanic Commutator*, p. 48.

107 *"something of the grandeur"* Foster, *Titanic Reader*, p. 33.

108 *"blade douche"* Beveridge, *Titanic: Ship Magnificent*, p. 421.

109 *"We will beat the* Olympic*"* Elizabeth Lines, Limitation of Liability Hearings, October 27, 1913, TIP.

109 *"There will be no attempt"* New York Times, June 23, 1911, in Chirnside and Halpern, "*Olympic* and *Titanic:* Maiden Voyage Mysteries," ET.

109 *"one of those groups"* Lord, *Night Lives On*, p. 41.

110 *"with a leaning"* Luhan, in Kowsky, *Buffalo Architecture*, p. 136.

110 " *'Let us wander' "* Candee, "Sealed Orders."

111 *"As her bow"* Candee, in Bigham, "Life's Décor," ET.

111 *"a member of the city's most exclusive smart set"* Ibid.

112 *"dressing like the matron"* Ibid.

112 *"one for myself and the other"* Lord, *Night Lives On*, p. 41.

112 *"We are here to amuse you"* Ibid.

113 *"two famous men passed"* Young, in OBT, p. 428.

114 *"the fancy French poultry,"* *"the cooks before,"* and *"It is such good luck"* Ibid.

115 *"The* Titanic *was a good boat"* Toronto Telegram, April 19, 1912.

116 *"to be unseizable"* Woods, *Molson Saga,* p. 211.

117 *"a very pretty girl,"* *"vivacious good-looking niece,"* and *"two attractive sisters"* Sloper, *Life and Times,* p. 394.

117 *"You are in danger"* Ibid., pp. 396–97.

118 *"When are you going"* and *"You have forgotten"* Ibid., p. 396.

118 *"How little did I know"* Gracie, ST, p. 125.

119 *"the speed of the boat"* Williams, *"CQD."*

CHAPTER 9: DESIGNING WOMAN

122 *"One morning"* Etherington-Smith and Pilcher, *The "It" Girls,* p. 39.

123 *"crotchety, cranky invalid"* Ibid., p. 11.

124 *"white-corded silk dress"* Ibid., p. 18.

124 *"the two pretty red-headed girls"* Ibid., p. 18.

124 *"It was in black velvet"* Ibid., p. 24.

125 *"I decided that there was"* Ibid., p. 25.

126 *"In those days"* and *"I loosed upon"* Ibid., p. 73.

126 *"Half the women flocked to see them"* Ibid., p. 56.

127 *"the* crème de la crème*"* Glyn, *Romantic Adventure,* in Fowler, *The Way She Looks Tonight,* p. 72.

127 *"the oddest creature I had ever seen"* Etherington-Smith and Pilcher, *The "It" Girls,* p. 39.

127 *"masterpieces of"* Ibid., p. 88.

128 *"keeping the illusion,"* *"on this parade,"* and *"all hung with"* Ibid., p. 76.

128 *"I shall never forget"* Duff Gordon, *Discretions,* p. 73.

128 *"gallery of exquisite creations"* Washington Times, May 22, 1904, in Bigham, *Lucile,* p. 38.

128 *"There was never"* Duff Gordon, *Discretions,* p. 73.

129 *"If you are going to"* Etherington-Smith and Pilcher, *The "It" Girls,* p. 85.

129 *"most extraordinarily dull"* and *"deadly, deadly dull"* Ibid., p. 86.

132 *"I'm sure we can"* Ibid., p. 112.

132 *"The one thing that counts"* Ibid., p. 127.

132 *"Ours was a new playhouse"* Avery Strakosch, ed., "Fashions for the Famous: Dressmaking Days with Lady Duff Gordon," Bigham, *Lucile,* p. 76.

133 *"The dramatic performance"* Bigham, *Lucile,* p. 40.

133 *"We are so accustomed"* Bigham, *Lucile,* p. 61.

133 *"As business called me over"* Duff Gordon, *Discretions,* p. 161.

133 *"The designer was"* Bigham, "Saved from the Titanic," ET.

133 *"Everything aboard"* and *"pretty little cabin"* Duff Gordon, *Discretions,* p. 164.

134 *"One can only"* Etherington-Smith and Pilcher, *The "It" Girls,* p. 86.

134 *"regularly surrounded by"* Ibid., p. 164.

134 *"a sexual ambiguity"* Bigham, *Lucile,* p. 87.

135 *"smart to the last degree"* Ibid., p. 54.

135 *"the hum of voices"* and *"disaster swift"* Duff Gordon, *Discretions,* p. 162.

CHAPTER 10: A CALM SUNDAY

137 *"Time like an ever rolling stream"* From the sixth verse of "O God Our Help in Ages Past" by Isaac Watts, 1719.

137 *"quite one-half"* Brown, in OBT, p. 218.

137 *"bergs, growlers"* "Marconigrams Sent. . . . ," ET.

138 *"At my funeral"* Abbott, *Letters of Archie Butt*, p. 81.

138 *"as if I were in a summer palace"* Gracie, in ST, p. 119.

139 *"the Greek steamer"* "Marconigrams Sent . . . ," ET.

139 *"thought he was a minister,"* *"my boy,"* *"one big party,"* and *"a spirit of"* Harris, "Her Husband Went Down."

140 *"couldn't do,"* *"Mr. Freshy,"* *"I knew I couldn't,"* and *"childlike and lovable"* Bigham and Jasper, "Broadway Dame."

141 *"Life was all play"* Ibid.

141 *"If anything happens"* Geller, *Titanic: Women and Children*, p. 50.

141 *"Harry lost $430,000"* Bigham and Jasper, "Broadway Dame."

142 *"beat him with,"* *"toys in,"* *"flirting with,"* *"Man is,"* *"One of the women,"* and *"They have just"* Candee, "Sealed Orders."

143 *"two large icebergs"* "Marconigrams Sent. . . . ," ET.

143 *"I hope you are comfortable"* and dialogue, Emily Ryerson Limitation of Liability Hearings, TIP.

144 *"a wide blood-red band"* Rosenbaum 1934 memoir, Charles Pellegrino website.

145 *"took a header"* and following quotes Harris, "Her Husband Went Down."

145 *"how fondly"* Futrelle, in OBT, p. 288.

146 *"shining in pale"* and *"glittering frock"* Candee, "Sealed Orders."

147 *"I want everything dark"* Lynch, *Titanic: An Illustrated History*, p. 77.

147 *"In the elegantly"* Futrelle, in OBT, p. 287.

CHAPTER 11: THE LAST EVENING

149 *sat down with the Futrelles* May Futrelle describes dining with the Harrises on the last night in the "luxurious saloon after-deck," which likely means the restaurant.

149 *"It made me feel"* Harris, "Her Husband Went Down."

149 *"caviar, lobster, quail"* Douglas, in OBT, p. 278.

150 *"any claims"* and *"absolutely unfounded"* Ibid.

150 *"Mr. Widener, Major Butt and I"* Marian Thayer affadavit, cited in Davie, *Titanic: The Death and Life*, p. 520.

150 *"From the moment we met"* and all other quotes from Marian Thayer's letter to Taft OBT, p. 415. (See p. 309 for full text of letter.)

151 *Widener party actually lasted longer.* Daisy Minahan stated in her affadavit to the U.S. Senate Inquiry that the Widener party broke up at 9:25; William Sloper recalled seeing the captain on his way to the bridge after dinner at 10:00 p.m.

151 *"There is not much wind"* and dialogue with captain from Lightoller testimony, U.S. Senate Inquiry, TDH, p. 47.

152 *"did not know how,"* *"a method of control,"* and *"It would be"* Thayer, in OBT, p. 415.

153 *"everybody was so merry"* Futrelle, in OBT, p. 287.

153 *"clicked her satin heels"* Candee, "Sealed Orders."

153 *"made gay by"* and dialogue and *"How gay they were"* Ibid.

154 *"I have only one"* Duff Gordon, *Discretions*, p. 167.

156 *"heavy pack ice"* Lynch, *Titanic: An Illustrated History*, p. 80.

156 *this all-important message . . . went undelivered* Lightoller claimed that this message was not seen on the bridge, but whether it was delivered or not is unknown.

157 *"of a mummy case"* Seward, newspaper article, ET.

157 *"This is exactly what"* Eckley, *Maiden Tribute*, p. 105.

158 *"dancing motion"* Beesley, in ST, p. 26.

158 *"I must have looked"* Harris, "Her Husband Went Down."

158 *"hot grog"* Woolner, in OBT, p. 179.

158 *"very pretty young woman"* Sloper, *Life and Times*, p. 398.

160 *"the White Star, the Cunard,"* *"the pleasure,"* and *"an ominous feature"* Gracie, in ST, p. 118.

160 *two other Frenchmen and one American* Paul Chevré's bridge companions were the French aviator Pierre Maréchal, twenty-eight, a cotton dealer, named Alfred Omont, twenty-nine, from Havre, and the honeymooning Lucian Smith, twenty-four, from Huntington, West Virginia.

161 *"Say, old man"* and *"Keep out!"* Lynch, *Titanic: An Illustrated History*, p. 83.

161 *"Is someone there?"* Fleet, in TDH, p. 179–80.

CHAPTER 12: COLLISION AND AFTER

163 *a ferryboat striking the planks* Sloper, *Life and Times*, p. 399.

163 *"An iceberg just passed astern!"* Woolner, in TDH, p. 369.

163 *"An iceberg has ground"* Barkworth, "Barkworth's Account," ET.

164 *a thousand marbles* White, in TDH, p. 423.

164 *a giant hand was playing bowls* Duff Gordon, *Discretions*, p. 172.

164 *"What have we struck?"* and dialogue Boxhall, in TDH, pp. 132–33.

164 *stoker Frederick Barrett* TDH, pp. 527–28.

164 *"All up on deck"* Buckley, in TDH, p. 438.

165 *"I expect the iceberg"* and *"Just run"* Beesley, in ST, pp. 29–30.

166 *"What has happened?"* and dialogue Ismay, in TDH, pp. 3–4.

166 *"The ship is making"* and *"The mail hold"* Boxhall, in TDH, p. 136.

166 *Thomas Andrews, was already making his own inspection* Most accounts claim that Captain Smith asked Andrews to make an inspection, but it seems that Andrews was already inspecting the damage on his own. Steward James Johnson saw Andrews descending to the post office and Stewardess Annie Robinson saw a mail clerk fetch Smith and McElroy and overheard Andrews say, "Well, three have gone . . ."

167 *"The captain says"* Sloper, *Life and Times*, p. 400.

167 *"What has happened?"* Ibid., p. 400.

168 *"It will take more than an iceberg"* Hustak, *Titanic: The Canadian Story*, p. 91.

168 *"Why, she is listing"* and dialogue Peuchen, in TDH, p. 198.

168 *Smith opened his hand,* Gracie, in TDH, p. 407.

169 *"The order is"* and dialogue Peuchen, in TDH, p. 198.

169 *"Didn't I tell you"* Brown, in OBT, p. 219.

169 *"What for?"* and dialogue Russell [Rosenbaum] article.

170 *"I will be forced to report you"* Williams, "CQD."

171 *gone through it up to B deck* Buckley was in a forward cabin and went up a stairway to a first-class area, so this gate would likely have been at B deck.

171 *"had a look"* Sloan, in OBT, p. 397.

172 *"You had better"* and dialogue, Bride, in TDH, pp. 84–85.

172 *Have struck an iceberg* Foster, *Titanic Reader,* p. 72.

172 *"What are you sending?"* and dialogue Bride, in ST, p. 315.

172 *"Send SOS"* Bride's account makes it seem as if they began using *SOS* early on, but the first call from the *Titanic* using *SOS* was received by the *Mount Temple* and the *Olympic* at 12:57 a.m. *Titanic* time.

172 *not, as is often claimed, the first time* The SOS signal was introduced on July 1, 1908, and was first used in an emergency on June 10, 1909, when the SS *Slavonia* was wrecked off the Azores.

172 *"I'll never ride"* Sloper, *Life and Times* p. 404.

173 *"Oh, I suppose"* Quoted in Hays bio, ET.

173 *At twelve-forty Murdoch instructed* Lifeboat launch times and sequence are based on new research by Bill Wormstedt, Tad Fitch, and George Behe, in "Titanic: The Lifeboat Launching Sequence Re-examined" on the website wormstedt.com.

174 *"There is no time to waste"* Pitman, in TDH, 164.

174 *"Come along, ladies"* and dialogue, Pitman, in TDH, 164–65.

174 *"Can the men come too?"* and dialogue Behr, in OBT, p. 208.

175 *"You go ahead"* Pitman, in TDH, 165.

175 *"Lower away"* and *"If you will"* Lowe, in TDH, pp. 212–13.

175 *"Hebrew doctor"* Stengel, in OBT, p. 403.

175 *"They wouldn't send"* and Ryerson dialogue in Lynch, *Titanic: An Illustrated History,* p. 110.

175 *"Don't you hear"* Emily Ryerson, in TDH, p. 492.

175 *"Fire one"* Lynch, *Titanic: An Illustrated History,* p. 110.

176 *"Gentleman, the accident"* New York American, April 24, 1912, in Behe, "*Archie,*" vol. 3, p. 628.

176 *"desired to show"* Gracie, in ST, p. 129.

176 *"a strange unseeing look"* and dialogue Thayer letter to Taft, in OBT, p. 415.

177 *"to see the stars"* Spedden diary, *Titanic Commutator,* p. 48.

177 *"rather like a stupid"* Harper, in OBT p. 315.

177 *"You and mother"* Hustak, *Titanic: The Canadian Story,* p. 96.

177 *"At last the ropes"* Shutes, in Gracie, ST, p. 235.

CHAPTER 13: TO THE LIFEBOATS

179 *"Down below"* Candee, "Sealed Orders."

180 *"a splendid act"* Peuchen, in TDH, p. 196.

180 *"Have some iceberg!"* Candee, "Sealed Orders."

180 *"Why are we so calm?"* and *"We are"* Ibid.

180 *a little silver flask* Bigham, "Life's Décor," ET.

181 *Berthe kept insisting* Brown, in OBT, p. 219.

181 *pulled out a silver brandy flask* Hustak, *Titanic: The Canadian Story,* p. 94

181 *"We have been living"* Alfred Crawford, U.S. Inquiry, TIP, ET.

181 *"I am sure"* and *"I will not go"* Woolner, in TDH, p. 371.

181 *"throw the damn thing overboard"* Lightoller, in ST, p. 291.

182 *"You are going, too!"* Brown, in OBT, p. 219.

182 *"I can't manage"* and dialogue Peuchen, in TDH, p. 197.

182 *"One hundred and"* Toronto Evening Telegram, April 22, 1912.

182 *"Get down and"* and *"Hurry! This boat"* Peuchen, in TDH, p. 198.

183 *"none of us"* Lady Duff Gordon, British Inquiry, TIP.

183 *lavender silk kimono* Letter from Lucile, in OBT, p. 281.

183 *shoemaker Pietro Yantorny* Lucile later wrote to her sister Elinor that she regretted leaving her sable coat behind but was glad that she had worn her Yantorny mules. Pietro Yantorny (1874–1936) bragged that he was the most expensive shoemaker in the world, and his custom-designed shoes took years to make. It was said that he would refuse to make shoes for women with ugly feet.

184 *"Shouldn't we try"* and dialogue, Lucile, in TIP.

184 *"That is the funniest"* Stengel, in TDH, p. 399.

184 *how the boat shook* Barratt, *Lost Voices,* p. 159.

185 *"For God's sake man"* Farrell bio, ET.

185 *"a lot of Italians"* Lowe, British Inquiry, TIP.

186 *"shut up"* Lynch, *Titanic: An Illustrated History,* p. 121.

186 *"I am in charge,"* *"It's our lives,"* and *"He had been swearing"* in Kuntz, TDH, p. 199.

187 *"What are you"* Russell [Rosenbaum] article.

187 *"Put one foot"* Ibid.

188 *"great lighted theatre"* Barrett, in TIP.

189 *"How many of"* Douglas, in OBT, p. 279.

189 *"damned cowards"* Mennell, in Gracie, ST, p. 201.

190 *"No, I must"* and *"Walter, when you"* Douglas, in OBT, p. 279.

190 *"Ladies, you must"* Sloan, in OBT, p. 397.

191 *Come as quickly* Foster, *Titanic Reader,* p. 75.

191 *"She cannot help"* Lightoller, in ST, p. 294.

191 *acted like a mirror* Wilkinson, "Titanic's Silent Distress Signals: A New Look at a Minor Mystery," ET.

192 *"quite a group of people"* Ryerson, in OBT, p. 382.

192 *"Just tell us"* Stephenson, in OBT, p. 405.

192 *seen being dressed* Bonnell, in OBT, p. 210.

192 *Madeleine's pearls New York Evening Telegram,* April 22. 1912.

193 *"That boy can't go!"* and dialogue Ryerson, in OBT, p. 382.

193 *"Look after Father"* Hustak, *Titanic: The Canadian Story,* p. 87.

CHAPTER 14: THE FINAL MINUTES

197 *"Get out of this"* Woolner, in *TDH,* p. 372.

197 *a panicked Daniel Buckley* There is debate as to which lifeboat Buckley entered. Some believe it was Boat 14. But Buckley said an officer fired shots to clear the boat and that the *Titanic* sank fifteen minutes after it left, which points to Collapsible C.

197 *"Italian and other foreign women"* Woolner, in TDH, p. 373. "Italian" was the catchword at the time for any foreign person.

197 *"Are there any more"* New York Times, April 22, 1912.

198 *"dagoes"* Lightoller, in ST, p. 296.

198 *"You go first"* and *"Never mind"* Gracie, in ST, p. 134.

199 *"My God, woman!"* and following dialogue Harris, "Her Husband Went Down.".

199 *"Good-bye, sweetheart!"* Bigham and Jasper, "Broadway Dame."

199 *"He was motionless"* Harris, *Omaha News,* April 21, 1912, cited in Behe, *"Archie,"* vol. 3, p. 642.

199 *"wearing that same"* Harris, letter to John Millet, in OBT, p. 319.

199 *"Have you any message, Frank?"* Behe, *"Archie,"* vol. 3, p. 640.

200 *"Let's make a jump"* Woolner, in OBT, p. 180.

200 *"My God, it's my husband!"* Paterson Morning Call, April 23, 1912.

200 *"Jane!"* and *"Let me take"* Harris, "Her Husband Went Down."

200 *"pull like the deuce"* Woolner, in OBT, p. 181.

200 *"Look out for the suction!"* Harris, "Her Husband Went Down."

200 *May Futrelle later claimed* In a May 1912 article in *American Medicine* (OBT, p. 292) Mrs. Futrelle said she was in a lifeboat with Mrs. Harris, which would imply Boat D, but in a 1932 article she claimed otherwise. It seems most likely that she was actually in Boat 9.

200 *"For God's sake go!"* Times of London, April 20, 1912.

200 *"I know those hands"* Futrelle, in OBT, pp. 304–5.

201 *"I learned swimming"* Evening Banner, April 26, 1912, ET.

201 *"We have dressed"* and *"If anything should"* Etches, New York Times, April 20, 1912.

201 *"Aren't you going to"* Bullock, *"A Titanic Hero,"* p. 71.

201 *"he looked as if"* Kemish letter to Walter Lord, on Charles Pellegrino website.

202 *"in silence and"* Shelley letter, in OBT, p. 391.

202 *"at every stroke"* Harper, in OBT, p. 317.

203 *"was not an agreeable one"* and *"While I said"* Gracie, in ST, p. 136.

203 *Frank Millet had written* Engstrom, *Francis Davis Millet*, p. 4.

203 *"Has any passenger"* Gracie, in ST, p. 137.

203 *"You look out"* and *"Let's clear out"* Bride, in ST, pp. 316–17.

206 *"an utter nightmare"* and *"piling the"* Lightoller, in ST, p. 299.

207 *"It was as though"* Unnamed passenger quoted in *Philadelphia Press*, April 19, 1912, cited in Behe, *"Archie,"* vol. 3, p. 644. Historian George Behe suspects the unnamed passenger may have been Robert Daniel.

207 *"The stern then seemed"* Thayer, Sinking of the S.S. Titanic.

207 *"She's gone."* Lightoller, in ST, p. 300.

207 *"She's gone, lads"* Lynch, *Titanic: An Illustrated History*, p. 139.

207 *"we raised our hats"* Walter Hawksford, letter to his wife.

208 *"the most horrible"* Gracie, in ST, p. 150.

208 *"the most fearful"* Woolner, in OBT, p. 181.

208 *"a sound…as will haunt"* Harris, in OBT, p. 321.

208 *"a wild maniacal chorus"* Harper, in OBT, p. 318.

208 *"immediately their massed"* Sloper, *Life and Times*, p. 403.

208 *"every possible emotion"* Beesley letter, in Barratt, *Lost Voices*, p. 162.

209 *"a man in the uniform"* Unnamed stoker in *New York Tribune*, April 19, 1912, in Behe, *"Archie,"* vol. 3, p. 648.

209 *"a heavy moan"* Candee, "Sealed Orders."

CHAPTER 15: VOICES IN THE NIGHT

211 *"Appeal to the officer"* Etches, in TDH, p. 359.

211 *"If any of us"* Gladys Cherry letter, in OBT, p. 244.

211 *"It would have been sheer"* Woolner, in OBT, p. 181.

211 *"came as a thunderbolt"* and *"no-one in"* Beesley letter, in Barratt, *Lost Voices*, p. 162.

212 *"I thought it was"* George Harder, in TDH, p. 447.

212 *"seamen or possibly steerage"* Smith, in OBT, p. 399.

212 *"suicide"* and *"thinned out"* Lowe, in TDH, p. 222.

212 *"You ought to be"* and *"Jump"* Minahan, in TDH, p. 496.

213 *"It is no use"* Peuchen, in TDH, pp. 199–200.

213 *"What's the use"* and *"the little blighter"* Charlotte Collyer, in OBT, p. 253.

213 *The rescued man was actually Chinese* It is believed that his name was Fang Lang, and he was a thirty-two-year-old fireman from Hong Kong.

214 *"short shrift"* and *"grated on"* Gracie, in ST, p. 160.

214 *"Look out"* Lynch, *Titanic: An Illustrated History*, p. 145.

216 *"Just fancy"* and dialogue down to *"At any rate"* Duff Gordon, *Discretions*, p. 175.

217 *"Rebellion to tyrants"* Wojtczak, "Elsie Bowerman: Feminist and Barrister," ET.

217 *"Soy, don't you know"* and *"I know who"* Brown, in OBT, p. 221. The "Cockney" accent Mrs. Brown identified may have simply been a working-class English accent.

217 *"treasured above all"* Young, in OBT, p. 429.

217 *"were just like little canaries"* Helen Bishop, in Geller, *Titanic: Women and Children*, p. 59.

218 *"would have killed us"* and *"That icy air"* Cherry, in Bigham, "A Matter of Course," ET.

219 *"Should the worse"* Barratt, *Lost Voices*, p. 150.

219 *"There is a steamer"* and *"All you men"* Gracie, in ST, p. 166.

220 *"Come over"* Gracie, in ST, p. 167.

220 *"We can see a ship"* and following dialogue Lynch, *Titanic: An Illustrated History*, p. 152.

220 *"They were a party"* Harper, in OBT, p. 182.

221 *"sank into the bottom"* Harris, in OBT, p. 322.

221 *"That is a falling star"* Brown, in OBT, p. 221.

221 *"No, she is not"* Gracie, in ST, p. 180.

221 *"Where those lights"* Ibid.

221 *looked like giant opals* Duff Gordon, *Discretions*, p. 177.

221 *glistened like rock quartz* Futrelle, in OBT, p. 306.

221 *"Oh Muddie, look"* and *"the tragedy of"* Spedden diary, *Titanic Commutator*.

222 *"I have only"* and dialogue, down to *"Thank you, mister"* Lynch, *Titanic: An Illustrated History*, p. 150.

223 *"clung to each other"* Duff Gordon, *Discretions*, p. 178.

223 *"had been dreadful"* and *"we were all charmed"* Spedden letter, in OBT, p. 178.

223 *"woman of substantial size"* and *"Look at that"* Harper, in OBT, p. 319.

224 *"No. If you will leave me"* Lynch, *Titanic: An Illustrated History*, p. 156.

224 *"a young man of six"* Harris, in OBT, p. 322.

225 *"What difference"* Harris, "Her Husband Went Down."

226 *"our brave and heroic"* and *"did not tarry"* Brown, in OBT, p. 222.

227 *"Could not another"* and *"Was it not"* Lightoller, in ST, p. 303.

227 *"This is the last"* Futrelle, in OBT, p. 306.

CHAPTER 16: THE SHIP OF SORROW

229 *"Please don't!"* Futrelle, in OBT, p. 307.

229 *"the shock and finality of it"* Ibid.

229 *Reverend Father Roger Anderson* is described by *Carpathia* passenger Charles Hutchinson as being an Episcopal monk.

229 *"speechless, half-clad"* Brown, in OBT, p. 222.

230 *"Deeply regret advise you"* and *"Captain, do you think"* Lynch, *Titanic: An Illustrated History,* p. 159.

231 *"Minarets like cathedral"* Rostron, *Loss of the Titanic.*

231 *"nature's implacable strength"* Candee, "Sealed Orders."

231 *"half-frozen"* Spedden diary, *Titanic Commutator.*

232 *"The rats swim"* Engstrom, *Francis Davis Millet,* p. 6.

233 *"Frank D. Millet, whom I loved"* Ibid., p. 7.

233 *"Have just heard fearful rumor"* Strouse, *Morgan,* p. 647.

235 *"Unto Almighty God"* Book of Common Prayer Service for Burial at Sea. The four men buried at sea are believed to have been: W. F. Hoyt, first-class passenger; Abraham Harmer [David Livshin], third-class passenger; S. C. Siebert, steward; and P. Lyons [William Lyons], sailor.

235 *"the inquisition"* Lightoller, in ST, p. 303.

236 *"I can't do"* and *"Please excuse"* Hyder, "Excuse Sending . . . Am Half Asleep," ET.

236 "Titanic *foundered"* Franklin, US Senate Inquiry, in TIP.

237 *"All that day"* Duff Gordon, *Discretions,* p. 181.

237 *"the poor foreigners"* Iversen, *Molly Brown,* p. 35.

238 *"Are you the one"* and *"all her models"* Rosenbaum, *Women's Wear Daily,* April 19, 1912, p. 1.

239 *"Canadian girlfriend"* Sloper, *Life and Times,* p. 405.

241 *"the two young men"* Gracie, in ST, p. 144.

242 *"I don't think I could"* George Behe's Titanic Tidbits website.

242 *"helped in seeing"* Cherry, in Bigham, "A Matter of Course," ET.

242 *"The number of widows"* and *"We spend our time"* Spedden, April 18 letter, in OBT, pp. 178–79.

243 *"Madam, we"* and *"unburdened their"* Brown, in OBT, p. 224.

243 *"pathetic"* and *"as if it were a blot"* Ibid., p. 225.

243 *"Do not grieve"* and *"he would run"* Harris, "Her Husband Went Down."

244 *"proved himself a brave man"* Lightoller, in OBT, p. 169.

244 *"a subject of universal"* Toronto Star, April 17, 1912.

244 " 'Poor Butt' " *Washington Times,* cited in Behe, *"Archie,"* vol. 3, p. 657.

244 *"the employees of"* Ibid., p. 660.

245 *"The scene in front"* Barratt, *Lost Voices,* p. 197.

245 *"In the humbler homes"* London Daily Mail, April 18, 1912, cited in Eaton and Haas, *Titanic: Triumph and Tragedy,* p. 206.

245 *"and you can imagine"* Barratt, *Lost Voices,* p. 197.

CHAPTER 17: TWO CONTINENTS STIRRED

247 *"Please take me"* to *"reporter was on the pier"* Mary Adelaide Snider, "Through the Needle's Eye How Woman Writer Went," *Toronto Evening Telegram,* April 1912, cited in Dupuis, "And Mind You're a Nurse."

248 *"shouting all sorts of"* Spedden diary, *Titanic Commutator.*

249 *"A deep sigh"* Marshall, *Sinking of the Titanic,* p. 126.

249 *"Archie was like"* Behe, *"Archie,"* vol. 3, p. 660.

250 *"the black-hulled ship"* Snider, *Toronto Evening Telegram,* April 1912, cited in Dupuis, "And Mind You're a Nurse."

250 *"I never saw a sadder face"* Dobbyn letter, in Barratt, *Lost Voices*, p. 153.

250 *"a colossal piece"* Lightoller, in ST, p. 303.

251 *"I have come alone"* Harris, "Her Husband Went Down."

251 *"My God!"* Engstrom, *Francis Davis Millet*, p. 6.

251 *"Carelessness, gross carelessness!"* and *"The captain knew"* Brewster, "Sinking Sensation."

251 *"stalwart, sunburnt"* Snider, "With Orphaned Babe in Arms," *Toronto Evening Telegram*, April 1912, cited in Dupuis, "And Mind You're a Nurse."

251 *"I have a clear,"* *"It was my training,"* and *"If there is room"* Brewster, "Sinking Sensation."

251 *"quite equal to"* Dupuis, "And Mind You're a Nurse."

252 *"William T. Sloper, son of"* Sloper, *Life and Times*, p. 408.

252 *"Well, we might as well"* New York American, April 19, 1912.

253 *"sincere grief"* and *"More than"* U.S. Inquiry, TIP and TDH, p. 2.

255 *"Your conduct deserves"* U.S. Inquiry, Day 1, TIP and TDH, p. 36.

255 *"nothing but a complete farce"* Lightoller, in ST, p. 304.

255 *"a gentleman from"* London Globe, cited in Wade, *Titanic: End of a Dream*, p. 189.

255 *"it may be humiliating"* Wade, *Titanic: End of a Dream*, p. 189.

256 *"has stirred two continents"* Toronto Globe, April 18, 1912.

256 MAJOR PEUCHEN BLAMES *Toronto World*, April 20, 1912.

256 *"I have never"* Toronto World, April 22, 1912.

256 *"The men of our race"* Toronto Globe, April 22, 1912.

256 *"those women who go"* Wade, *Titanic: End of a Dream*, p. 71.

257 *"any personal or"* and *"I am here, sir"* Peuchen, U. S Inquiry, Day 4, TIP.

257 *"Votes for women"* Poem by Clark McAdams, in Foster, *Titanic Reader*, p. 240.

257 *" 'Women first' "* Iversen, *Molly Brown*, p. 43.

258 *"They speak of the"* White, U.S. Inquiry, Day 11, TDH, p. 426.

258 *"a flock of sea gulls"* Ruffman, *Titanic Remembered*, p. 28.

258 *Astor's body was found mangled* "The Two Deaths of John Jacob Astor," George Behe's Titanic Tidbits website.

259 *"We are so used"* Letter of John Alfred Parsons Millet, cited in Behe, *"Archie,"* vol. 3, p. 686.

259 *Meanwhile, Major Blanton Winship* Blanton Winship (1869–1947) later became a major general and was appointed military governor of Puerto Rico in 1934. Winship treated nationalist demonstrators in Puerto Rico very harshly and was the subject of an attempted assassination in 1938 and removed from his post in 1939.

260 *"never did I know"* and *"It always seemed to me"* Behe, *"Archie,"* vol. 3, p. 689.

260 *"made her escape"* Rosenbaum, *Women's Wear Daily*, April 19, 1912.

261 *"All over the [train] station"* Duff Gordon, *Discretions*, p. 192.

261 *"shuts himself in the library"* Duff Gordon letter, in OBT, p. 283.

261 *"a fashionable matinee"* New York Times, May 22, 1912.

261 *"the air was rent"* Duff Gordon, *Discretions*, p. 173.

261 *"There were many things"* British Inquiry, Day 10, TIP.

262 *"not to try,"* *"that you considered,"* and *"The witness's position"* British Inquiry, Day 11, TIP.

262 *"Torquemada never"* Ashmead Bartlett, *The Academy*, in Duff Gordon, *Discretions*, p. 200.

262 *"the very gross charge"* British Inquiry, Final Report, TIP.

262 *"A great deal of the mud"* Duff Gordon, *Discretions*, p. 203.

262 *"he would merely have"* British Inquiry, Final Report, TIP.

263 *"might have saved many"* Ibid.

263 *"without doubt be negligence"* Ibid.

264 *"there was no such thing"* Bigham and Jasper, "Broadway Dame."

265 *"practically lost her reason"* *Harrisburg Leader,* April 21, 1912, in Geller, *Titanic: Women and Children*, p. 59.

266 *"I simply did"* *Denver Times,* April 21, 1912, in Iversen, *Molly Brown*, p. 38.

268 *"evil has come with the good"* Woodrow Wilson, Inaugural Address, March 4, 1913, from bartleby.com.

268 *"It takes a terrible warning"* Smith, U.S Inquiry, in Iversen, *Molly Brown*, p. 40.

POSTSCRIPT: *TITANIC* AFTERLIVES

274 *"one of the outstanding"* Harris, "Her Husband Went Down."

276 *"She's too mean"* Iversen, *Molly Brown*, p. 38.

280 *"The era of elaborate ornamentation"* Cecil Beaton, *The Glass of Fashion*, p. 162, in Bigham, *Lucile: Her Life by Design*, p. 235.

280 *"She had to learn"* Melanie Abrams, "Lady Duff Gordon: Fashion's Forgotten Grande Dame," *Telegraph,* February 21, 2011.

282 *"Louis, how do you"* Lord, *A Night to Remember,* p. 167.

282 *"Mrs. Harris was rich, racy"* Hart, *Act One,* cited in Geller, *Titanic: Women and Children*, p. 49.

283 *"I have had four"* Geller, *Titanic: Women and Children*, p. 52.

283 *"The lady was"* *Variety,* September 1969, cited in Bigham and Jasper, "Broadway Dame."

284 *"immigrants of the Latin race"* Lowe, U.S. Inquiry, Day 5, TIP.

285 *"Greatly upset by loss"* Strouse, *Morgan*, p. 647.

286 *"the backlash of"* and *"Years after"* Brewster, "Sinking Sensation."

287 *"I'm accident prone"* Geller, *Titanic: Women and Children*, p. 74.

APPENDIX A

Frank Millet's Letter to Alfred Parsons
ON BOARD R.M.S. "*TITANIC.*" APRIL 11, 1912

Dear Alfred:

I got yours this morning and was glad to hear from you. I thought I told you my ship was the *Titanic*. She has everything but taxicabs and theatres. Table d' hote, restaurant à la carte, gymnasium, Turkish baths, squash court, palm gardens, smoking rooms for "Ladies and Gents," intended I fancy to keep the women out of the men's smoking room which they infest in the German and French steamers. The fittings are in the order of Haddon Hall and are exceedingly agreeable in design and color. As for the rooms they are larger than the ordinary hotel room and much more luxurious with wooden bedsteads, dressing tables, hot and cold water, etc., etc., electric fans, electric heater and all. The suites with their damask hangings and mahogany oak furniture are really very sumptuous and tasteful. I have the best room I have ever had in a ship and it isn't one of the best either, a great long corridor in which to hang my clothes and a square window as big as the one in the studio alongside the large light. No end of furniture, cupboards, wardrobe, dressing table, couch, etc., etc. Not a bit like going to sea. You can have no idea of the spaciousness of this ship and the extent and size of the decks. The boat deck has an uninterrupted space as long as our tennis court almost, and the chair decks are nearly as wide as our large courtyard, or quite. 500 people don't make a show on the decks. Queer lot of people on the ship. Looking over the list I only find three or four people I know but there are a good many of "our people" I think and a number of obnoxious, ostentatious American women, the scourge of any place they infest and worse on shipboard than anywhere. Many of them carry tiny dogs and lead husbands around like pet lambs. I tell you the American woman is a buster. She should be put in a harem and kept there.

Yes I had a devil of a time in Rome and if this sort of thing goes on I shall chuck it. I won't lose my time and temper too. I think Mead will resign. Lily will tell you about her, the B . . . she makes trouble everywhere and he, poor wretch has to dangle about her day and night. I pity him.

I wrote from Paris the day we arrived. I couldn't tell where we should stop because I didn't know whether Lily would go to the Grand or not. We found it excellent.

Yours always
Frank

APPENDIX B

Marian Thayer's Letter to President Taft
(from the William Howard Taft papers, Library of Congress)

Dear Mr. Taft:

In my own grief I think often of yours and feel I must write to tell you how I spent the last Sunday evening with Major Butt—for we all cherish news of last hours—and we spoke much of you.

How devoted he was to you and what a lovely, noble man he was!

We were dining in the restaurant with the poor Wideners & from the moment we met never moved from each other for the rest of the evening.

Never before have I come in such close contact immediately with anyone. He felt the same & we both marveled at the time at the strangeness of such a thing, for we both realized it while actually opening our innermost thoughts to each other.

He told me much about his mother and their letters, his sister-in-law, you, and someone else he loved but I do not [Theodore Roosevelt].

He spoke with deep enthusiasm of leaving his mark and memorial of truth to the world with those letters which should be published after he had gone.

He made an engagement for the next afternoon as I was going to teach him a method of control of the nerves through which I had just been through with a noted Swiss doctor knowing it would be a very wonderful thing for him if he could just get hold of it for he was very nervous & did not know how he was going to stand the rushing life he was returning to, and we were going to work so hard over it the rest of the time on board.

He said I was just like his mother and opened his heart to me & it was as though we had known each other well for years.

It was the strangest sensation and felt as tho' a veil was blown aside for those few hours eliminating distance between two who had known each other always <u>well</u> long, long before and had just found each other again—I believe it.

Otherwise we could not have met just then and talked as we did.

That night about 12:10 I saw him again and for the last time.

As Mr. Thayer, my son and I had come from dressing in our staterooms & were standing in the hall near the door he came towards us with a strange, unseeing look on his face. I caught hold of his coat and said, "Major Butt, Major Butt, where are you going? Come with me" & he replied "I have something to do but will come then" and went in the direction of the staterooms & I said to myself, "He has gone for his letters."

And what of those letters? He told me he had had duplicates made of all. Did he mean while he was abroad and that he had them all with him or are they safe with someone in Washington? I must hear.

Oh Mr. Taft, is there any chance of seeing either my husband or him here again in this life? My reason tells me no but how can we give up all hope until some days yet go past of this cruel torture.

Oh how he loved you and how frightfully you will miss his care— such a true, devoted, close more-than-friend.

I am sorry for you.

My brief deep knowledge of that lovely personality (I cannot call him acquaintance) is very, very strong & strange to look back upon, and as I say we both at the time remarked and greatly marveled at it.

It was meant to be for some reason & I am compelled to write you.

Believe me, with the deepest sympathy and grief.

Sincerely,

Marian I. M. Thayer

P.S. Today is my husband's fiftieth birthday. Oh he is young to go and leave us he so loved.

April 21st, 1912

BIBLIOGRAPHY

BOOKS

Abbott, Lawrence F. *The Letters of Archie Butt*. New York: Doubleday, Page & Company, 1924.

————. *Taft and Roosevelt, The Intimate Letters of Archie Butt*, volumes 1 and 2. Port Washington, NY: Kennikat Press, originally published 1930, reissued 1971.

Anthony, Carl Sferrazza. *Nellie Taft: The Unconventional First Lady of the Ragtime Era*. New York: HarperCollins, 2005

Archbold, Rick, and Dana McCauley. *Last Dinner on the Titanic*. New York: Hyperion, 1997.

Auchincloss, Louis. *The Vanderbilt Era*. New York: Scribner, 1989.

Austen, Roger, edited by John W. Crowley. *Genteel Pagan: The Double Life of Charles Warren Stoddard*. Amherst: The University of Massachusetts Press, 1991.

Baker, Paul R. *Stanny: The Gilded Life of Stanford White*. New York: The Free Press, Macmillan Inc., 1989.

Ballard, Robert D., with Rick Archbold. *The Discovery of the Titanic*. New York: Warner Books, 1987.

————. *Lost Liners*. New York: Hyperion, 1997.

Barratt, Nick. *Lost Voices from the Titanic*. London: Palgrave Macmillan, 2010.

Beard, Patricia. *After The Ball*. New York: HarperCollins, 2003.

Beaton, Cecil. *The Unexpurgated Beaton Diaries*. London: Weidenfeld & Nicolson, 2002.

Behe, George. *"Archie": The Life of Major Archibald Butt from Georgia to the Titanic*, volumes 1, 2, and 3. Raleigh, North Carolina: Lulu.com, 2010.

————. *On Board R.M.S. Titanic: Memories of the Maiden Voyage*. Raleigh, North Carolina: Lulu.com, 2011.

————. *Titanic: Psychic Forewarnings of a Tragedy*. London: Patrick Stephens, 1986.

Beveridge, Bruce, Scott Andrews, Steve Hall, and Daniel Klistorner. *Titanic: The Ship Magnificent*, volumes 1 and 2. Stroud UK: The History Press, 2008.

Biel, Steven. *Down with the Old Canoe: A Cultural History of the Titanic Disaster.* New York: W.W. Norton and Company, 1996.

————. *Titanica: The Disaster of the Century in Poetry, Song and Prose.* New York: W.W. Norton and Company, 1998.

Bigham, Randy Bryan. *Lucile: Her Life by Design.* San Francisco: MacEvie Press, 2011.

Bisset, James. *Tramps and Ladies: My Early Years in Steamers.* New York: Criterion Books, 1959.

Bradley, James. *The Imperial Cruise.* New York: Little, Brown, 2009.

Brewster, Hugh, and Coulter, Laurie. *882 1/2 Amazing Answers to Your Questions About the Titanic.* New York: Scholastic Inc., 1998.

Bullock, Shan F. *"A Titanic Hero": Thomas Andrews, Shipbuilder.* Reprinted by 7 C's Press, Titanic Historical Society, 1972.

Butler, Daniel Allen. *Unsinkable: The Full Story of RMS Titanic.* Mechanicsburg, PA; Stackpole Books, 1998.

Butt, Archibald W. *Both Sides of the Shield.* Philadelphia: J.B. Lippincott Company, 1905.

Candee, Helen Churchill Hungerford. *Angkor the Magnificent.* New York: Stokes, 1934, reprinted 2010 by DatAsia Inc.

————. *How Women May Earn a Living.* New York: The Macmillan Company, 1900, reprinted by General Books, 2009.

Collier, Peter, with David Horowitz. *The Roosevelts: An American Saga.* New York: Simon & Schuster, 1994.

Cowles, Virginia. *The Astors: The Story of a Transatlantic Family.* Worthing, UK: Littlehampton Book Services, 1979.

Davie, Michael. *Titanic: The Death and Life of a Legend.* New York: Henry Holt and Company, 1986.

Davis, John H. *The Guggenheims, 1848–1988: An American Epic.* New York: Shapolsky Publishers, Inc.,1978.

Dodge, Washington. *The Loss of the Titanic: An Address Given Before the Commonwealth Club, San Francisco, May 11, 1912.* Springfield, Massachusetts: 7 C's Press, Titanic Historical Society.

Duff Gordon, Lady (Lucile). *Discretions and Indiscretions.* New York: Frederick A. Stokes, Co., 1932.

Eaton, John P., and Charles A. Haas. *Titanic: Destination Disaster.* New York: W.W. Norton and Company, 1994.

————. *Titanic: Triumph and Tragedy.* New York: W.W. Norton and Company, 1994.

Eckley, Grace. *Maiden Tribute: A Life of W. T. Stead.* Philadelphia: Xlibris Corporation, 2007.

Ellmann, Richard. *Oscar Wilde.* London: Hamish Hamilton, 1987.

Engstrom, Peter. *Francis Davis Millet: A Titanic Life*. East Bridgewater, MA: Millet Studio Publishing, 2010.

Etherington-Smith, Meredith, and Jeremy Pilcher. *The "It" Girls*. London: Hamish Hamilton, 1986.

Exman, Eugene. *The House of Harper: The Making of a Modern Publisher*. New York: Harper & Row, 1967.

Foster, John Wilson, ed. *The Titanic Reader*. London: Penguin Books, 1999.

Fowler, Marian. *In a Gilded Cage: From Heiress to Duchess*. Toronto: Random House, 1993.

————. *The Way She Looks Tonight: Five Women of Style*. Toronto: Random House, 1996.

Gale, Robert L. *The Gay Nineties in America*. Westport, CT: Greenwood Press, 1992.

Geller, Judith. *Titanic: Women and Children First*. New York: W.W. Norton and Co., 1998.

Hardwick, Joan. *Addicted to Romance: The Life and Adventures of Elinor Glyn*. London: André Deutsch Ltd., 1994.

Homberger, Eric. *Mrs. Astor's New York*. New Haven: Yale University Press, 2002.

Hustak, Alan. *Titanic: The Canadian Story*. Montreal: Véhicule Press, 1998.

Hyslop, Donald, Alistair Forsyth, and Sheila Jemima, eds. *Titanic Voices: Memories from the Fateful Voyage*. Southampton: Southampton City Council, 1994, 1997 edition, Sutton Publishing Limited.

Iversen, Kristen. *Molly Brown: Unraveling the Myth*. Boulder, Colorado: Johnson Books, 1999.

James, Henry. *Picture and Text*. Reprinted by the Dodo Press, 2011.

Jessop, Violet, edited by John Maxtone-Graham. *Titanic Survivor*. New York: Sheridan House, 1997.

Kaplan, Justin. *When the Astors Owned New York*. New York: Penguin, 2007.

Katz, Jonathan. *Love Stories: Sex Between Men Before Homosexuality*. Chicago: University of Chicago Press, 2001.

Kavaler, Lucy. *The Astors: A Family Chronicle of Pomp and Power*. New York: Dodd, Mead, 1965.

King, Greg. *A Season of Splendor: The Court of Mrs. Astor in Gilded Age New York*. Hoboken, NJ: John Wiley & Sons, 2008.

Kowsky, Francis R. *Buffalo Architecture: A Guide*. Buffalo: Architectural Guidebook Corporation, 1981.

Kuntz, Tom. *The Titanic Disaster Hearings: The Official Transcripts of the 1912 Senate Investigation*. New York: Pocket Books, 1998.

Langford, Gerald. *The Murder of Stanford White*. New York: Bobbs-Merrill, 1962.

Langtry, Lillie. *The Days I Knew.* New York: H. Doran, 1925.

Larson, Erik. *The Devil in the White City.* New York: Vintage, 2003.

Lee, Hermione. *Edith Wharton.* New York: Random House, 2007.

Lehr, Elizabeth Drexel. *"King Lehr" and the Gilded Age.* New York: J.B. Lippincott Company, 1935.

Lessard, Suzannah. *The Architect of Desire: Beauty and Danger in the Stanford White Family.* New York: The Dial Press, 1996.

Levinson, J. C., Ernest Samuels, Charles Vandersee, and Viola Hopkins Winner, eds. *The Letters of Henry Adams,* vols 1–6. Cambridge, MA: The Belknap Press at Harvard University Press, 1986.

Lewis, Alfred Allan. *Ladies and Not-So-Gentle Women.* New York: Viking-Penguin, 2000.

Longworth, Alice Roosevelt. *Crowded Hours.* New York: Charles Scribner's Sons, 1933.

Lord, Walter. *The Night Lives On.* New York: William Morrow, 1986.

———. *A Night to Remember.* New York: Holt, Rinehart & Winston, 1955. Bantam edition, 1956.

Lynch, Don. *Titanic: An Illustrated History.* New York: Hyperion, 1992.

Lynch, Don, and Ken Marschall. *Ghosts of the Abyss.* Boston: Da Capo Press, 2003.

Marshall, Logan. *The Sinking of the Titanic.* Philadelphia: C. Winston, 1912; Halifax: Nimbus Publishing, 1988.

Millet, Francis Davis. *A Capillary Crime and Other Stories.* New York: Harper & Brothers, 1892.

———. *The Danube from the Black Forest to the Black Sea.* New York: Harper & Brothers, 1893.

———. *The Expedition to the Philippines.* New York: Harper & Brothers, 1899.

Marcus, Geoffrey. *The Maiden Voyage.* New York: Viking, 1969.

Moffat, Wendy. *A Great Unrecorded History: A New Life Of E. M. Forster.* New York: Farrar, Straus and Giroux, 2010.

Mooney, Michael Macdonald. *Evelyn Nesbit and Stanford White: Love and Death in the Gilded Age.* New York: William Morrow, 1976.

Morris, Edmund. *The Rise of Theodore Roosevelt.* New York: Random House, 1979.

———. *Theodore Rex.* New York: Random House, 2001.

O'Donnell, E. E. *The Last Days of the Titanic.* Dublin: Wolfhound Press, 1997.

Paterson, John. *Edwardians, London Life and Letters, 1901–1914.* Chicago: Ivan R. Dee, 1996.

Patterson, Jerry E. *The First Four Hundred.* New York: Rizzoli, 2001.

Pellegrino, Charles. *Her Name, Titanic, The Untold Story of the Sinking and Finding of the Unsinkable Ship.* New York: McGraw-Hill, 1988.

Rostron, Arthur H. *The Loss of the Titanic.* Ludlow, MA: 7 C's Press for the Titanic Historical Society, 1975, first published 1931.

Ruffman, Alan. *Titanic Remembered: The Unsinkable Ship and Halifax.* Halifax: Formac Publishing, 1999.

Sharpey-Schafer, Joyce. *Soldier of Fortune, F. D. Millet, 1846–1912.* Utica, New York: 1984.

Skinner, Cornelia Otis. *Elegant Wits and Grand Horizontals.* Boston: Houghton Mifflin Company, 1962.

Sloper, William T. *The Life and Times of Andrew Jackson Sloper.* Privately printed, 1949.

Smith, Harriet Elinor, ed. *Autobiography of Mark Twain,* vol. 1. Berkeley: University of California Press, 2010.

Spedden, Daisy Corning Stone, and Leighton Coleman. *Polar the Titanic Bear.* Boston: Little, Brown and Co., 1994.

Stead, Estelle. *My Father: Personal & Spiritual Reminiscences.* London: William Heinemann, 1913.

Stead, William T. *Hymns That Have Helped.* Charleston, SC: BiblioLife reprint, 2009.

———. *If Christ Came to Chicago.* Chicago: Laird & Lee, 1894.

Stenson, Patrick. *"Lights":The Odyssey of C. H. Lightoller.* London: The Bodley Head, 1984.

Strouse, Jean. *Morgan: American Financier.* New York: Random House, 1999.

Stuart, Amanda Mackenzie. *Consuelo and Alva, Vanderbilt.* New York: HarperCollins, 2005.

Tharp, Louise Hall. *Saint-Gaudens and the Gilded Era.* Boston: Little, Brown, 1969.

Thayer, John B. *The Sinking of the S.S. Titanic.* Springfield: 7 C's Press reprint for Titanic Historical Society, 1974, first published 1940.

Unger, Irwin, and Debi Unger. *The Guggenheims: A Family History.* New York: HarperCollins Publishers, 2005.

Uruburu, Paula. *American Eve: Evelyn Nesbit, Stanford White and the Crime of the Century.* New York: Riverhead Books/Penguin Group, 2008.

Wade, Wyn Craig. *The Titanic: End of a Dream.* New York: Rawson Associates, Scribner Book Company, 1979; Penguin Books, 1980.

Wharton, Edith, edited by Roxana Robinson. *The New York Stories of Edith Wharton.* New York: New York Review of Books, 2007.

Whyte, Frederic. *The Life of W. T. Stead,* volumes 1 and 2. London: Jonathan Cape Ltd., 1925.

Wilson, Derek. *The Astors.* London: Weidenfeld & Nicolson, 1993.

Winocour, Jack. *The Story of the Titanic as Told by Its Survivors: Lawrence Beesley; Archibald Gracie; Charles Lightoller; Harold Bride.* New York: Dover Publications Inc., 1960.

Woods, Shirley E, Jr. *The Molson Saga.* Toronto: Doubleday Canada, 1983.

UNPUBLISHED SOURCES

"CQD." An unpublished memoir by Richard Norris Williams, courtesy of the Williams family.

Hawksford, Walter, letter to his wife, private collection.

Millet Letters to Charles Warren Stoddard. Charles Warren Stoddard Collection, Special Collections Research Center, University of Syracuse Library.

Russell, Edith [Rosenbaum]. "By The Grace of God—And Fashion" speech, 1924, courtesy of Randy Bryan Bigham; April 1, 1934, *Titanic* account, Charles Pellegrino website.

Simpson, Marc. *Reconstructing the Golden Age: American Artists in Broadway, Worcestershire, 1885–1889.* Dissertation, Yale University, 1993.

ARTICLES FROM MAGAZINES. JOURNALS, AND WEBSITES

Abrams, Melanie. "Lady Duff Gordon: Fashion's Forgotten Grande Dame." *Telegraph,* February 21, 2011.

Barkworth, Algernon. "Barkworth's Account." ET.

Behe, George. "The Music of the *Titanic*'s Band" and "The Two Deaths of John Jacob Astor." George Behe's Titanic Tidbits website.

Bigham, Randy Bryan, and Gregg Jasper. "Broadway Dame: The Life and Times of Mrs. Henry B. Harris." *Titanic Commutator* 36, no. 193–195.

Bigham, Randy Bryan. "Life's Décor," "Madame Lucile: A Life in Style," "A Matter of Course," and "Star Turn," from ET. "Lady Duff Gordon: Saved from the *Titanic*," *Titanic Commutator* 15, no. 1.

Brewster, Hugh. "Sinking Sensation." *Toronto Life,* May 1997.

Candee, Helen. "Sealed Orders." *Collier's,* May 4, 1912.

Chapman, Earl. "Gunshots on the *Titanic*." ET.

Chirnside, Mark, and Sam Halpern. "*Olympic* and *Titanic*: Maiden Voyage Mysteries." ET.

Dupuis, Michael. "And Mind You're A Nurse." *Herstoria,* issue 7, Autumn 2010, pp. 46–49.

Halpern, Sam. "*Titanic*—From Daunt's Rock to a Collision." Titanicology website.

Harris, René. "Her Husband Went Down with the *Titanic*." *Liberty,* April 23, 1932.

Hyder, Jemma. "Excuse Sending . . . Am Half Asleep." ET.

James. Henry. "Our Artists in Europe." *Harper's New Monthly*, June 1889.

Kamuda, Ed and Karen. "The Courtship and Wedding of Madeleine Talmage Force and Colonel John Jacob Astor." *Titanic Commutator* 35, no. 192.

Louden-Brown, Paul. "Ismay and the *Titanic*." Titanic Historical Society website.

Molony, Senan. "A Tender Named America," "Bruce Ismay and the Ring's Taunt," "The Fleecing of Hugh Woolner," and "The Riddle of the Sphinx." ET.

Mulpetre, Owen. "W. T. Stead & the Titanic." Attacking the Devil website.

Pellegrino, Charles. "Astor, Straus, Futrelle." Charles Pellegrino website.

Rosenbaum, Edith. Article in *Women's Wear Daily*, April 19, 1912.

Ryerse, Phyllis. "Rich Man and Poor Man: The Story of the Ryersons on the *Titanic*." *Titanic Commutator* 14, no. 2.

Spedden, Margaretta Corning Stone, and Leighton Coleman. "Excerpts from the Daily Journal of 'Daisy' Spedden." *Titanic Commutator* 16, no. 3.

Ticehurst, Brian. "Marconigrams Sent and Received by Captain Smith on the *Titanic*." ET.

Warchol, Clara B. "Edward Kent, *Titanic* Hero." *Titanic Commutator*, December 1976.

Wilkinson, Paul. "*Titanic*'s Silent Distress Signals: A New Look at a Minor Mystery." ET.

Wormstedt, Bill, Tad Fitch, and George Behe. in "Titanic: The Lifeboat Launching Sequence Re-examined." Wormstedt.com.

Wormstedt, Bill, and Tad Fitch. "Did an Officer Commit Suicide on *Titanic*?" *Titanic Commutator* 30, no. 173.

———. "*Titanic* Lifeboat Occupancy Totals," wormstedt.com.

Wojtczak, Helena. "Elsie Bowerman: Feminist and Barrister." ET.

ACKNOWLEDGMENTS

My first acquaintance with the remarkable circle of people devoted to the study of the *Titanic* dates back to 1986, when I began working on Robert Ballard's book about the discovery of the wreck. Twenty-five years later, I was delighted to be able to call once again on the expertise of that same circle, now greatly enlarged. Ed and Karen Kamuda of the Titanic Historical Society have been outstanding conservers of the lost liner's history since 1963 and I'm grateful for their assistance with research and photographs and for the many articles in the organization's magazine, *The Titanic Commutator.* I have also had the pleasure of working on several books with the THS's historian, Don Lynch, who has an astonishingly comprehensive knowledge of the lives of those who made the fatal voyage. For this book, Don generously reviewed each chapter, caught many potentially embarrassing errors, pointed me towards useful new information, and shared photographs from his collection.

George Behe, a past vice-president of the THS, has also put in years of assiduous research on the *Titanic* and I am very grateful for his unflagging kindness and assistance. His scholarly three-volume biography of Major Archibald Butt, *"Archie": The Life of Major Archibald Butt from Georgia to the Titanic,* is invaluable to anyone interested in the life of this intriguing man, or the history of the White House during the Theodore Roosevelt and Taft administrations. Another of George's books that I found to be of inestimable help is *On Board RMS Titanic,* a useful compilation of first-person accounts of the disaster. George also carefully reviewed various drafts of the text, though any errors in it are mine alone.

In articles and books, Randy Bryan Bigham has documented the lives of some of the ship's most extraordinary women: Lucy Duff Gordon, Renée Harris, Helen Candee, Dorothy Gibson, and Noëlle Rothes, among others. Randy generously shared his extensive research and picture collection with me, and provided excellent suggestions and welcome encouragement as he read each chapter. He also gave me prepublication access to his book, *Lucile: Her Life by Design*.

The life of Frank Millet has now been properly chronicled in a definitive biography by Peter Engstrom entitled *Francis Davis Millet: A Titanic Life*. I'm indebted to Peter for sharing his book in manuscript form, and for giving me a guided tour of East Bridgewater and the Millet studio. In Broadway, Worcestershire, John Noott kindly provided accommodation at Farnham House, another Millet residence, and Lord Birdwood gave me a tour of Russell House, the artist's second home in Broadway, while Richard Tae welcomed me to the Abbots Grange which was once a studio for Millet and the Broadway colony. I'm also grateful to John Lamoreau for sharing his Millet letters and to Shelley Dziedzic for her research and photos of both Frank and his friend Archie Butt.

For editorial suggestions I must thank my early readers, Larry Muller and Marian Fowler, and also my agent Beverly Slopen, editors Brad Wilson and Charlie Conrad, assistant editor Miriam Chotiner-Gardner, production editorial director Mark McCauslin, and copy editor Richard Willett. Thanks also go to Tad Fitch for reviewing the chapters concerned with the loading of the lifeboats. I also drew on a convincing new lifeboat loading sequence, which Tad worked on with Bill Wormstedt and George Behe, that is available on Bill Wormstedt's website. Sam Halpern and Geoff Whitfield provided insight into how the daily on-board betting pool was operated and Michael Poirier also reviewed the text and provided suggestions and photographs. Special thanks to Michael Dupuis for sending me his article about Mary Adelaide Snider. Artist Ken Marschall, a longtime friend and illustrator of many *Titanic* books, also provided photographs from his collection. Thanks also to Gord Sibley for his advice.

It's a privilege to have been able to quote from an unpublished memoir by R. Norris Williams, and I'm grateful to the Williams family for that and for the rare photograph of Norris with his father, Charles Williams. Leighton H Coleman III, with whom I once worked on the children's book *Polar the Titanic Bear*, allowed me to quote from the diaries of Daisy Spedden, to which he holds the copyright, and to reprint a photograph of Daisy with her son and his nurse. Thanks also go to the Adlard family.

The Internet has become a highly effective tool for *Titanic* researchers, and the websites I have listed in the bibliography were particularly helpful. George Behe and Don Lynch have also provided a most useful service by posting transcripts from the two *Titanic* inquiries and the Limitation of Liability hearings on the Titanic Inquiry Project site. But above all, I owe a debt to Philip Hind and the Encyclopedia Titanica website. To have such a comprehensive repository of *Titanic* information available only a click away is something I've been grateful for on a daily basis. And although the contributors to ET are too numerous to name, I do wish to single out the following people: Earl Chapman, Mark Chirnside, Michael Findley, Dave Gittins, Philip Gowan, Sam Halpern, Mike Herbold, Alan Hustak, Daniel Klistorner, Senan Molony, Luke Owens, Inger Sheil, Michael Standart, Brian Ticehurst, David Whitmire, and Helena Wojtczak.

I'd like to thank Michael Levine for launching me into the sea lanes of *Titanic* publishing by introducing Al Cummings and myself to Robert Ballard in 1984. Thanks also to Bob Ballard for his undersea explorations of the *Titanic* and other lost ships and for happy collaborations on a long list of titles. Finally, the warmest of thanks go to my partner, Phillipp Andres, for his patience and support during the writing of this book.

PHOTOGRAPH AND ILLUSTRATION CREDITS

American Academy of Arts and Letters Collection, New York City, 4 (bottom), 155 (bottom right)

Atlanta History Center, 153

Author's Collection, 93 (right), 125, 162 (top), 178 (top), 189, 196 (top)

Bancroft Library, University of California, 49

Brown Brothers, ii, 16 (bottom)

Canada Science & Technology Museum, 177

Davison & Associates, 62 (bottom)

Don Lynch Collection, 26 (left and right), 84, 115

George Behe Collection, 90 (bottom), 151 (left), 196 (bottom)

Getty Images, 35, 37, 62 (top)

Gregg H. Jasper Collection, 139 (bottom)

International Tennis Hall of Fame & Museum, 18

Irish Examiner, 67, 71, 74

Ken Marschall Collection, 136 (top and bottom), 148 (top)

Leighton H. Coleman III Collection, 106 (bottom)

Library of Congress Prints and Photographs Archive, 9, 11 (top right and bottom), 43 (top and bottom), 57, 79 (top and bottom), 93 (bottom), 96, 130, 139 (top), 151 (right), 162 (bottom), 202, 225, 228 (top and bottom), 234 (top and bottom), 240, 246 (top and bottom), 254 (top and bottom), 255, 265, 267

Mary Evans Picture Library, i, 143, 165, 210, 213, 239, 243

Mike Poirier/NARA Collection, 190

Museum of the City of New York, Byron Collection, 28 (top), 90 (top), 93 (top), (106 (top), 113 (bottom), 155 (top)

National Museums of Northern Ireland, Collection Harland & Wolff, Ulster Folk & Transport Museum, 11 (top left)

New York Public Library, Astor Lenox and Tilden Foundations, Print Collection, Miriam and Ira D. Wallach Division of Arts, Prints and Photographs, 77

Randy Bryan Bigham Collection, 22, 28 (bottom), 102, 113 (top), 120 (top and bottom), 148 (bottom), 155 (bottom left), 159, 170, 192, 218, 266,

Syracuse University Library, Special Research Center, Charles Warren Stoddard Collection, 48

Thomas Jefferson University Archives and Special Collections, Scott Memorial Library, Philadelphia, PA, 32

Titanic Historical Society Collection, endpapers, 4 (top), 16 (top), 64, 178 (bottom), 215

University of Pennsylvania Archives, 206

Wellington County Museum & Archives, Fergus, Ontario, ph16199, 123

Woods Hole Oceanographic Institute, xii

Worcestershire Record Office, Ref. No. x705:1235 BA11q302/xiiii, 46

INDEX

ABOUT THE AUTHOR

HUGH BREWSTER was born in London, England, but spent his teen years in Guelph, Ontario, in a house near Summerhill, the girlhood home of *Titanic* passenger Lucile, Lady Duff Gordon. As a young editor at Madison Press Books in Toronto he met Dr. Robert Ballard in 1984 and worked with him to produce the international bestseller *The Discovery of the Titanic*. Nineteen other nautical books followed, including *The Discovery of the Bismarck, Lost Liners, Polar the Titanic Bear,* and *Last Dinner on the Titanic.* Brewster also worked with Don Lynch and Ken Marschall on *Titanic: An Illustrated History,* a book that proved useful to James Cameron's epic movie, and he later compiled the tie-in to Cameron's 3D film *Ghosts of the Abyss.* Brewster is also the author of *Inside the Titanic, 882½ Amazing Answers to Your Questions About the Titanic,* and *Deadly Voyage* and has written twelve award-winning books for young readers. *The Other Mozart* was hailed as "history at its best" by the *San Francisco Chronicle,* and *Carnation, Lily, Lily, Rose* was chosen as one of the best of 2007 by the *Washington Post* and nominated for several of Canada's top literary awards. Hugh Brewster lives in an Edwardian neighborhood in Toronto just around the corner from the house that was the last address of Major Arthur Peuchen.